Educating Veterans in the 21ˢᵗ Century

Douglas Herrmann
Charles Hopkins
Roland B. Wilson
Bert Allen

wp24

ISBN: 1-4392-3782-4
ISBN-13: 9781439237823

To order additional copies, please contact us.
BookSurge
www.booksurge.com
1-866-308-6235
orders@booksurge.com

Dedication

This book is dedicated to all who have served; especially those who have made the ultimate sacrifice, and those who returned with medical problems that continued, sometimes known or unknown to others, long after their discharge. We are grateful to them for their faithful service.

Table of Contents

Foreword

By
Steve Kime

President of the Servicemembers Opportunity
Colleges (Retired)
Vice President of the American Association of
State Colleges and Universities (Retired)
Past Chair and current member of the Veterans
Advisory Committee on Education
Captain, U.S.N. (Retired)

This is a timely book. Congress awakened in 2008 to the plight of the
GI Bill. It took a war hero, former Secretary of the Navy, and current Senator
to hold reveille on Capitol Hill. Senator James Webb's new GI Bill is inspiration to all of us to look hard at how veterans fare in their attempts to get an
education.

The World War II G.I. Bill was widely recognized as one of the most
successful pieces of legislation in U.S. history. Thousands of the nation's future leaders used the G.I. Bill to get an education. Those veterans, many now
gone, lived out their lives recognized as The Greatest Generation.

It was downhill from there. Subsequent veterans of Korea, Vietnam,
Afghanistan, Iraq, and the lesser conflicts in between have not enjoyed the
educational support they deserve from either the government or the people.
The wars themselves were controversial, and the warriors suffered. In a sense
it was a case of the nation cutting off its nose to spite its face, because development of the human potential of those who had served in conflict was a
proven, productive national investment.

Though G.I. Bill benefits have waxed and waned over the last half-century, veterans seeking education have had to do with less than they deserved and far less than needed for young adults, many with families, to go to college. Their financial strain has been accompanied by physical and mental handicaps for many veterans disdain from some fellow students and even faculty who would not serve, and sometimes from unhelpful or unsympathetic college administrations. Of course, this dark picture is not accurate everywhere or at all times, but many veterans have encountered elements of it.

It is difficult to chronicle the educational experience of a group that is widely dispersed and intent on blending back into the population. Information on veterans has been in short supply for those who know that there are problems and seek to correct them.

This book is important. It fills a genuine need. As we continue to fight a global war on Terror and implement the new GI Bill, we need to understand the world that veterans face when trying to go to college.

S. K.

Preface

Presently, in the early twenty-first century, American Veterans need the help of higher education in order that they may be successful in obtaining a college degree. The new GI Bill will definitely help them deal with the financial costs of college. However, veterans also need help with a variety of unique problems that most other students will not encounter. These unique problems discourage veterans from continuing their studies in many cases.

The purpose of this book is to inform American society, veteran organizations, and the higher education academic community, about the problems unique to veterans and to propose how colleges and universities could make changes to help eliminate these problems. This book reviews little known facts about the challenges that veterans face when they begin college. After reviewing these challenges in detail, we propose solutions that higher education can implement to give veteran a better chance of getting a degree.

Higher education needs to address problems that did not trouble the preponderance of veterans prior to the Korean War due to the sheer volume of veterans and the American support given to veterans up until this point. However, since the Vietnam War, veterans have been comparatively small in number on college campuses, creating difficulties for veterans as they seek a college degree. This book has been written to help higher education's institutional leaders as they assist veterans in obtaining a college degree. The book should be informative especially to professors and administrators in higher educational institutions who want to know how they may facilitate veterans who study at their institution.

The authors of this book, who are veterans, wish to point out that they believe virtually everyone in academia is patriotic and wants to treat veterans fairly while they seek a college degree. However, the book is intended to call attention to the problems of veterans in college so that educators can help eliminate these problems. The college problems of veterans presented in this book were first pointed out to the authors by veterans who were students, by faculty members or college administrators.

Who Might Benefit From Reading This Book

In addition to helping college professors and college administrators eliminate the college problems of veterans, the content of this book may also help the people of this nation, government leaders, leaders in veteran service organizations, and veterans become aware of these problems. The content of this book should be informative to members of the federal and state governments who are responsible for assisting veterans in some capacity. The book also may be useful to State Certifying Officials and Program Administrators who seek to identify those schools that do or do not merit certification (Veterans Education Association, 2006).

Finally, it is also the hope that the content of this book can help veterans who can use it as a guide to higher education, and to better understand the successful ways to obtain an education. Additionally, veterans may benefit from this book in order to realize what benefits, programs and rights they have, what they should have, what they are up against to get an education, and how to better overcome the obstacles they face.

It may be noted that different readers may have different reasons for reading this book. For readers who would like to know more about a particular problem, articles in both the scholarly and popular press that reported a problem are cited. Examples of college problems that were pointed out by veterans while attending college are also included.

Most of the content of the book will be useful to faculty and administrators, but it may also be useful to legislators at the national, state, and local levels. The authors hope that this book will lead to legislation that will help veterans with the factors that discourage them from getting a college degree or from completing one. It is possible that older veterans in veteran's service organizations (e.g., American Legion; Disabled American Veterans; Veterans of Foreign Wars; Vietnam Veterans of America; Vietnam Veterans Institute) whose members are concerned with the education of younger veterans will be interested in this book also.

Two introductory chapters and the four closing chapters address the various problems in general that veterans encounter in college. Each of the other ten chapters focuses on a different kind of problem. However, some of the specific problems depend on how other problems are addressed. Readers interested in a specific kind of challenge may read the chapter that focuses on this problem. However, readers interested in how a specific kind of problem affects other problems may want to read one or more of the other chapters. Of course, readers who want to fully appreciate the "veterans' higher education problems" will want to read the entire book.

Sources

Academic sources are cited where appropriate. In addition, the authors have consulted other members of academia and other veterans about the issues addressed in this book.

About the Authors

Three authors have spent all or nearly all of their professional lives teaching at the college level. Two authors (Herrmann and Hopkins) are emeriti professors from Indiana State University. One author has also had a long career in college teaching at Milligan College and is not far from retirement (Allen). One author (Wilson) retired from the military after almost 21 years of service and recently obtained a BA and MA in Linguistics at Indiana State University.

All four authors are veterans. The first author is a Marine Corps veteran of the Vietnam War; the second author is a WWII veteran of the 44th Infantry Division, Seventh Army; the third author is a Marine Corps veteran with 16 years of service overseas; and the fourth author is an Army Vietnam veteran. While in the military, two authors received a purple heart (CH, BA).

All four authors have first hand experience with the problems discussed here. Each was a veteran when he obtained a college degree after serving in the military. All of the authors obtained part of their education with the support of the GI Bill. Three of the authors provided, as part of their professional duties, advice to veterans about the problems they encountered in higher education.

Acknowledgements

All four authors are grateful to college administrators, professors, and non-veteran students who genuinely support veterans who are students in college and the service men and women who are on active duty. We are especially grateful for the advice of veterans who have been or currently are students.

Doug Herrmann expresses his gratitude to veterans he has known as students in college. These veterans include: John Candelaria, a student at Indiana State University (ISU), who founded of the Veterans Education and Transition Society at ISU; past presidents of this society: Jonathan Alberts and Drew Hauber; Director of ISU's Vet to Vet program, Jessica Saunders; veterans who studied at ISU: Dannie Perry, Sunshine and Kurt Phares; Matthew Harmon; Deborah Bolin. He is grateful as well for advice on issues discussed here from professors and administrators who are veterans: Mike Caress, Air Guard veteran; David Vancil, Vietnam Veteran; Kevin Hoolahan, Vietnam Veteran; Bob Huckabee, Army Reserve Veteran and veteran of the Iraq War; John Gartland, Army Reserve Veteran and Robert English, Air Guard.

Herrmann has learned about aspects of the issues reviewed in this book from leaders in Academia such as Steve Kime, Lloyd Benjamin, Jack Maynard, Cathy Baker, Bob English, Mike Caress, and Daniel Bradley. Also certain members of the DVA have advised him: VA Employees: Angela Chastain, VA licensed clinical social worker; Dianna Cooper-Bolinsky, licensed clinical social worker; Steve Herman, Director of the Indiana Vet to Vet program; Eric Lewis, Education Liaison for the VA; Leann Wenzel, Psychiatric Nurse Practitioner; Keith Wilson, Director of Education Services, DVA Central Education Office; and Dennis Douglas, Assistant Director. Deputy Director of Education Services, DVA Central Office; and Tom Applegate, Director of the Indiana Department of Veterans Affairs. Similarly various colleagues have advised him: Roger Peterman. Army veteran; Jay Simmerman, Elizabeth Ransom, Ashley Reese, Angela Duncan, David Ellington, Army veteran, Doug Gibbens, John C Gilliland, Mike Miner as well as several guard members: Sergeant Neil Brown, First Sergeant Madden, and Lt. Col. Pam Moody. Also ISU Staff has aided our efforts: Bernie Anderson, Toni Bollinger, and Nancy Rankin. David Witcher and Jim Stever have been instrumental in determining how to publish this book. Finally, Zachary Herrmann has influenced my views on how veterans are treated in college.

The "copy-editor" author, Charles Hopkins' acknowledges the three co-authors who have become colleagues. He also expresses his gratitude to two high-school teachers at Lebanon, Indiana – Mary McIntire and Mary Ann Tauer—who began the development of his feel for writing and how it gets completed, must also be acknowledged. The reality of the "real world" must also be acknowledged with the wish that it is reflected in this book about some very important people.

Roland B. Wilson expresses his gratitude to Dexter Jordan for his help in transferring his military credits to academic credits, and to Dr. Ron Dunbar and the professors in the Department of Languages, Literatures, and Linguistics who guided and helped him in the pursuit of his Master's in Linguistics. The motivation to write this book is due to the gravity of its nature and the hope of positive impact for the dedicated and deserving service members and veterans who he was proud to have served with, who are too many to name, but none of who are forgotten. Their sacrifice, selflessness and love for their families and country remain forever unparalleled anywhere in this world.

Bert Allen acknowledges the service and dedication of several fellow servicemembers: LT John Farley and SGT Uriel Banuelos, both of whom were wounded severely at Fire Support Base Pershing six kilometers north of Trang Bang, Vietnam, on January 10, 1969; Father Donato Silveri, who was on that date a Chaplain for artillerymen of the 25th Infantry Division and who came to the aid of four wounded cannoncockers still under enemy fire, risking his own life; Steve Giles, a compassionate and genuine psychologist to Vietnam and other veterans as well as a mentor to me; Pat Arnow, who guided me in the editing and writing for Now and Then Magazine's tribute to Appalachian veterans; Marshall Conkin, a friend who served his nation fully as a Marine during the Vietnam War; Marshall's oldest child, Johnny Conkin, a Marine who served his nation well during the Iraqi War of the early 21st Century, and Mike Speer, a Marine from Redfield, Kansas, who loved his men and who was killed by an enemy round while going to the aid of some of his men in Fallujah, Al Anbar Province, Iraq, April 9, 2004.

This book was published in cooperation with the Vietnam Veterans Institute.

Review and Commentary

by
J. Eldon Yates*

After reading **Educating Veterans in the 21st Century** I was astonished that the current generation of American veterans are facing many of the stigmatisms and stereotypes that thwarted the sprit and efforts of Vietnam veterans returning to college.

Educating Veterans in the 21st Century is an important and necessary scholarly work. It is designed to assist professors and all those charged with providing quality academic experiences and educational opportunities for students to assure that they are fully extended to America's veterans as well.

The book cites obstacles identified by the current generation of veterans and offers instructional guidance to assist professors and administrators to remedy the issues. Hence, veterans are provided an optimal learning environment and an opportunity for integration into the culture of campus life.

* J. Eldon Yates is the Chairman of the Vietnam Veterans Institute

Once upon a time in the land of hushabye,
Around the wondrous days of yore,
They came across a sort of box,
Bound up with chains and locked with locks
And labeled 'Kindly do not touch its war'

from THE BOX
by Lascelles Abercrombie (1881-1938)

Chapter 1
The Need to Help Veterans with Their College Education

The authors have written this book because we believe that veterans who are students in higher education currently need help from professors, college administrators, staff members, and fellow students in order that veterans obtain a college degree. Veterans need help because a variety of problems have arisen for them in college in the past three decades following the Vietnam War.

Many citizens feel that the new GI Bill will essentially eliminate any problems of veterans and put them on a fast track to get a college degree. The new GI Bill will definitely help veterans with the costs of college. However, money alone will not ensure that veterans avoid problems in college. Veterans need help with problems that other students will not encounter. The additional problems that they encounter discourage them and lead them to perform less well in their pursuit of a college degree. In some cases the discouragement leads some veterans to drop out of college.

The Scope of Veterans Problems in College

Veterans' problems extend much farther than the financial burden that the new GI Bill addresses. The problems that veterans encounter belong to the same categories of problems that non-veterans encounter: selecting an appropriate college; making the transition to college life; acquiring the academic skills needed in college; adjusting to the culture of a college; interacting with professors, administrators, and other students; financing college; obtaining transfer credits; participating in college educational programs; maintaining one's health; and finding employment on graduation. However, as reported by veterans to the authors, the problems in these categories challenge and affect veterans differently from how they challenge and affect non-veterans.

Why Veterans College Problems Have Yet to be Addressed Today

The problems of veterans in higher education have not been recognized until recently. Few in higher education know about these problems other than the veterans who are in school today. Most professors and college administrators do not know about the problems of veterans because these professors and administrators are not veterans themselves, thus preventing them from being able to anticipate or recognize these problems. Many of the remaining professors and administrators are unaware of these problems because they do not realize that their actions treat veterans poorly. Some professors and administrators are aware of these problems but do not talk about them because they do not see it as their responsibility to help mistreated veterans. However, some other professors and administrators deliberately mistreat veterans but do not talk about their negative behavior. Like others in higher education, the authors were unaware of these problems until they became involved in advising veterans about their college education.

Veterans constitute less that 3% of students on most campuses. There are many other student groups who are much larger and/or attract attention to their problems easily due to their highly visible special interests. Veterans, due to their nature, usually do not talk about the problems they encounter, or complain, as they merely want to get their degree and start a career as soon as possible, and, in many cases, to support a family that they acquired while in the service. In addition, even if they wanted to complain, the likelihood that a professor or administrator would help them is small.

The Origins of Veterans' College Problems

We personally know many professors and administrators who have gone out of their way to help veterans. Nevertheless, because they do not know about the military experience of veterans, professors and college administrators sometimes follow bureaucratic procedures and educational practices that inadvertently create problems and barriers for veterans. In addition to these problems, a small number of educators mistreat veterans as a protest to the actions of the government. We propose later in this book how those educators who are angry with the government may protest in more productive ways than by treating veterans poorly.

What this Book Might Achieve

The authors believe that this book demonstrates not only that veterans have problems that should be eliminated, but also that the elimination of these problems will need the cooperation of educators, leaders in society, and leaders in veterans organizations who are able to rectify the situations that lead to the problems. The authors believe that once educators are properly informed, they will help eliminate what might be called the **veterans-education problem**. Then they can assist veterans in achieving the education that they seek.

Some Historical Background for this Book

America's veterans have participated in approximately 40 conflicts of the United States. Especially well-known conflicts include: the Revolutionary War, the War of 1812; the Civil War; the Spanish-American War, World War I; World War II; the Korean War; the Vietnam War; Desert Storm; Somalia, Bosnia, and the current War on Terror. Several of these conflicts resulted in thousands of our service men and women being killed and many more wounded, often disabled. Most recently, more than 4300 service members have died in the War on Terror and several thousands more have returned with wounds and disabilities.

The Challenge to a Previous Generation of Educators

American higher education is in a similar situation today as it was during, and shortly after, World War II. While that war was being waged, many university educators and persons in government grappled with the **veterans-education problem**. Educators and members of government recognized that higher education was needed to determine the future of veterans in American society. It was feared that a large number of unemployed veterans would affect the American economy negatively. Some program was clearly needed to meet the financial needs of veterans in order to avoid the economic problems evident in the depression (Dickson & Allen, 2004; Gaines, 1945/2004; Mettler, 2005; Winter, 2005).

Also a program was needed that would enable veterans to join society as productive participants. Veterans would clearly need to be retooled in order to return to American society (Bolte, 1945). During World War II, many technologies had advanced. If veterans were to gain employment in American society, they would need additional education and/or training in the new technologies. Considerable discussion was devoted to determine how veterans might be given a college education (Bedford, 1946; Cartright, 1944; Clark, 1998; Commission on Post-War Training and the Adjustment, 1942; Educational Policies Commission, 1944; Grinnell, 1946; Webb & Atkinson, 1946).

Besides financial and employment considerations, returning veterans would have to undergo a transition from military to civilian life. Educators specializing in the social sciences and history were looked to in order to develop programs that would help veterans with the social aspects of this transition (Bolte, 1945; Cartright, 1944; Rogers & Wallen, 1946; Todd, 1949).

Discussions among educators during and just after World War II revealed that some of them were in favor and some against the idea of having veterans in higher education (Clark, 1998; Gaines, 1945/2004; Ross, 1969; Wector, 1944; Weller, 1944). Some argued that veterans would not be sufficiently prepared to succeed in college. Others were concerned about whether typical college students would have difficulty getting along with veterans who largely originate from lower socioeconomic strata. Nevertheless, as you know, Congress passed the first GI Bill that addressed both the financial and educational needs of veterans at that time (Gaines, 2004). In 1944, President Roosevelt signed into law the "Serviceman's Readjustment Act," better known as the "G.I. Bill of Rights" and commonly referred to as the GI Bill.

Eventually, many professors and administrators came to recognize veterans as capable of succeeding in higher education (Love & Hutchison, 1946). Moreover, veterans were seen by many educators as being more mature than the younger non-veteran students (Fine, 1947). Over time, the GI Bill came to be praised for rendering higher education in America more democratic and less dominated by elitist attitudes (Adams, 2000; Avery, 1946; Clark, 1998; Olson, 1974; Serow, 2004; Washton, 1945; Winter, 2005). Twice the GI Bill has been modified substantially; these revisions are discussed in detail in the second chapter.

The Challenge to the Current Generation of Educators. Fortunately, higher education today does not have to address all of the issues about veterans considered during World War II. To begin with the GI Bill has become a customary benefit of those who have served in the military. Nevertheless, higher education today still has a variety of problems that affect the likelihood of successfully educating returning veterans.

Until recently, veterans (as well as those on active-duty military, in the National Guard, and in the Reserve) have been relatively rare on college campuses. Where they did enroll, they looked for and found whatever assistance they needed from someone in their college community who at least knew about some of the veterans' needs. However, many veterans now from the War on Terror have decided to seek a college degree. There are too many veterans for the small number of colleges and universities who had been helping veterans. As a result, many veterans currently do not receive the needed help and guidance with their college problems.

Too Few Veterans Attend and Complete College

The difficulties veterans experience when attending and completing college are clearly evident in available statistics. Approximately 65%of the general population has had some college education and 29% of the general population has obtained a Bachelor's or higher degree. In contrast, approximately 41 % of veterans attend college and 15 % of veterans obtain a Bachelor's or higher degree. The current estimate of veterans attending college, 41.9% represents a recent increase in veterans who have received some college education. Previous estimates of obtaining some college were about 24% (approximately 40% of veterans used their educational benefits for some kind of education, from the end of World War II through the end of the Vietnam War). Undoubtedly, even with increased interest in a college education by veterans, a substantially smaller proportions of veterans than non-veterans attend college or graduate. These statistics are summarized in 1.1 and their origins are provided in the notes to the table.

Table 1.1
The Percentages of Veterans and Non-veterans
Who have Attended College and those who have Completed College

	Some College	Obtained a College Degree
Non-veterans	65.8% a	29% b
Veterans	41.9% c	15% d

Note: a - The Bureau of Labor Statistics reported in October of 2006 that
a - 65.8 % of high school graduates from the class of 2006 enrolled in college.
b - Wikipedia on the web reported 29 % of the general population received
a Bachelor's degree or higher in 2006. c - The percent of veterans who
currently receive some college education was estimated to be 41.9%. This
percentage was computed by multiplying the current rate of veterans' usage
of educational benefits (69.9%, K. Wilson, 2006) by the proportion of
veterans who use their educational benefits to attend college (approximately
60%, reported on the 2004 National Survey of Veterans). d - the percentage
of veterans who obtain a college degree, 15%, as reported by Judge (2004).

Exploring the Problems of Students in College

Veterans experience the same categories of problems in college that
non-veterans experience. However, they sometimes experience other aspects
of these problems that non-veterans do not experience. In some cases, veterans are unable to eliminate or solve the problems that are unique to them
without help.

Currently, some veterans:

Do not apply for college when they should, or
Attend college but progress slower than necessary toward a college
degree, or
Attend college but do worse in their courses than they should, or
Drop out of college when they should not.

The authors identify nine kinds of problems that confront all students
who attend college. A good education optimizes the learning process for all
students by eliminating these problems. The nine kinds of problems are:

- **Selecting a College or University.** All students have to cope with the problem of selecting a college or university that is appropriate for his or her background. Such selection requires careful attention to a variety of characteristics of higher educational institutions.

- **Transition Problems.** All students must make an adjustment to their new surroundings and lifestyle prevalent in college. To optimize this adjustment, colleges and universities sometimes instruct students how to make this difficult adjustment.

- **Academic Problems.** All students must improve their academic skills in order to succeed academically. Colleges and universities try to provide students with these skills but some students must make a greater effort than other students to acquire these skills.

- **Campus-Culture Problems.** College students need to cope with the problem of learning how to interact successfully with professors, college administrators, younger students and older students. The nature of the interactions that should be learned by students follows the customs of a college's or university's culture. The degree to which a culture facilitates learning is sometimes called its climate. The better the climate and the more able a student able to cope with the climate, the better the academic performance of a student.

- **Educational-Program Problems.** All students need to learn about their school's curriculum and how to take the courses required to obtain the kind of degree they want. Colleges offer a variety of programs e.g., orientation, advisement that guide students to learn what courses they must take in order to graduate. Through various educational programs, students learn the names of courses and sequences of related courses that must be taken in order to obtain each specific degree. However, students must discover and learn such information in order to meet the curricular requirements of their school.

- **Financial Problems.** All students must find the financial resources required to pay for a degree. A student learns best when he or she knows that a way has been developed to meet the costs of getting a degree. However, students must meet these financial costs if they want to obtain a degree from their schools,

10

- **Transfer Problems**. These days, many students begin college with credits obtained elsewhere. Transfer of these credits gives students confidence when starting college and helps them get a leg up on meeting degree requirements. However, getting transfer credits is not always easy. When a school refuses to give transfer credit for work done elsewhere, a student will need to figure out how to persuade his or her school to award the credits for which a student is eligible.

- **Health Problems**. Students learn best when they are healthy, both physiologically and psychologically. Consequently colleges and universities maintain health services that may attend to the health problems of students. To maintain health, students must learn to use their college or university health service or to obtain medical care outside of school.

- **Employment Problems for Students at Graduation.** Career centers help students define their career goals and decide which college programs will enable them to achieve these goals. Students need to determine how a career center may assist them in identifying their career goals. Moreover, as students approach graduation and afterwards, they will try to land a good job. Doing so requires a student to learn the ins and outs of the job market and how their school's career center may help them. Figuring out how to get the best job possible is the ultimate problem of all students.

Professors and administrators do their best to ensure that all students eliminate these problems. They know that students learn best when these problems do not trouble them.

Problems of Veterans in College

Veterans have the same nine kinds of problems that other students have. However, veterans also encounter some problems in ways that are not problems to non-veteran students.

Veterans need to, and have the right to know what problems they will encounter in college that are specific to veterans. They have the right to know how a college: selects veterans to become students and how it provides help for veterans to: make the transition to college; acquire the academic skills needed in college; adjust to the culture of the college; learn how to interact well with professors, administrators, and students in college; successfully finance a college education; obtain transfer credits; participate productively in college programs; maintain their health; and find employment on graduation. A veteran needs to have some understanding of how each of these problems specific to veterans may be eliminated.

Most non-veterans in college-preparatory programs in high school are educated at that time how to deal with these nine problems. Non-veterans are also assisted in dealing with these problems as they are encountered in college. Sometimes they are provided additional assistance by family members who have attended college, fraternities or sororities to which they belong, and friends with a college background. Veterans, however, usually have not taken a college-preparatory program in high school, and normally have had a long time between high school and the start of college due to time in the service, that makes academic life a bit more difficult. Also, many veterans come from first college generation families and may not have relatives who had attended college or live too far away. Veterans are disinclined to join fraternities or sororities, and their friends are usually other veterans on campus. Despite these considerations, they have the right to be provided assistance not only comparable to non-veterans, but tailored to their needs.

Eliminating the College Problems of Veterans

In order that veterans are not discouraged from seeking a degree, they need help with eliminating certain problems associated with getting an education. The help they need will require the attention of college administrators and professors. Because veterans constitute less than 3% of the student body at most schools, the nature of their problems generally require the careful consideration of the professors and college administrators at the schools attended by veterans.

Although few educators are familiar with the college problems of veterans today, higher education possesses the expertise and ability to correct these problems by educating veterans and other participants in the education process. In addition, higher education also consists of professional organizations that serve to assist the process of higher education. For example, higher education organizations include the American Council on Education, the American Association of University Professors, and the Association of Colleges and University Administrators. These organizations possess expertise that could be marshaled to eliminate many of the college problems of veterans.

The Process of Eliminating the College Problems of Veterans

Besides reviewing the current problems that veterans encounter while seeking a degree, this book suggests ways that professors and college administrators may eliminate these problems. Each chapter ends with suggestions about what higher education may do to eliminate problems based on a particular category.

Sharing the knowledge of particular problems with professors and administrators, as well as students can eliminate many problems. For example, several problems can be shared through paper publications and through web courses along with knowledge on how to correct them. We also propose that pamphlets and/or web courses be given that can provide information needed about veterans service organizations concerned with the education of the veterans. Paper publications and web courses may additionally be used to instruct veterans about how to eliminate their problems.

The Plan for this Book

This book is comprised of three sections that examine the nature of the college problems of veterans and how some college administrators and professors in America's higher education can eliminate these problems. The first section of the book begins with an introduction about the need for this book. Chapter 1, this chapter, explains the kinds of problems and potential solutions to these problems by the three sectors of society as discussed above. Chapter 2 reviews the history of veterans and the education of veterans. Knowledge of the history of veterans and their education will be helpful for professors and college administrators to understanding the psychology of many veterans and the assumptions that veterans hold about the education they expect in college.

The second section has 10 chapters. Chapter 3 begins by providing a list of the specific problems that veterans have reported at various institutions. Then each of the chapters 4 through 12 addresses one of the nine kinds of problems and how each problem may be eliminated.

The third section examines broader issues on how to improve the education of veterans. Chapter 13 reviews the consequences of not eliminating the problems encountered by veterans in higher education. Chapter 14 proposes ways for helping veterans feel comfortable in higher education. Chapter 15 discusses how to improve higher education's overall approach to America's veterans. Chapter 16 addresses student veterans only and explains how veterans can eliminate their problems. The Epilogue presents an Educational Bill of Rights for veterans and discusses the responsibilities for veterans while they are students in college.

Summary

This chapter proposed that veterans, like all students, encounter a variety of problems in college. The chapter begins by discussing the scope of the problems encountered in college and then explains how these problems are different for students who are veterans and non-veterans. Some of the historical background for the book was presented as knowledge that would be useful for educators participating in the education of veterans today. Statistics that describe the lower attendance rate and degree completion were reviewed. The process for eliminating these problems for veterans was considered. Finally, the plan for the book was laid out as consisting of three sections with two or more chapters in each section. It was proposed at several points in the chapter that the college problems of veterans can be largely eliminated.

Chapter 2

The History of Efforts to Educate America's Veterans

The practice of giving veterans help in order to attend college is fairly recent in U.S. history. Education was not a necessity for veterans in the late 1700s, the 1800s, and in the 1900s prior to World War II. In those years, veterans returned to their farms or to the jobs they held before joining the military.

Manufacturing, business, and commerce became increasingly more technical in the middle of the 20th century. World War II itself was fought with technologies that no one had conceived a few years before the war. When the veterans returned after World War II, they came back to a more technical world than when they left. It was clear that America needed to educate these new veterans in order that they become able to find useful work needed by society. At the same time, society could benefit from the contributions of veterans due to their education, as well as their military experience.

Purpose of this Chapter

The goal of this chapter is to provide knowledge about veterans and about the veterans' education movement. This knowledge may help professors educate veterans and help administrators provide services for veterans. When an educator interacts with a veteran, it cannot be assumed that the student who is a veteran is the same as a non-veteran student of the same age. A veteran carries attitudes and beliefs acquired in military service. In addition, veterans are also products of different parts of society. An awareness of these factors can enable an educator to give the best education to students who are veterans.

Accordingly, this chapter begins with a quick review of the history of our military. This knowledge will help explain why a veteran's communication habits are different from those of non-veterans. Second, a veteran's ability to handle college, financially and otherwise, is a function of past and present government programs and private sector programs. Thus, the chapter reviews the history of the programs that have contributed to veterans seeking a college degree. Third, the chapter concludes with a brief assessment of what is known about the problems of veterans. Knowledge of the veterans' education movement and of the factors underlying the recent problems of veterans can assist educators in appreciating the bureaucratic and social challenges that must be dealt with by their students who are veterans.

America's Military History

Veterans are proud of their service. Any professor or college administrator who has not served in the military can teach and interact better with veterans by knowing some of the history in which veterans take pride. Veterans are aware that countless Americans have defended our democratic values to help keep the peace in our nation and in nations around the world. Veterans know that many American servicemen and servicewomen have fought bravely under the most horrific conditions. In many cases, some of today's students are veterans who have done so.

America's veterans have risked or sacrificed their lives for more than 230 years to protect the freedoms established by the founders of our great nation (Department of Veterans Affairs, 2004). Our service men and women have participated in one or more of approximately 40 conflicts in which the United States has been involved. Table 2.1 lists the major conflicts in which America has been involved and the number of American military killed in action (KIA) in those conflicts (The numbers in this table originate from several sources: Congressional Research Service, 2008; Marley, 1998, and presented at several web sites). When a professor or an administrator interacts with a student who is a veteran, this student feels that he or she is part of this history.

Different Kinds of Efforts to Help Veterans

A variety of ways have been developed to help veterans, regardless of when or where they have served. Many veterans serve during peacetime, but this fact should not lead to a conclusion that these veterans have not made a sacrifice for our country.

Table 2.1
The Wartime Sacrifices of American Military Men and Women

Name of War		Killed in Action
Revolutionary War	1775-1783	4,435 c
War of 1812	1812-1814	2,260 c
Naval War with France		
(Undeclared)	1798-1801	20
War with the Barbary		
Pirates	1801-1805	
	and 1815	35
Mexican War	1846-1848	1,711
Civil War	1861-1865	
Union		360,000
Confederate		260,000
Spanish American	1899-1902	1,000
Philippine Islands	1899-1902	1,053
Indian Wars	1817-1898	
Indigenous peoples		45,000
Europeans and		
descendants		19,000
China Relief Expedition	1900-1901	13
Pacification of Nicaragua,	1912-1913	55
Interventions in Mexico	1914-1917	22
Pacification of Haiti and the		
Dominican Republic	1915-1918	26
World War I	1914-1918	53,402 c
World War II	1939-1945	292,131 (291,55
Korean War	1950-1953	33,651 (33,68:
Vietnam War	1961-1975	47,378 (47,410
Lebanon Peacekeeping	1982-1984	263
Panama	1989-1990	24
Desert Shield/Desert Storm	1990-1991	339
Somalia,	1992-1993	19
Yugoslav Wars	1991-2001	unknown
Afghanistan, Iraq, War		
on Terror as of	2001-2009	
March 31, 2009		more than 4300

Note: When possible, the numbers presented in this table have been
confirmed by two sources ("c") is put alongside of these numbers.

They will have given up early and valuable years of adulthood to our
country's defense. Many will have also experienced hazardous duty in many
unknown locations of various durations. Veterans who have served in combat

in some capacity will have had life threatening experience over a period of days, months, or years.

Veterans of peacetime and wartime need to make an adjustment after discharge. Different parts of society have sought to help veterans with this adjustment. Veteran service organizations, veteran support organizations, commercial veterans-assistance organizations, and the federal government have provided different kinds of assistance to veterans.

Veterans Service Organizations. After U.S. military conflicts, veterans have sought each other's company to: discuss their experiences, help each other make the transition to civilian life, and to share in the camaraderie that fellow veterans provide each other. Many of these informal veteran gatherings led to the formation of chartered veterans' organizations. Table 2.2 lists the major veterans' organizations founded by American veterans.

Professors and college administrators who have not served in the military should know that students who are veterans might belong to one or more of these organizations. These organizations continue to provide veterans with advice in the preparation of and management of a claim to the VA for medical assistance such as disability compensation, rehabilitation and educational funds, or other benefits (Dillingham, 1952; Roche, 2000). In some cases, a professor or an administrator may suggest that a veteran who is a student contact a veteran's service organization for advice on financial matters.

A new veteran service organization emerged in the 1990's. Called Veterans to Veterans (Vet to Vet), this organization consists of meetings of veterans in which all manner of veteran issues may be discussed anonymously. No membership fee is required. Those who attend generally find it beneficial to participate on one or more occasions (Straus, 2005). Also new organizations have been formed for veterans who work in academia (Academic Veterans Association) and for college educators who want to help veterans obtain a college degree (College Educators for Veterans in Higher Education).

Table 2.2
The Veterans Organizations Established After Major Conflicts

War	Society	Year
Revolutionary War	Society of Cincinnati	1783
Civil War	Grand Army of the Republic	1866
	United Confederate Veterans	1866
Spanish American War	United Spanish War Veterans	1898
World War I	Veterans of Foreign Wars	1913
	American Legion	1919
	Disabled American Veterans	1920
	Marine Corps League	1923
	Military Order of the Purple Heart	1932
World War II	American Veterans of World War II	1944
	Blinded Veterans of America	1945
	American Ex-Prisoners of War	1945
	Paralyzed Veterans of America	1946
Vietnam War	Vietnam Veterans of America	1972
	Vietnam Veterans Institute	1981
Korean War	Korean War Veterans	1985
	National Veterans Foundation	1992
War on Terror	Iraq and Afghanistan Veterans of America	2006

Note: The first President of the Society of Cincinnati was George Washington

Organizations that Support Members of the National Guard and Reserve. The jobs of members of the Guard and Reserve are protected when they are called to active duty by a law called the Uniformed Services Employment and Reemployment Rights Act (USERRA; U.S. Department of Labor, 2006). If a Guard member or reservist has a job at the time of deployment, his/her job must be held for up to five years until this person returns from active duty or deployment. If an employer violates this law, such as by firing a Guard member or Reservist who is about to be deployed or is returning from deployment, an organization the Employer Support of Guard and Reserve (ESGR, 2007) informs the employer of the legal consequences of failing to comply with USERRA (Department of Labor, 2006).

Commercial Veterans-Assistance Organizations. Several commercial veterans' organizations depend on fees paid to them to serve veterans and/or members of the active duty military. Some of these organizations function as web businesses. For example, Military.Com provides information about veteran-friendly colleges that have paid Military.Com to be listed among veteran-friendly colleges.

Veterans/Student Organizations. After past wars, veterans' organizations were established at some colleges and universities to escape from an academic environment that was still hostile to veterans (McDaniel, 2006). For example, after the Vietnam War veterans' organizations of students were established at Indiana State University, Indiana University, and Ivy Tech College campuses in Indiana; Pennsylvania State University; the University of Connecticut; and the University of Virginia. In 2008 the Student Veterans of America was established to provide veterans with a great deal of information for veterans about their rights on campus (Powers, 2008a,b). Also a non-Greek fraternity of veterans, known is Omega Delta Sigma, was formed. Fortunately, it has generally been found that the college/university organizations shielded veterans from anti-military attitudes and made them feel more welcomed.

Government and Private Sector Assistance to Veterans Education

After America's major conflicts, the American government has developed programs to help veterans and to express the nation's gratitude to them for their contributions to the nation's defense (VA History In Brief, 2006a,b). The Continental Congress offered a pension for U.S. military service in the Revolutionary War. In 1865, President Lincoln called upon Congress "to care for him who shall have borne the battle and for his widow and his orphan." Subsequently veterans were assisted by a series of agencies (the U.S. Veterans' Bureau, the Bureau of Pensions of the Interior Department and the National Home for Disabled Volunteer Soldiers) which eventually led to the Veterans Administration (VA) in 1930 and the Department of Veterans Affairs in 1988, which became a cabinet-level department in 1989. A brief history of the Department of Veterans affairs may be found in a report of the Veterans Administration (2007a); a more complete history of government efforts to help veterans may be found in the history of the Veterans Administration

(2007b). That part of the history presented here is concerned with the higher education of veterans.

The GI Bill

Origins and Development. On June 22, 1944, President Franklin D. Roosevelt signed into law the "Serviceman's Readjustment Act," better known as the "G.I. Bill of Rights." Under this legislation, the federal government provided World War II veterans with education, vocational training, loan guarantees for homes, farms, or businesses, unemployment pay, and assistance in job searches. In the 60-plus years since the first GI Bill was signed, more than 21 million veterans and family members have received education and training from the VA and later the Department of Veterans Affairs (Bound & Turner, 2002; Greenberg, 2004; Stanley, 2003)

In 1985, the Montgomery GI Bill (MGIB) became the newest federal program to provide education and training to our nation's veterans. This form of the GI Bill became the first to require servicemen and women to pay into the program while on active duty. The contributory nature of the MGIB was expected to give veterans an incentive to use their GI Bill funds. Unfortunately, this feature of the MGIB prevented veterans who did not have the presence of mind, or extra funds, to contribute to the MGIB, especially when they were young (from 17 to 21). So they were unable to receive any educational support after discharge.

Although few of today's veterans are aware of it, the GI Bill was controversial at first. The GI Bill did not originate only out of a desire to help veterans. It also was conceived to address the financial needs of veterans that were very apparent in the depression (Dickson & Allen, 2004; Gaines, 1945/2004; Mettler, 2005; Washton, 1945; Winter, 2005). Discussions at the end of World War II both favored and disfavored the idea of having veterans on campus (Clark, 1998; Gaines, 1945/2004; Ross, 1969; Wector, 1944; Weller, 1944). Some argued that veterans would not be sufficiently intelligent to succeed in college. Some were concerned about whether the typical college students would have difficulty getting along with those veterans who originate from a lower socio economic strata.

After World War II, veterans were recognized by many faculty and professors, as being more mature than the younger non-veteran students (Fine, 1947). Additionally, the GI Bill came to be praised as making higher education in America more democratic and less elite (Adams, 2000; Avery, 1946; Clark, 1998; Olson, 1974; Serow, 2004; Winter, 2005).

Veterans of the Korean and Vietnam wars received similar, but less extensive, benefits (Adams, 2000; Bound & Turner, 2002; Greenberg, 2004; Harris, 2005; Mettler, 2005; O'Donnell, 2002; Stanley, 2000, 2003). Generally, the GI Bill led many veterans to become educated (Lipsett & Smith, 1949; Todd, 1949; Washton, 1945). In all, since World War II, more than 21 million veterans and family members have received education and training from the VA. It should be noted that despite this large number, less than half of the veterans from any conflict have made use of their educational benefits (Department of Veterans Affairs, 1994; benefits (Veterans Administration, 1991; Veterans Information Service, 2003). The lowest use of educational benefits was that of Vietnam veterans (Teachman, 2005). Recently there was agreement that GI Bill does not provide veterans enough financial support for the costs of attending school (Adams, 2000; Asch, Kilburn, & Klerman, 1999; Ashby, 2002; Colloquy Live, 2005; Massey, 2000; Walters, 2006; Webb, 2007 and many others).

The First New GI Bill. In 1985, the Montgomery G.I. Bill (MGIB) required servicemen and women to pay into the program while on active duty. The contributory nature of the MGIB was expected to give veterans an incentive to use their MGI Bill. For those veterans who paid into the program, the Montgomery GI Bill provides up to 36 months of educational benefits for college, business, technical, correspondence or vocational courses, apprenticeship or job training, or flight school. The new 9/11 GI Bill does not require service members to contribute to their GI Bill account. Those service members who contributed prior to August of 2009 will be have their contribution returned.

Administration of the GI Bill On Campus. Many schools have representatives of the Registrar or Bursar of the college who validate a veteran's enrollment so that he or she can receive GI Bill benefits. In some cases, these university officials will steer veterans to other offices that they need help from. On some campuses, an administrator is there who is designated to help veterans with their problems.

The VA approves or disapproves a higher educational institution as being able to approve or disapprove students as recipients for GI Bill. Approved institutions have certifying officials who approve veterans who apply for GI

Bill for attending that school. Certifying Officials typically belong to the Association of Veterans Education.

The Second New GI Bill. For many years, people in and out of government recognized that the MGI Bill did not provide adequate support for the costs of college (Anderson, 2004; Dyhouse, 2004; Gelber, 2005; Kime, 2006, 2007a,b; Webb, 2007; Partnership for veterans education, 2006; Trewyn, 1998; Young, 2005). While education has helped many service men and service women become upwardly mobile in our society (Massey, 2000), education does not improve a veteran's earning power as much as it does for non-veterans (Angrist, 1993; Anonymous, 2001; Berger, & Hiersch, 1983; Cohen, Segal, & Temme, 1992; Langbert & Wells, 1982; Pedan, 1987). Veterans programs should not be cut (Miami Times, 2005). Many veterans do not use MGIB (Snyder, 2002), possibly because they do not know how to apply for financial aid (Gilroy. 2007). Consequently, Congress passed a new version of the GI Bill in 2008 (Department of Veterans Affairs, 2008; Post 9/11, 2009).

As America became involved in a new kind of war of terror (Greer, 2005), an inequity became apparent between the Guard/Reserve GI Bill and personnel in the active duty military component that needs to be resolved. A "total force MGIB" was proposed to treat all military personnel in the same way if the length of service is equal. Portability of education benefits for members of the Guard and Reserve is necessary if they are activated for at least one year under contingency operations orders. The problem was that, although they become 'veterans' after their activation, they were not permitted to use any of their MGIB benefits in civilian life after separation from the Guard/Reserves. The new Post 9/11 GI Bill attempted to correct for such inequities (VA Pamphlet, 2008; IJAV, 2008).

VA Affiliated Veterans Education Organizations

Research, Training, and Employment Support. The VA encourages research on education of veterans. Not-for-profit organizations that conduct such research include the: National Association of Veterans' Research and Education Association (NAVREF, 2006); National Association of Veteran's' Program Administrators (NAVPA, 2006); and the National Veterans Training Institute. The Veterans' Employment & Training Service (VETS) provides veterans and transitioning service members with information that enable them to find employment and succeed in the workplace by protecting their employment rights and meeting labor-market demands with qualified personnel. Also, the e-VETS Resource Advisor assist veterans as they are preparing to enter the job market.

Veterans' Advisory Committee on Education. This committee was formed in the 1990s to provide advice on education and training to the Secretary of Veterans Affairs regarding programs for veterans and servicemembers, reservists and dependents of veterans. This advice concerns immediate and long range needs and may pertain to administrative changes and legislative proposals. The committee is made up of eminent people in education and was established by statute under Chapters 30, 32, 35, and 36, Title 38, and Chapter 1606 of Title 10, United States Code.

Servicemembers Opportunity Colleges (SOC)

A Need for Higher Educational Support of Veterans. During the Vietnam War and at its end, many Americans protested the continuation of the War (Anderson, 2002; Allen, Herrmann, & Giles, 1995; Appy, 1992; Batteiger, 1993; Bonior, Champlain, & Kolly, 1984; Brady & Rapport, 1973; Burkett, 1998; Capps, 1982; Caputo, 1978; Card, 1983; Dolan, 1989; Emerson, 1972; Goldman & Fuller, 1983; Greene, 1989; Herr, 1978; Helmer, 1974; Horne, 1981; Karnow, 1983; Kovic, 1984; Macpherson, 1984; Mason, 1990; O'Brian, 2003; Rollins, 1993; Rollins & Yates, 1995; Santolli, 1981; Strange, 1974; Thompson, 1997; Thorn & Payne, 1977; Van Devanter & Fuey, 1991; Yates, 1993, 2004). More than 100 books about the Vietnam War may be found on the Web. The protests against the war were especially intense at many colleges and universities where veterans were not welcomed (Burkett, 1998; Dolan, 1989; Magruder, 2002, 2003; Mason, 1990).

Many Americans believed after the war that the poor treatment of veterans was unfair. Moreover, many in government feared that active-duty service men and women, as well as veterans, would have a difficult time obtaining proper instruction and academic services on college campuses where protests were common. As a result, to facilitate the education of service members and veterans, the Department of Defense (DoD) established a program called the Servicemembers Opportunity Colleges (SOC) in 1972. The members of this organization consisted of institutions that promised to offer the same services to active duty military and veterans as offered to non-veteran students (Servicemembers Opportunity Colleges, 2004). Today, SOC consists of more than 1800 colleges and universities. SOC is cosponsored by the American Association of State Colleges and Universities (AASCU) and the American Association of Community Colleges (AACC), in cooperation with other educational associations, the Military Services, the National Guard, and the Coast Guard. SOC is funded by the Department of Defense (DoD) through a contract with AASCU that is managed for the DoD by the Defense Activity for Non-Traditional Education Support (DANTES), (SOC 2007).

Requirements for Membership. Each SOC higher educational institution is required to submit documents that demonstrated that it accepts credits transferred from other accredited institutions, and that its credits in turn are generally accepted by other accredited institutions. A SOC institution must correctly deal with academic residency requirements for active-duty service members. A SOC institution uses the ACE Guide for the evaluation of educational experiences in the Armed Services to determine the academic credit for appropriate learning acquired in military training and experience applicable to a veteran's program (Mullane, 2005). SOC institutions facilitate the admission and enrollment of qualified service members. These institutions also accept previously successful postsecondary study as part of the service member's or veteran's program requirements and nationally standardized tests. SOC institutions are supposed to correctly evaluate transfer credits earned through distance learning from accredited institutions.

Veterans Centers and Higher Education of Veterans

As noted above when discussing the formation of SOC, Vietnam veterans were treated poorly when these men and women returned home from the war (Burkett, 1998; Dolan, 1989; Mason, 1990), making them reluctant to attend college (Magruder, 2002, 2003; Mason, 1990). Due to this unfair treatment, a second program was established to help veterans adjust to civilian life and acquire a college education. This program consisted of establishing centers around the country in the early 1980's to help Vietnam veterans make the transition to American society and, where appropriate, persuading them to go to college (House Committee on Government Operations, 1981). Although these centers were created first to help Vietnam veterans, they have helped veterans of any subsequent war or military combat (e.g., Somalia) cope with emotional and physical problems acquired while serving in a war.

The Educational Mission of Centers

It became apparent to those who visited a center in the 1980's and 1990's that many Vietnam veterans did not want to be further educated or trained. Many of the Vietnam veterans who did attend college dropped out and never completed a degree. This reluctance to attend college or remain in college was mostly attributed to veterans feeling unwelcome on campus. Consequently, many veterans understandably did not want to attend college because, if they did, they would be most likely subjecting themselves to insults and derision from anti-war faculty, administrators, and students. The Vietnam veterans who did go on to college had many experiences of rejection on the campuses they attended.

This reluctance to attend college or remain in college was well known among Vietnam veterans and staff of the Veteran Centers. The staff members, who had clinical responsibilities in the Veteran Centers, found it difficult to encourage veterans to go to college when staff members themselves experienced harassment when they studied for their degrees or went on campus. Veterans who attended college in this period tended not to self-identify themselves as veterans for fear that they would be socially spurned and that some of those educators who were vocal about their opposition to war would not be as fair in grading veterans as in grading non-veterans.

Societal Efforts to Establish a New Rhetoric about Veterans

After the Vietnam War, many politicians, celebrities, other public figures and citizens concluded that America had learned that, regardless of their political affiliation or stance on war, people should not attack those service men and women who are sent to defend the nation. Society concluded that it was unfair to blame our military and veterans for participating in a war that the public disapproved.

Unfortunately, some politicians, celebrities, and other public figures have recently concluded that they could again voice anti-war attitudes if they claim that they supported the troops while being opposed to a particular war. Nevertheless, many in our military and veterans as well, believe that such claims embolden the enemy and encourage them to attack American forces more often and more aggressively. Also claims to support the troops, while opposing a war, give the military no more cover than it had before and it was held by many veterans to dishearten soldiers, sailors, airmen, and marines, making them more error prone in battle (Baars, 1992; Hoffman, Roesner, & McCandles, 2006).

Efforts to Defuse Rhetoric About Veterans. No social program was developed during or after the Vietnam era to neutralize the rejection of veterans by faculty, administrators, and students. Eventually, one social change by the federal government seemed to have helped many Americans to cease holding negative attitudes towards America's military and veterans. The change involved eliminating the Selective Service System draft young males and made the military an all-volunteer force. By exempting American males from obligatory military service, the voicing of anti-war attitudes became largely unnecessary.

Many of the protesters during the Vietnam War, who frequently did not serve in the military, received educational deferments, became educated, and joined the faculties of many colleges and universities that veterans must attend today. These professors sometimes speak with pride of their role as protestors of the Vietnam War. On hearing anti-military sentiments, some veterans who attend college even now tend not to self-identify themselves as veterans for fear that they would be socially spurned.

Recent Problems of Veterans in College

The Burdens of Veterans in College

Common Burdens. Veterans of any war have found it challenging to return and go to school for additional training and education. Veterans have less time and energy to devote to their studies than non-veterans because veterans have to make more of an effort to adjust to college than their civilian counterparts. This difference in time and energy results in veterans finding college more difficult than non-veterans.

Current Burdens of Veterans. After World War II, Korea, and Vietnam, professors and administrators were familiar with veterans and some of their problems. However, as the Vietnam War faded in the memories of Americans, fewer and fewer professors and administrators understandably were familiar with the college problems of veterans. Alternatively, in the past few years, the number of complaints about such problems has been on the increase (Herrmann, 2007a,b; Herrmann, Raybeck, & Wilson, 2008). Despite claims to support our troops, recently there are more reports than in previous years that some faculty, administrators, and students sometimes engage in actions that make veterans feel uncomfortable (Magruder, 2005a). They make veterans feel this way by engaging in anti-war protests (Campus Antiwar Network, 2003, 2004; Gillman, 2002; Hall, 2007; Hall & Schweizer, 2005; Herrmann, 2007a,b; Johnson, 2007; Lehrer, 2002; Magruder, 2005b; Marklein, 2007; Penzenstadler, 2007; Petrovic, 2006; Pierre, 2003; Rosenzweig, 2002; Sinner, 2008; Sparta/Gannett, 2008; Students for a Democratic Society, 2008; Steigmeyer, 2009; Traina, 2004; Wilkes-Edrington, 2007; R. Wilson, 2006; You Tube, 2003), by protesting the presence of recruiters on campus (365 Gay.Com, 2007; Butchjax, 2005; Brown, 2006; Democracy Now, 2005; George, 2005; Lane. 2005; LawMemo, 2006; Maclean & Roller , 2005; Malladi, 2005; Malkin, 2008; Mangan, 2005; Mears, 2005; North, 2005; Traina 2004; see Lederman, 1997). Recent trends have also been to protest the presence of ROTC facilities on campus (Hohmann, 2007; Lewin, 1990; Parade, 2008). In addition, there have been some reports that the number of veterans who feel uncomfortable on campus is substantial (Herrmann, 2007a,b). Some veterans are reported to avoid college all together because they feel they are not welcomed there (McDaniel, 2006).

Alternatively, the overall post-Vietnam atmosphere has been less hostile to veterans in recent years than in the several years after the Vietnam War. Apparently, the inclination to treat veterans poorly has decreased as the memories of that war have faded. Additionally, the anti-terror feelings of Americans since 9.11.01 may have also made it more acceptable recently to consider what should be done for our veterans while they seek a degree. Some articles have proposed that veterans are treated well on campus today (Gruder, 2008; Heller, 2006; McDaniel, 2006; Nelson, 2006; Harmeyer, 2007; Lanigan, 2007). Nevertheless, while some articles indicated that veterans are well received and treated better on some campuses than veterans were received and treated after the Vietnam war, four times as many articles report campus activities that make veterans feel uncomfortable on campus (anti-war protests, protests of recruiters on campus, and protests of the presence of ROTC on campus).

Why the Burdens of Veterans Have Escaped Attention. Why hasn't more attention been given to veterans problems in higher education before now? Several organizations might have recognized these problems but have not reacted. Certifying officials, members of National Association of Veterans Program Administrators (NAVPA, 2006), who are responsible for verifying whether a veteran is properly enrolled at a college, might have been expected to detect the educational challenges facing veterans. The VA office of Research and Development has solved many veterans' medical problems but has not focused on the veterans-education problem. The US House of Representatives Committee on Veterans Affairs or the US Senate Committee on Veterans 'Affairs have given considerable attention to the financial problems and transfer problems of veterans in college but have yet to address the other categories of problems. Veteran's service organizations have yet to pay serious attention to these problems. However, the important point is not why the higher-education problems of veterans have gone unnoticed until recently. Instead, the important point is how to rectify the problem now that it is evident.

What Colleges and Universities Can Do To Use Knowledge About the History of Veterans and Government Programs to Help Veterans

Because veterans are a minority on campus, they tend to feel different than non-veteran students and non-veteran professors and administrators. This feeling of isolation makes them feel excluded from the educational process occurring there. Colleges and universities can take steps to prevent this from occurring by familiarizing professors and administrators with the military history that veterans are a part of.

The recent memories of non-veterans out of high school are different from the recent memories of veterans. Non-veterans out of high school still reflect on high school, their prom, and their last summer before college. In contrast, veterans reflect on their military training, recent duty assignments, past deployments and family. If a professor or administrator knows or recognizes that a student is a veteran, he or she can help that veteran become a better student simply by showing awareness and respect for his or her military background.

Summary

Improving the attendance of veterans to college and the rate of degree completion can do a great deal to ensure that veterans make the best use of their veteran education benefits and have a successful life. This chapter reviewed knowledge that professors and college administrators can use in interacting with veterans. The chapter began by briefly summarizing the military history of America, a history that veterans feel part of whether or not they have served in combat. The chapter also reviewed the history of the government and private sector assistance provided to the educating of veterans. Finally, information about the recent college problems of veterans was examined. Knowledge of the history of American military conflicts, the veteran education movement and the recent problems of veterans can help educators to better understand the bureaucratic and social burdens that are encountered by their students who are veterans. This knowledge should facilitate the teaching of veterans and the providing of services needed by veterans.

Section II.

Factors that Discourage Attending and Completing College

Chapter 3

Problems Reported by Veterans in Higher Education

The purpose of this chapter is to acquaint the reader with the kinds of complaints veterans have been raising about their college experience. Many veterans have reported to the authors having encountered problems that have discouraged them from attending or completing college.

Below are 57 specific problems that were reported to the authors by veterans. They are presented here in a non-verbatim form. As may be seen, these problems are numerous and diverse. These problems are presented below according to the nine categories of problems discussed in Chapter 1 and examined in the remaining nine chapters of this section: selecting a college, making a transition to college, acquiring academic skills, adjusting to a college's culture, finding out about the educational programs of a school, meeting the financial requirements of a school, successfully transferring credits, maintaining one's health, and finding employment on graduation.

The wording of some problems appears to indicate that the school is the source of the difficulty encountered. The wording of other problems indicates that a professor, administrator, or student creates the difficulty. The authors point out that it is always possible that a veteran raises a complaint that he or she believes to be true but in actuality may not be. For example, a miscommunication between veterans and educators may make a problem out of a situation that actually is not problematic. Nevertheless, real or imagined, problems interfere with the academic performance of veterans and make it less likely that a veteran will eventually obtain a degree. Therefore, a first responsibility of this book is to identify the problem or problems that different veterans experience. The second responsibility is to develop ways to eliminate these problems.

Specific Problems of Veterans per Category

Note: 'School' below stands for a college or university.

I. Selection of a College or University to Attend—Some schools fail, or seem to fail, to provide correct information pertinent to the selection of a college to attend.

1. My school appeared to be friendly before I enrolled but has not turned out to be friendly.

2. I could not find a book or web site that explains whether the school I am attending would be good for veterans such as me.

3. My school told me that as a veteran I would get lots of financial aid and scholarships but I have not.

4. My school told me that as a veteran I would get all of the transfer credits approved by military but that has not turned out to be true.

5. My school told me that as a veteran I would be able to major in the topic of my military occupational specialty but I have not been able to do so.

III. Transition—Some schools fail, or seem to fail, to provide veterans with information that may help them with adjustment problems in college.

6. My school does not inform veterans about the culture at this school and how a veteran can fit into that culture.

7. My school does not inform veterans about the administrative problems that they may encounter at their school.

III. Acquiring Academic Skills—Some schools fail, or seem to fail, to provide veterans with help with acquiring academic skills.

8. My school does not make allowances for the lack of a college preparatory program in their background when deciding whether to admit veterans.

9. My school does not provide veterans with preparatory instruction in academic skills before entering college (such as how to take notes, to learn in class, to participate in laboratories for courses that require them, to learn outside of class, to make use of study groups outside of class, to learn from a tutor when necessary, to take exams, quizzes, multiple choice, essay, write term papers, academic standards regarding cheating and plagiarism).

10. My school does not provide veterans with appropriate tutoring in academic skills or in course material after entering college.

11. My school does not take into account a veteran's military occupational specialty when providing veterans with advice about what courses to take.

IV. Campus Culture—Some schools fail, or seem to fail, to educate veterans about their campus culture, leading veterans to sometimes be upset by events on campus.

12. A professor or some professors at my school openly make false negative statements in class about military service.

13. A professor or some professors at my school do not give veterans help during class while non-veterans are given help. For example, some professors do not answer questions raised by students in class whom the professor knows are veterans.

14. A professor or professors at my school gives lower grades to veterans than they expected.

15. Administrators at my school say anti-military or anti-veteran comments to students knowing they are veterans.

16. Administrators at my school give veterans the brush off or ignore them.

17. At my school, when a veteran files a grievance, it generally fails more often than do the grievances of non-veteran students.

18. Non-veteran students say disrespectful and slanderous things to veterans about military service at my school.

19. Non-veteran students at my school ask inappropriate questions about hazardous duty or combat experiences of mine. (Such as, "what does it feel like to kill someone?").

20. A professor, administrator, and/or non-veteran student at my school sometimes made prejudicial assertions about veterans. (For example, "veterans are stupid" or "veterans are killers.")

21. At my school some professors give veterans a brush off or ignore them in class or after class.

22. At my school some professors fail to give students academic help once they know these students are veterans.

V. Educational-Program Problems – Some schools fail, or seem to fail, to provide veterans with information that they need to participate in standard educational programs.

23. My college's orientation program does not present any specific information to help veterans.

24. The explanation of a student's curriculum provided by my school does not address how veterans might design a plan of study.

25. My advisor at my school is not prepared to enable veterans to major or minor (MOS related) in the specialty that they acquired while in the service.

26. Advisors at my school do not advise a veteran about course selection while taking account of prior military training and experience

27. The administrators, professors and staff at my school assume that all veterans are in the Upward Bound program.

28. My school does not provide training in study skills that have been designed specifically for veterans.

29. Some professors at my school have penalized Guard members for missing class in order to attend drills.

VI. Financial Problems—Some schools fail, or seem to fail, to provide veterans with appropriate financial-aid procedures and information.

30. My school requires a veteran to use his or her GI Bill to pay for all of tuition and fees as soon as possible after enrolling, or lose enrollment.

31. My school subtracts GI Bill from the financial aid that a veteran could receive.

32. My school does not include a veteran's costs of living (meals and transportation) in the total costs of an education.

33. The financial aid offices of my school provide little or no financial aid to recently discharged veterans because these veterans received pay in his or her last year of military service, pay that a discharged veteran no longer receives. (Schools that use this financial procedure do not do so for veterans who do not start college in a year after they leave the service).

34. My school does not have scholarships tailored to the background of veterans.

35. My school does not provide assistance in finding financial support for veterans who have a family.

VII. Academic-Credit Problems—Some schools fail, or seem to fail, to provide veterans with appropriate procedures to transfer their credits to the school's academic credits.

36. My school gives veterans little or no transfer credit for their military training and experience.

37. My school does not give veterans academic credit for the physical education they received in the military.

38. My school does not give appropriate academic credit and a grade for work completed by members of the Reserve or the National Guard or Reserve prior to being deployed before a semester ends.

39. My school will not re-admit some Guard or Reserve members after deployment, requiring reapplication to continue enrollment at this school.

40. My school will assign a withdrawal for the courses taken by Guard members or Reservists at the time of deployment without asking whether he or she wanted a withdrawal for these courses.

41. My school will assign a withdrawal for the courses taken by Guard members or Reservists at the time of deployment but not give a refund for the courses that were not taken.

42. My school will assign an incomplete for the courses taken by Guard members or Reservists at the time of deployment without asking whether he or she wanted an incomplete for these courses

43. My school will assign a low grade for each course taken at the time of deployment without allowing the Guard member or Reservist to take an incomplete in these courses.

44. My school will assign a low grade for an incomplete, started by Guard members or Reservists before deployment and finished after deployment, without allowing for enough time to finish the incomplete.

VIII. Health Problems—Some schools fail, or seem to fail, to provide needed health care for military service-connected or possibly service-connected disabilities.

45. My school does nothing to help students who have physiological and emotional disabilities that have been determined to be service connected by the VA.

46. My school does nothing to help veterans who have physiological and emotional disabilities that arise in college but may be due to military service.

47. My school's health service will not treat me on an emergency basis for any disability that may have arisen because of military service.

48. My school's health service will not treat symptoms of PTSD because they believe that their school was not responsible for treating veterans with their medical problems.

49. My school's health service will not treat symptoms of a concussive head injury because they believe that their school was not responsible for treating veterans with their medical problems that were service-connected.

50. My school's health services will not treat symptoms of stress and other illnesses of the family of veterans because they believe that their school was not responsible for treating the families of veterans with their medical problems).

IX. Employment Problems for Veterans at Graduation – Some schools fail, or seem to fail, to give veterans all of the help they need for finding a job after graduation.

51. My school's career center will not search for jobs for which military training and experience are relevant for veterans who graduate.

52. My school's career center will not have alumni who are veterans help veterans who graduate find jobs but they do have alumni who primarily are non-veterans help non-veteran graduates find jobs for them.

53. My school's career center counselors are not familiar with resources to help veterans find jobs (such as employers who are veterans, and military-related

web sites, such as VeteranEmployment.com, Military Connection, Military Exits, and Military Job Zone).

54. A staff member at my school's career center has told me that I should rely primarily on the VA to find me a job.

55. The staff members at my school's career center are not familiar with the skills that veterans offer employers (e.g. problem-solving ability, interpersonal skills, communication ability, and leadership ability).

56. The career center at my school offers less help to veterans than to non-veterans on how to find a job.

57. The staff of my school's career center does not know how to help veterans plan for a career while taking account of the veteran's military background.

Problems that Demand the Most Attention

The preceding list consists of numerous problems that a veteran may encounter as he or she seeks a degree. There are several caveats that apply to this list. The authors do not claim that this list is exhaustive. In other words, we cannot claim to have heard all possible complaints of veterans. The authors found that no one veteran reported encountering a great number of these problems. Similarly not all veterans at a school reported experiencing the same problems. No particular problem appears to occur at all schools. Some higher educational institutions probably do not confront veterans with problems.

Any problem in one of the nine categories demands attention when it deters any veteran from working to get a college degree. It might be assumed that the problems that demand the most attention are the ones that are most commonly experienced by veterans. Unfortunately almost no research has addressed the frequency with which different problems are encountered by veterans.

The little research that is available involved asking CEOs, or their representatives, of colleges and universities in Indiana how often different categories of problems had been the target of complaints made by members of the National Guard at their school (Herrmann, 2007a). This research found that about 31% of the schools that responded to the survey (61% of Indiana school) had heard some complaints. The percentage of schools reporting complaints was: 25% concerning difficulties in obtaining transfer credits; 23% concerning how educational programs were not responsive to them; 19% concerning a campus climate that was unfriendly to those with a military background; 17% concerning difficulties in adjusting socially on campus; 15% concerning difficulties in getting health care on campus; and 8% concerning administrative difficulties that arose when they were deployed. As may be noted, the survey did not address all of the nine categories of veterans' problems in college. In addition, the survey did not address particular problems within these categories. Research is needed that may assess the frequency with which each of the 57 problems is encountered by veterans.

Another study examined how often reports of services are appropriate for service members and veterans (Sternberg, MacDermid, Vaughan, & Carlson, 2009). In general, this study found that certain services were being provided infrequently and certain schools provided fewer services than other schools.

What Colleges and Universities Can Do About Specific College Problems of Veterans

Elimination of a veteran's college problem(s) requires first determining if any problem occurs on campus. Then professors and administrators can start to help eliminate a veteran's problems at their school. A college or university may determine whether their veterans are voicing essentially the same problems listed here by listening to the concerns expressed by their veterans. To help with this, surveys are presented later in the book that may be used to assess veterans' problems on a campus.

The following chapters present information that educators can use to address the category to which a veteran's problem may belong. Each succeeding chapter presents suggestions at its end of the chapter about what might be done to eliminate the problems discussed in the chapter.

Summary

Veterans have reported encountering various problems in the nine categories discussed in Chapter 1. This chapter has presented 57 problems reported by veterans. The authors found that no one veteran reported encountering a great number of these problems. Similarly not all veterans at a school reported experiencing the same problems. It was noted that some veterans might believe that they had a certain problem but this may not have been the case. Nevertheless, even when reports are not valid, they constitute a basis for poor morale on the part of the veterans who make the reports. Elimination of the problems of veterans at a particular school requires that some determination of whether these problems actually occur, or are believed to occur, at that school.

Chapter 4
Selection of a College or University to Attend

Veterans face a confusing situation when they decide to apply for college. Some schools appear to not want veterans on their campus. Other schools appear to want veterans very much. This brief chapter reviews this situation, how schools may differ in their treatment of veterans, and how colleges and universities may help veterans make the right choice of a school.

Selecting a school to attend is very difficult for veterans. They do not have a guidance counselor to advise them about the schools they consider. A very small number of schools employ dishonest individuals who will promise anything to veterans in order to get them to enroll. Alternatively, a small number of schools will make an honest effort to persuade veterans to attend.

Veterans need counselors, similar to a high school guidance counselor, to advise them where to go to college. Veterans should not be limited to state sponsored schools due to limitations in the funding available to veterans. Instead, they should also be able to attend private, high status schools supported by scholarships as well based on good counseling.

Selection of a Veteran-Friendly School

Veterans face a confusing situation when they decide to apply for college. Ideally, veterans want to study at a veteran-friendly school or at least the most veteran-friendly school that provides the education of the specialty that a veteran wants. Next we describe what constitutes a veteran friendly school and a veteran-unfriendly school.

Veteran-Friendly Schools
Some colleges and universities cater to veterans. Veteran-friendly

schools are generally identifiable. These schools typically have a substantial number of their professors and administrators who are veterans. Veteran-friendly schools typically have individuals who either volunteer or are on the staff to advise veterans about their problems and help them eliminate the major problems.

These schools normally do not confront veterans with the different kinds of problems that are discussed in this book. Veterans have their GI Bill paid without difficulty. Their financial aid is not based on an estimate of total cost of education that has been reduced by their GI Bill. They are awarded academic credits for their military credits without having to fight the school for these credits. The school may also offer some scholarships and/or grants for veterans.

A veteran-friendly school's educational programs inform veterans about what they need to know. Their campus climate is, of course, clearly friendly toward veterans. Professors, administrators, and other students do not say insulting things to them about the military or veterans. Advisors know about military occupational specialties and provide career advice that takes account of the student's MOS, should the veterans want to pursue a degree in a program that is similar to what they performed while in the military. The health services of veteran-friendly schools treat the emergency needs of veterans' service-connected medical problems. The career centers conduct employment searches for soon-to-be or new graduates in a manner that takes account of the graduate's military background, as well as the veteran's major or minor.

Veteran-Unfriendly Schools

These schools normally do not openly state that they do not want or welcome veterans on their campus or that they will not be helpful to veterans, but veterans discover that the school is unfriendly after being there for a while. Nearly all veteran-unfriendly schools had a reputation for not wanting the military or veterans on campus during and after the Vietnam War. Many colleges still cling to the veteran unfriendly reputation, or at least do not go out of their way for veterans. Some schools may even try to frighten them away by clinging to their anti-military reputation.

What complicates this further is that many Vietnam-era professors are still teaching or acting as administrators in public as well as private schools.

Some of these professors and administrators still proudly boast about their anti-military activities that they engaged in during their youth. Also many of the younger professors have developed anti-military attitudes while teaching under the influence of Vietnam era faculty. Veterans who nevertheless enroll in veteran's unfriendly schools while being aware of the schools' reputation later discover that their school is indeed unfriendly worse than expected. These schools offer few if any of the rights, benefits and help that veterans have at veterans friendly schools or that students enjoy at any school.

These unfriendly schools typically offer no scholarships for veterans and their educational programs offer no information for veterans. The campus cultures are also unfriendly toward veterans. Many professors and administrators insult the military or veterans, and similarly students make veterans feel unwelcome. Advisors do not know about military occupational specialties and do not provide career advice that ignores military backgrounds. The schools' health services refuse to treat emergency needs of veterans' medical problems unless they are enrolled in the health program for students. The career centers conduct an employment search for soon-to-be or new graduates in a manner that does not consider military backgrounds which decreases the number of opportunities available for veterans.

Seemingly Veteran-friendly but actually Veteran-unfriendly Schools

Some schools present themselves as veteran friendly but are not. These schools try to enroll veterans in order to obtain the money GI Bill pays them. Some of these schools engage in other shoddy business practices and are dishonest to veterans. For example, they may claim to provide a major in which a veteran is interested in, but actually do not. They also may claim to transfer all the veteran's military credits that are in line with ACE guidelines, but actually do not. In some cases, veterans are asked to sign a contract that promise that they will get all of their education at the school, rendering them indebted for the whole amount of education.

Schools That Atone for How Academia Treated Veterans after the Vietnam War. Most members of academia recognize that veterans were treated badly by higher education after the Vietnam War. They admit that they mistakenly treated the Vietnam veteran badly because they objected to the war when the object of their protest should have been the government and neither the military nor veterans. Because academia recognizes its mistaken treatment of veterans after Vietnam, professors, college administrators, and staff claim to have rehabilitated themselves and to treat veterans of today fairly.

However, this new good treatment of veterans is sometimes superficial. As discussed recently in the Chronicle of Higher Education, veterans still encounter a variety of problems at many of today's colleges and universities (Herrmann, Raybeck, & Wilson, 2008). This book examines the problems recognized in the Chronicle article and many more problems that occur in higher education today.

The overt hostility encountered by Vietnam veterans occurs far less frequently on campus today – but it still does occur. The hostility may be less direct. Instead of physical protest, some professors now lecture in class about how America should not be involved in the current war and/or that the behavior of today's military is shameful.

Many problems encountered by today's veterans arise out of administrative ignorance of the needs of veterans. Ignorance can be forgiven to a point. Unfortunately, when veterans point out these problems, professors and administrators often deny the existence of these problems; and they do not make an effort to correct the problem. In other words, today's colleges and universities may not be overtly anti-veteran but when it comes to helping veterans with their problems, many of their professors and administrators fail to eliminate these problems. While they may not be overtly anti-veteran, their lack of assistance to veterans makes them appear to be this way. This book reviews both the intentional and unintentional problems that veterans encounter in college today.

Determining Whether a School is Veteran-Friendly

Sources about What Colleges Are or Are Not Veteran Friendly. There are no such sources. Veterans should be advised independently where to go to school. Veterans should be planning to attend the best schools possible. However, with few exceptions (Harmeyer, 2007) this class of schools currently does not actively seek out qualified veterans to attend them.

Veteran-Friendliness Must be Estimated from Certain Information. It is difficult at any one point in time for a veteran to know for sure whether a school is truly anti-military. One indicator that a school is anti-military is conspicuous to veterans: a recent rejection of a ROTC program by the school. Approximately 800 colleges and universities have ROTC programs (GoArmy.Com., 2007). That leaves many schools that do not have such a program (Hohmann, 2007).

Another indicator is whether a school has prohibited military recruiters from working on campus (Brown, 2006; Lane. 2005; Lederman, 1997; Petrovic, 2006: Traina, 2004). The Solomon Act prohibits funding to schools that prohibit recruiters from working on campus, although this act has been challenged (Train, 2004). Yet another indicator is the school's history regarding having had protest movements in the past or in the present. Many colleges and universities were the context for protests during the Vietnam era (Magruder, 2002; Mason, 1990; Trewyn & Stever, 1995). Some colleges and universities are the scene for protests today (Hall & Schweitzer, 2005; Magruder, 2002, 2005b). The bottom line here is that a history of protests at colleges and universities in the past or present makes veterans feel uncomfortable while attending such institutions.

The Admission Process

Veteran and non-veteran students do not compete to get into college on a level playing field. Non-veteran students are prepared by their high school and their parents to get into the best college possible. Non-veteran students acquire exposure in high school to what courses are like in college. They are instructed by their school on what they need to do to increase their chances for college. They get advice on what schools at which they have a good chance of being accepted. Many non-veteran students take courses to prepare for college-entrance exams.

Few veterans acquire exposure in high school to what courses are like in college because veterans typically do not take a college-preparatory program when in high school. Consequently, they were not groomed for college in high school on what they need to do to increase their chances for college. Few veterans get advice about where to apply for college or take courses to prepare for college-entrance exams. Veterans also have a disadvantage of having many years off between studying in high school and then wanting to go to college so their study skills may not be as sharp.

Consequently, veterans tend to be assessed by colleges as not having a good potential or less potential than their non-veteran applicants. Therefore, even if a veteran and a non-veteran possess similar native intelligence, the veteran is less likely to be accepted by a good school as a non-veteran.

Financial Problems of Veterans in the Admission Process

On leaving the service, veterans are not encouraged to apply for the best school, as are their non-veteran counterparts when in high school. The Ivy League and top tier state and public schools do not seek veterans to apply nor offer them scholarship or incentives to apply. Because they do not have the funds to apply to Ivy League schools, some first tier state schools, and private schools, veterans usually do not apply for or get admitted into those schools.

Veteran Educational-Support Businesses

Various businesses make money by advertising for schools that claim they are military friendly. Some of these schools appear to be an extension of the federal government or to have the blessing of the U.S. military. Presently, there is no national system that evaluates colleges and universities, although the SOC schools require its members to promise to treat active-duty military and "veterans" appropriately (Servicemembers Opportunity Colleges, 2004).

The VA web site lists some schools as "approved," but does not explain what approved means. This does not mean that the school has been approved because the school is veteran friendly. All that the VA approval means is that the school has been approved to certify whether a student is a veteran. A VA approved school will be in some cases a veteran unfriendly school.

College Application Centers Needed for Veterans

High school students have advisors and special programs that help them prepare and apply for the most appropriate college. Veterans have no such system but one is much needed. No branch of the military provides advice to active duty personnel about how to plan specifically for a college education after they eventually are discharged or retire. Active duty personnel should be advised early in their first tour of duty about college entrance exams and about the benefits of preparing for these exams well ahead of taking them.

However, every branch of the military has education specialists who brief service men and women on active duty, as they are about to be discharged or retire. Unfortunately, these briefings do not address the particular criteria that these personnel should consider when selecting a college, how to prepare for such college or colleges, and whether a particular school may be appropriate for them. Veteran Centers of the federal DVA or state VA could take on this task of such advising, with the addition of properly trained staff. Colleges and universities should also prepare to advise veterans on their choice of school.

What Colleges and Universities Can Do to Help Veterans Select the Appropriate College or University

Veterans, like other students, base their selection of a college in part on what various schools tell them about themselves. However, veterans need both the information that non-veterans have and also information that apply specifically to them. Colleges and universities can help veterans with making their choice of a school to attend by discussing with them how their school helps veterans obtain a degree. Veterans need an accurate review of what it is like for them who attend a school regardless of what the school is like otherwise. Veterans will primarily base their selection of a school on whether they will receive a good education in the major that they hope to pursue, the transfer of any earned credits they had from their military careers, financial ability to attend and quality of life on campus. They will adjust to a school better if they are aware of the kinds of problems they may encounter.

Eventually, the authors hope that a system is developed to provide veterans with the information they need about how various schools help veterans and that advise veterans about what schools would be best for them. For example, such a system might indicate the kinds of help available to veterans and explain whether the school provides majors and minors that are based on a veteran's military occupational specialty. Such a system is needed for advising veterans about what schools would be best for them and also for alerting veterans to the kinds of dishonest promises that may be made to them.

Summary

Selecting a college or university to attend is much more difficult for most veterans than it is for non-veterans. Some schools clearly want veterans on their campus while others do not. A very small number of schools are dishonest and will promise anything to veterans in order to get them to enroll. Almost no expensive, private, high status schools attempt to recruit or provide aid to veterans. Veterans need an advisor, similar to a high school guidance counselor, to counsel them on their choice of a school to attend. Such a system would indicate whether a school provides majors and minors that are based on a veteran's military occupational specialty and the kinds of problems veterans might encounter on campus.

Chapter 5
Making a Transition From Military life to College Life

Professors, college administrators, non-veteran students, and members of society in general know that making the transition to civilian life is difficult. Many movies have touched on this transition experience, for example, the movie "From Here to Eternity." The transition of veterans to college life has not received the same attention but this transition is just as taxing. Professors and college administrators, who have not been in the military, still remember the stress of their own transition to college. However, there are many aspects of veterans' transition from the military to civilian life and to college life that would be unfamiliar to a professor or a college administrator unless he or she had served in the military earlier in life

The Purpose of this Chapter

This chapter has the goal of conveying what the transitions are like for veterans. It is hoped that the knowledge in this chapter will enable professors and college administrators to help veterans who study at their institutions with their transition from military to college life (Allen, 1987, 2003). Many veterans have a period of time elapse between discharge and entering into college. So before covering a veteran's transition to college life, our first consideration here is a veteran's transition from military to civilian life. This transition will be difficult for all veterans (Quillen-Armstron, 2007; Stiglitz & Bilmes, 2008), especially for combat veterans and disabled veterans. It is more difficult for veterans who were drafted than those veterans who voluntarily entered the military (MacLean, 2005). It has been asserted that the transition for veterans today is easy (Heller, 2006), but very rarely is this the case (Hall & Schweizer, 2005; Magruder, 2005b; Mears, 2005; Petrovic, 2006, Trewyn & Stever, 1995).

Subsequently, the chapter reviews what the transition is like when a veteran heads off to college or university. Those veterans who wait several months, a year or two before beginning college will have already made the transition from the military to civilian life, but they still will have to make the transition from civilian life to college life, which involves several more transition tasks. Besides coping with an unfriendly climate on many campuses, veterans must start adjusting to the academic demands of college. Many veterans will also have to improve their study skills and broaden their understanding of learning.

The Transition to Civilian Life

As noted above, it is well known to many non-veterans that a veteran's transition from military life to civilian life is not easy (Bascetta, 2002; Berry, 1977; Coeyman, 2001; Cornelius, 1993; Enzie, Sawyer, & Montgomery, 1973; Leisner, 1995; Stiglitz & Bilmes, 2008; Wector, 1944; Weller, 1944). Transition tasks include ceasing to depend on the military to take care of the many problems of a service member.

Transitions Made by all Veterans

Sometimes transition tasks are nearly overwhelming, especially for those veterans who have a spouse and family. To begin with, veterans have to move to a new location and adjust to a new situation. In addition, there are things to be learned about the cost-of-living in the "civilian world." Many in the military world disparage civilians and the civilian world, so veterans might see themselves entering not only a foreign culture, but also one that may harbor hostility toward them. Consequently, the new veterans will need to acquire new skills in order to live successfully.

Financial Transition. Veterans have to adjust some of their financial habits and learn to purchase certain products in local stores that often cost more than at Post Exchanges (PX) or Base Exchanges (BX). Civilians have to make their purchases at several locations. When veterans were on active duty, they purchased what they needed at one place, which is at the PX or BX.

Transition in Health Care. Similarly, most medical services are on base when in the service, so recently discharged veterans have to find where these services can be found in the town or city where they may live. The purchase of medical insurance can be a formidable task, both in fiscal and cognitive terms, for anyone. The costs for medical care and insurance are just as expensive and daunting for veterans. A student veteran can take advantage of college health insurance for himself or herself, but private insurance will still be needed to be purchased for family members. The language in which insurance information is conveyed and the lengths of brochures, pamphlets, leaflets about the coverage, the limits of coverage, the items which are covered/not covered, and the limitations to hospital and prescription plans are overwhelming.

Social Transitions. The transitions that veterans must make socially when leaving the military and entering civilian life are considerable. Veterans discover that a certain proportion of the people they encounter have anti-military prejudice. For example, a politician recently suggested that young people could be sent into combat if they do not apply themselves in school (Anonymous, VFW (2007b; Fields, 2006). Even disabled veterans are sometimes treated disrespectfully (Gelber, 2005).

Almost all veterans at times need to modify their behavior. For example, the language they used routinely in the military must be suppressed or avoided (military terms, military acronyms, military slang). Generally, they must get out of the habit of using acronyms, such as NCOIC (Non-commissioned officer in charge); E9 (the highest enlisted rank). They need to eliminate or modify the way they show respect and deference as they did in the military. Indeed, a military attitude may be perceived negatively by both student peers and authority figures in higher education. For example, simple military bearing by a veteran student can sometimes be viewed by non-military persons as being disrespectful to an authority figure because this bearing can make a veteran appear to be too macho, up-tight, or superior.

Adjusting to How Civilians Treat Them. Besides modifying military habits, veterans need to learn that civilians may treat them differently from the way they were treated when they were in the military. Veterans need also to learn that civilians might know about certain events that veterans are unaware of. For example, veterans may learn that they do not know about certain news events that occurred while they were on active duty, especially when they were overseas and more so when they were in a war zone (the Rip van Winkle effect).

Transitions that Must be Made by Combat Veterans

Most people expect that combat veterans will have additional transition steps to take that non-combat veterans do not have. Strong bonds are created among those who have served in combat and even at times with the people of the countries who were protected by those who served. In addition, combat veterans sometimes discover that they wish that they could have done more in a conflict, stayed with their fellow service members or even stayed longer in a combat zone in order to make more of a contribution to a conflict.

It is not unusual for returning veterans to feel survivor guilt where they fear for their comrades and native citizens left behind in a combat zone because they no longer could save the lives of comrades or help protect them. It is not unusual for combat veterans to still feel some of the traumatic stress of war well after (post) they experienced it, i.e., posttraumatic stress (PTSD). For example, memories of war may spontaneously come to mind because something they see or hear reminds them of a particular day or situation when they were in combat. It also is not unusual for unwanted memories to appear in veterans' dreams.

Some veterans will be troubled enough by the posttraumatic stress that they need treatment at a VA Clinic or VA Hospital. Others affected by post-traumatic stress may go untreated for a variety of reasons. Characteristics of post traumatic stress, according to the Diagnostic and Statistical Manual of the American Psychiatric Association, include, but are not limited to: a startle reaction to sudden loud noises resembling those heard in combat; brief times of "checking out" when familiar sounds, smells, feelings of the place of combat or trauma arise (as in a hospital helicopter passing overhead); irritability, truncated emotions (preventing positive, upbeat feelings due to guilt of being safe when comrades are still in a place of threat or wounded or dead); feelings as if no one understands his or her experiences; feeling a need for support in managing emotions (Boscarino, 2006; Figley, 1978a,b, 1988; Kubany, Leisen, & Kaplan, 2000; Kubany, Haynes & Abueg, 1996; Lanham, 2005; Muran, & Motta, 1993; Powell & Doan, 1992; Roca & Freeman, 2001; Shepard, 2003; Strange, 1974).

Transitions that Must be Made by Disabled Veterans

Most people expect that veterans who become disabled because of service including combat will have additional transition steps to take that non-combat veterans do not. Sometimes these disabilities are not obvious or detectable by others. Like many people who become disabled, some veterans who are disabled due to military service or combat have to struggle with attitudes about how they became disabled, about the nature of that disability, and about how others should or should not treat them. Struggling with these attitudes can make life difficult for disabled veterans until they are able to cope with them. For example, disabled veterans sometimes discover that persons do not know how to treat disabled people or that finding emergency care for their disabilities is often difficult.

Transitions Made in Becoming Employed or when Returning to Employment

Unemployment among veterans, especially younger veterans and minority veterans, remains higher than the national average (House Committee on Veterans' Affairs, 2004; Pedan, 1987). The challenge of adjusting to the workplace is formidable (Drier, 1995; Farley, 2005). Nevertheless, veterans who want to become employed before beginning college need some help in trying to locate a job. The Veterans' Employment & Training Service (VETS; 2007) provides veterans and transitioning service members with information that enables them to find employment and succeed in the workplace by protecting their employment rights and meeting labor-market demands with qualified applicants. Also, see Realifelines, National Veterans Training Institute, and the e-VETS Resource Advisor who assists veterans as they are preparing to enter the job market.

In addition, each person who leaves military service may receive a copy of a Corporate Gray transition guide. There are separate guides for veterans from the Army, Navy and Air Force. Previous editions of the Corporate Gray guides have received outstanding reviews. They are sold through major bookstore chains, military exchanges, and at career transition seminars worldwide. Even with these guides and assistance, many veterans remain unemployed, and the need to help veterans find work remains high.

Some veterans return to take a job that they had before they joined the service. However, other veterans may discover that their former employer has given their job permanently to someone else. When this occurs, a veteran may make a complaint about this and obtain help in getting a job back. Making a permanent replacement after deployment is against the Uniform

Services Employment Re-employment Rights Act (USERRA), so the employer could face a fine or even jail time. This is an employment problem that non-veterans almost never experience because they rarely take a leave of absence without the permission of an employer and when they do, their leave of absence is rarely as long as a deployment that may be several months or even years.

Members of the Employer Support for Guard and Reserve (2007), mentioned in the last chapter, can aid veterans in the necessary negotiations with their former employer. Veterans who go back to work after a deployment of less than five years are guaranteed, by law, to return to the same job that they had when they left. An employer may hire a replacement for the Reserve or Guard member but this employee has to know that the employment is temporary until the Reserve or Guard member returns. If a Reserve or a Guard member is denied employment by his or her previous employer, that member can contact the Employer Support of Guard and Reserve in his or her state or county for assistance in getting his or her job back.

Transition Assistance Provided by the Military and VA

Each military branch of service provides some transition training just prior to discharge. However, this training usually just touches on the major issues (i.e. how to get a job, write a resume and where to get basic information about colleges and universities). There are so many transition tasks it is understandable that transition assistance varies in content and delivery across the military branches (Bascetta, 2002). Moreover, it is difficult to convey to a service man or woman about to be discharged about what the various transitions will be like. Hearing about the changes and experiencing them are two different matters to consider.

After discharge, a veteran may obtain some transition assistance from the Veterans Administration (VA). The VA has had a long history of providing veterans with various benefits. Since 1989, the Department of Veterans Affairs (VA) has continued to extend VA benefits (Veterans Administration, 1991; Veterans Information Service, (2003). Information for new veterans is available on a special VA web page at <www.vba.va.gov/EFIF>. These efforts include counseling about VA benefits through the Transition Assistance Program (TAP). This program involves a nationally coordinated federal effort to assist military men and women to ease the transition to civilian life through employment and job training assistance. The goal is to foster continuity of care between the military and VA systems and to speed up VA's processing of applications for compensation. A pre-discharge physical may sometimes be conducted under VA disability examination protocols either by VA medical centers, contract medical examiners or military personnel. A problem with the VA transition program is that the system is overloaded with veterans and it lacks the trained personnel and resources to handle the current level of service members and veterans.

Veterans can obtain a three-day seminar from the VA about benefits and entitlements. VA's goal for TAP services is to ensure that service members are aware of their VA benefits and to provide assistance as needed. For those leaving active duty due to medical problems, the outreach effort is intensified to ensure a full understanding of the VA compensation process, vocational rehabilitation and employment program. They also conduct benefit briefings at other military pre-separation and retirement programs, and provide outreach to members of Reserve and National Guard units. The counselors who hold these briefings work directly with offices on military installations that provide education, medical, family and personal counseling, and casualty assistance. Returning Reserve and Guard members also can attend a TAP or a DTAP workshop. Briefings are presented for personnel stationed in the United States and around the world in such places as Guantanamo Bay; in Europe (England, Germany, Spain, Italy); Central America (Panama); the Far East (Korea, Japan, Okinawa); Iceland and the Azores. Briefings are sometimes given also on large naval ships.

The Disabled Transition Assistance Program (DTAP) provides comparable help for veterans with disabilities. Each VA medical facility and benefits regional office has a person whose responsibility is to coordinate activities to help meet the needs of these returning combat service members. The DTAP program for disabled service members offers vocational rehabilitation and employment assistance at major military medical centers where such separations occur and at other military installations.

In addition, the VA has a number of benefit counselors at key military hospitals who help severely wounded service members to make their transition to civilian life. For further information about current initiatives for today's veterans, see Pathway Home (2007). The VA operates a Discharge System from which recently separated and retired military personnel can receive information on VA benefits and services. Special businesses also send information concerning VA education, home loan guaranty, and insurance benefits.

The Department of the Army has implemented its own transition services, called the Army Career and Alumni Program (ACAP). There are many ACAP sites both in the United States and overseas; see <www.armyds3.org> for information on special service for combat veterans and severely disabled soldiers. This information can also help families cut through some of the red tape so they can more easily tap into services available to them through the military and VA.

Veterans are able to apply for service-connected disability compensation from the VA more quickly than was possible in the past. The VA adjudicates claims efficiently, sometimes within 60 to 70 days of discharge, by examining service members under VA protocols as part of the discharge process. This is the "goal" of the VA, but claims still lag far behind with some veterans, especially those who have been in the system for years reporting their claims, taking years to process. However, most recently the VA's national average processing time has been reduced for new claims requiring a disability rating if a service member is found to be disabled. Once disability claims are processed for veterans and a rating is given, applicable vocational rehabilitation and employment services may be initiated in a timely manner.

Sources on the Transition to Civilian Life

Veterans can find a lot of information about the transition to civilian life in some excellent books (see Cornelius, 1993). Also the advice given to an earlier generation may be found useful (Weller, 1944). Recently, there are also many new sites for veterans to access via the Internet that are too numerous and changing to be listed in this book.

The Transition to College

The VA provides assistance for the transition to civilian life but not for the transition to college life. It is generally held that the transition to college was smooth for veterans of World War II (Lipsett & Smith, 1949), although some of those veterans encountered some of the same kinds problems discussed in this book despite the welcome given them by the public at large

(Weller, 1944). Some college administrators and professors know about the difficulty of the transition from military to civilian life. There are several factors that affect the transition of veterans to college life.

Being a Minority

At most schools, veterans must adjust to being part of a minority, a very small minority. They are commonly less than 3 percent of all the students at a particular school. Although some minority groups have recognized help and status on most campuses, veterans do not. It is usually difficult for any non-vocal minority group that is this small to attract the attention and help of college administrators and professors.

Financial Burdens

Veterans have more financial burdens than non-veteran peers right out of high school. Many veterans have financial responsibility for a spouse and children when starting college. They have to pay costs of college because their parents no longer support them financially. As a result, they often must take on employment, more so than non-veteran peers.

Age and Bearing of Veterans

Veterans are less familiar than younger non-veteran students, who recently graduated from high school, with aspects of college because college tasks and social life are routinely discussed in high school. For example, non-veteran students know more than veterans about such aspects as college requirements for a degree, including those for general education, for a major course of study, and for a minor course of study.

Some professors, administrators, and staff tend to treat young veterans who are in their first year in college as if they had just graduated from high school because some young veterans often look similar to young non-veterans. The expectation of established members of the academic community on campus is that young students just entering school are naïve about the culture and the world beyond high school. As a result, some people on campus behave in a paternal or maternal manner toward veterans. Such treatment makes veterans uncomfortable. Veterans who had difficulty adjusting to the military tend to have difficulty adjusting to college (Price, 1980).

Veteran-Friendliness of Schools

Veteran Friendly Schools. As discussed in Chapter 4, some schools appear friendlier to veterans than other schools. As might be expected, the transition is easier to a veteran-friendly school than it is to a veteran-unfriendly school. The transition is easier because veteran friendly schools have staff and services that help veterans become accustomed to college life and the academic responsibilities of college.

Veteran Unfriendly Schools. Although many administrators, faculty, and students want veterans to feel welcomed at their college or university, a vocal minority makes many colleges and universities appear anti-military and anti-veteran (Brown, 2005; Hall & Schweizer, 2005; Magruder, 2005b; Mears, 2005; Petrovic, 2006). The transition of veterans to a veteran-unfriendly school never ends because anti-veteran situations may emerge at any time, even in a school that is only mildly veteran-unfriendly. Veterans must reconcile themselves to the anti-military climate of their schools if they are to remain and obtain a college degree. The transition at a veteran-unfriendly school may cost the veteran financially because a school's business practices involve requiring payment of fees that are not necessary (Winter, 2005). Some students may not welcome veterans because they are seen as competitors academically and socially (Clark, 1998; Fine, 1947).

Obtaining transfer credits can be much more difficult when staff avoid helping veterans (Wenger, Ruffle, & Bertalan, 2006). It also may result in much wasted time because bureaucratic procedures may not work out or take a great deal of time. For example, these procedures may lead a veteran to discover that certain programs are not available as promised. Transfer credits promised to a veteran may not materialize.

The transition may be especially difficult for veterans who attend veteran unfriendly schools that appear to be veteran friendly. The transition to these schools may be difficult because the initial treatment may mislead the veteran to feel secure and not recognize treatment that actually is unfriendly. This false sense of security may be especially persuasive when attending schools that claim they are atoning for how they treated veterans in the past, such as after the Vietnam War.

Academic Adjustment in General

Academic Preparation of Veterans for College. Veterans sometimes have difficulty adjusting academically to college because they have poorer academic skills than non-veterans who start college right after high school. Academic skills of veterans, such as for studying, test taking, reading, and writing, may be rusty due to their years away from a traditional study setting. Veterans sometimes have had lower grades in high school than non-veteran peers because they knew they were going to join the service.

Similarly, veterans may not have taken as many college prep courses as non-veterans. Because veterans take fewer college preparation courses prior to college enrollment, they sometimes have lower college aptitude scores than non-veteran students who attend college just after high school. Just because college aptitude scores are lower for veterans than non-veterans, it should not be concluded that veterans are not as intelligent or academically inclined as non-veterans.

Study Skills. For the reasons just discussed, veterans often need instruction in study skills prior to college or as they begin college (Diyanni, 1997; Herrmann, Raybeck, & Gruneberg, 2003; Mayer, 1999). They need to learn how to carry out a variety of academic tasks, as well as choosing a career and plan a career path.

Absence of Transition Help for Veterans

Lack of Campus Assistance. Colleges or universities rarely have a staff member officially designated to help veterans with their transition. If veterans belong to another minority due to race, sex, sexual preference, or religion, their minority status may be of help if the school has a system to help the other minorities. Most schools have programs for non-traditional students that generally include people older than the traditional non-veteran student right out of high school. Nevertheless, most schools fail to recognize that veterans are non-traditional students, despite the fact that the Defense Department recognizes people with a military background as non-traditional students (Defense Activity for Non-Traditional Education Support Agency, 2004).

Absence of Transition Programs. Almost no colleges or universities have programs specifically aimed at helping new veterans with their difficult process. For example, all colleges have some kind of orientation program every year for new students but these programs target non-veterans. However, no orientation program addresses the unique challenges that veterans have to adjust to—such as the transition problems listed above.

Lack of College Manuals. Many books have been written on how new college students may survive the challenges of seeking a college degree. However, none has been written on how veterans may survive the challenges that non-veterans encounter and the challenges unique to veterans. There are excellent books that address the financial aid issues of veterans (Caudell, 2005; Hunter & Tankovich, 2007) but these books do not address the challenges facing veterans that are unique to them. For example, these books do not tell veterans how to handle a professor or administrator who makes anti-military comments to them.

Preparation for the Transitions that are Unique to Veterans

Veterans lack a great deal of information that would help them when they begin their college education. At the time of discharge, no one in the military warns a service man or woman that, if they decide to attend college, they will encounter a variety of problems because of their veteran status. The different kinds of information that they lack are:

- No one warns a veteran prior to enrollment that a particular college or university may have an anti-military reputation in general (Chapter 4).
- Veterans are aware that they will experience some stress as they make the change from military life to college life. However, no one warns a veteran just what this experience will be like (Chapter 5).
- A veteran most likely feels that the academic skills are not as sharp as the non-veterans students, especially students just out of high school. However, no one warns a veteran just how their academic skills are deficient (Chapter 6).
- No one warns a veteran of the formidable social obstacles that he or she will encounter when getting to college. He or she is not told that relationships may be tense with professors, with college administrators, and with non-veteran students (Chapter 7).
- No one warns a veteran of the problems they will encounter various educational programs (Chapter 8) that do not include information for veterans. No one warns a veteran of the problems he or she will encounter with the selection of a major or that it may

be difficult to study in the field of his or her occupational specialty.

- A veteran is not warned of financial problems that are not covered by the GI Bill and that financial aid is not as good for veterans as it is for non-veterans (Chapter 9).
- No one warns a veteran that obtaining transfer credit for military training and experience is often very difficult (Chapter 10).
- No one warns a veteran that obtaining help with health problems due to military service is often complicated and sometimes difficult (Chapter 11).
- No one warns a veteran that he or she will get less help relevant to her or his background than is given non-veterans when seeking employment on or near graduation (Chapter 12).

What Colleges and Universities Can Do About The Transition Problems of Veterans

If a college or university wants to help veterans succeed in college, it must examine its reputation. If its reputation is veteran-unfriendly, it should establish a program of transitional education for veterans and make this program known to veterans. Transition training for veterans in college should address the transition tasks presented in this chapter, both for civilian life in general and transition tasks that pertain specifically to life at their college. A college or university's transition program would help veterans considerably if it offered counselors to help veterans with their adjustment on their campus. A transition program should involve an assessment of veterans' need for study-skills instruction and should advise veterans on how to obtain such instruction.

Summary

This chapter reviewed the considerable challenges that veterans must make in the transition from military life to college. First, veteran's transition from military life to civilian life was addressed. It was explained that veterans will most likely have more transition problems than non-veterans and that some veterans will have disabilities that will only add to their difficulties. It was noted that the VA provides some transition assistance when veterans ask but that assistance is only for the transition to civilian life. Second, the transition from military to college life was addressed. Several aspects of the transition to college were reviewed; such as having to relinquish military habits and to improve their study skills. The difficulty of the transition to college life was described as depending on the veteran friendliness of a college and whether a school provides transition help to veterans.

Chapter 6
The Academic Problems of Veterans

Veterans as a group differ from non-veteran students in their level of preparedness for coping with the challenges that arise after entering college. Thanks to the college preparatory program received by non-veterans in high school, they are more able than veterans to manage the academic and practical tasks of college. Many veterans have considerably more challenges and more needs for assistance than non-veteran student peers while seeking a degree.

Purpose of this Chapter

The purpose of this chapter is to call attention to the help that colleges and universities may furnish to veterans as they face their new challenges when they begin college. First, differences in student preparation for college between veterans and non-veterans are reviewed. Knowledge and skills are discussed that veterans must acquire to be competitive with non-veterans in college. Second, the chapter reviews how the high school experience facilitates the educational process more for non-veterans than for veterans. Proposals are made for how veterans could be better prepared early in their college experiences, to level the playing field for the two student groups. Additional help should continue through the college years. The help given to veterans will benefit for students as new challenges arise

Readiness for Studying in College

Non-veteran students arrive on campus with their high school study skills sharp, almost as sharp as they were a few months earlier in May or June when they graduated. Non-veteran students have been prepared in high school to know that there are many cognitive tasks to be performed as one works toward a degree. These tasks include studying, test-taking, writing reports, writing essays, as well as skills that support performance of the cognitive tasks including reading, skimming, and note-taking. In addition, practice for each skill may be provided.

Veterans are not as prepared for the many cognitive tasks of college. Unfortunately, veterans have not had experience with study skills from just a few years to twenty plus years. Moreover, veterans are not provided before or after being enrolled with sufficient assistance with: acquiring new learning skills such as taking notes in class, learning in class, learning outside of class from extracurricular activities, participating in study groups, being tutored on how to complete assignments, conducting laboratories, writing essays and reports in a college style rather than in military format, taking quizzes, and taking exams. Thus, veterans are not able to compete academically with traditional student peers until after the veterans have a chance to sharpen up skills needed to be successful.

Study Specific Skills

Veterans often have poorer academic skills than non-veterans. Thus, veterans need to "prep" their skills as they start college, or preferably just before school begins. However, instruction in study-skills programs at most colleges is not focused on the educational needs of veterans who are accustomed to training but not to the conceptual learning common in college (as discussed in greater detail in Chapter 8). Veterans need more instruction in tasks such as studying, test taking, reading, and writing than non-veterans who start college right after high school because veterans have not been in school for some or many years.

Broad Study Skill Preparation

Recent theories of learning and memory indicate that academic performance of any student depends on the status of his or her different processing modes. Central to academic performance are cognitive processes of learning, remembering, communicating, and thinking. Also central to such performance is how cognitive processes are supported by academic skills, such as reading, writing, and note taking (Mayer, 1999). However, many researchers have recently agreed that the cognitive processes involved in academic performance are affected by a person's physical and emotional state (Herrmann, Raybeck, & Gruneberg, 2002; Herrmann, Raybeck, & Gutman, 1993).

Veterans should be provided instruction, as they are educated about specific study skills, on how self care of health and effective learning and remembering. High school teaches students that their ability to respond to the physical and social environment also affects the cognitive processes. This relationship may not have been reviewed in military training in the same way that it applies to college learning. Consequently, veterans should be taught details of the relationship between self care of health and effective learning and remembering. For example, they should learn to recognize when and how stress undermines all manner of cognitive functioning.

In addition, veterans study skill instruction should also explain how academic performance is affected by sociological variables, such as class, income, and socio-economic status (Allen, Herrmann, & Giles, 1995; Appy, 1992; Klein, 1989; Langbert & Wells, 1982; Roth-Douquet & Schaeffer, 2006a, b). Instruction should explain how academic performance is affected by how a person succeeds socially and that social interactions themselves are affected by cognitive functioning and the broad skills that affect such functioning (Herrmann, 2008). This also includes the attitudes of professors toward veterans in the classroom and attitudes of students to war and to veterans in the classroom. It also includes how non-veteran students may or may not be inclined to interact with veterans.

College Transition Skill Preparation

As described in the previous chapter, veterans clearly have many transition tasks to deal with. They possibly have more transition tasks to deal with than they probably realize and certainly more than a student right out of high school. To the extent that veterans in general know about the many transition tasks, it is not surprising that many veterans decide to not use their educational benefits to attend college—as reported by the National Survey of Veterans (Department of Veterans Affairs, 1994, 2004; Drew & Creager, 1972). If an educator wants to help veterans succeed in college, these educators should try to establish a program of transitional education for veterans (Quillen-Armstrong, 2007). Transition training for veterans in college should especially address learning to adapt to the campus culture (discussed in greater detail in the next chapter).

Practical College-Skill Preparation

Veterans have not been prepared to know that there are many practical tasks to be mastered as one works toward a degree. These tasks include making decisions about: choosing a career, planning a career path, choosing a major and selecting courses to take. To the extent that a school's programs do not prepare veterans to make these decisions (as discussed in Chapter 8), veterans should be told to extract information from their advisors and focus on making these decisions on their own.

What Colleges and Universities Can Do to Improve the Academic Potential of Veterans

A college or university can improve a veteran's readiness and potential to compete academically through instruction on specific study skills, broad study skills, college transition skills, and practical skills that focus on designing their course of study in college. Most schools have experts in learning a culture and in the psychology of college learning and in education. These experts can develop a program to improve the specific and broad study skills of veterans. Schools who do not have these experts could arrange for another college or university to provide the appropriate experts. Experts should assess the level of competence of a veteran's study skills. Based on such an assessment, veterans should be advised to take a course in study skills, presented by his or her school, before and after entering college. Psychologists should develop a program of training to make the transition to college and provide instruction in the fundamental knowledge on how to design a program of study toward a career.

Summary

Most veterans are unable to compete academically with their non-veteran student peers until the veteran has had to acquire certain kinds of knowledge and skills. Training that veterans receive in the military does not rely on studying in the way that traditional students do, so veterans need help to acquire a different way of learning than they used in the military. This chapter explained how colleges and universities could provide veterans with instruction in the skills they will render them as ready for the classroom and academic responsibilities as their non-veteran counter parts. They need instruction in specific study skills such as test-taking skills, reading skills, writing skills, and note-taking skills. Instruction should also address the broad study skills of self-care that keep a student sharp. Veterans should also focus on learning to make the transition from the military to college life. Finally, veterans need to learn how to cope with practical college tasks of designing his or her college education.

Chapter 7

The Campus Culture for Veterans

Veterans have a variety of educational benefits available to them (Reston, 1997; Thirtle, 2001; Veterans Information Service, 2003). If veterans in general would take advantage of these benefits, college enrollments could increase substantially. However, as discussed in the preceding chapters, many veterans are aware that the culture on many campuses in the United States is too challenging for some veterans to adjust to. Consequently, fewer veterans use their education benefits than they could because they decide not to attend college or to remain in college.

Learning how to behave in a new culture

As discussed in the chapter on Transitions, veterans have to learn how to interact in a new culture when they enter higher education. This kind of learning provides several challenges to anyone coping with a new culture. More than any other sector of society (business, religion, law, medicine), academia has more to offer someone who wants to learn a new culture.

Certain academic disciplines, such as anthropology, linguistics, psychology, and sociology, have studied this kind of learning. Specialists in these fields can help anyone learn how to behave in a new culture. Additionally, many professors and administrations have experience with what it is like to learn a new culture. For example, many professors and college administrators have lived abroad for a year or more. They know what "culture shock" feels like. Their experience helps them appreciate what it is like to adjust to a new and different culture.

There are many aspects of a veteran's transition from the military to civilian life and to college life that are unfamiliar to professors or college administrators unless they have served in the military earlier in their lives. This chapter reviews three kinds of challenges that veterans must deal with because of the campus culture and then discusses the consequences of these challenges. First, veterans sometimes encounter difficulties because the behaviors they acquired while in the military mislead professors and administrators about the attitudes of veterans. Second, veterans sometimes feel unwelcome at their college or university because the speech and behavior of professors, administrators, and students made in protest to the government's diplomatic and military action. Third, veterans feel unwelcome when they encounter anti-veteran prejudices held by some professors, administrators, and students. Because of these three challenges, the academic problems of veterans suffer in various ways.

After these challenges have been discussed, the chapter considers the consequences of trying to learn the culture of their college. Specifically, the chapter focuses on how learning the college culture impacts on a veteran's academic performance. Finally, proposals are made about what educators and higher education in general can do to help veterans adjust to this cultural change.

Behaviors and Self-presentation of Veterans

When a person attempts to understand or "read" another person, the person doing the reading understands the attitude of the other person (Mehrabian, 1969; Nisbett, 2003). The attitude may be inferred from the other person's appearance or behavior. The attitude may be interpreted as indicating that the other person is co-operative or uncooperative.

For many professors, veterans are like any new group on campus who professors may not know how to read. Teachers who have not had a military background need to be briefed about the appearance of veterans, their posture, their communication skills and social skills. Some professors at most colleges and universities misread the countenance of veterans as reflecting negative attitudes that the veterans do not hold. As a result these professors are inclined to treat veterans in a way that does not show veterans the respect they deserve or expect.

Veterans Appear to be in a Non-veteran's Body

Younger veterans, the vast majority of veterans on campus, look like— or are similar to—the non-veteran students who are just a few years younger than the veterans. Faculty members are understandably thrown off by the appearance of young veterans who look like, but do not act like, non-veteran students. It is equally understandable that veterans may act differently than their non-veteran peers. Veterans have had challenging experiences that non-veterans have not had. Also many veterans have held leadership positions as a commissioned officer or noncommissioned officer and are comfortable around people in authority.

Veterans Military Carriage

Veterans tend to carry themselves better than non-veterans because of the training that veterans received in the military. Veterans have better posture than non-veteran students because they have been trained to walk erect and stand at attention when in the presence of authority figures. If a person does not take account of the fact that veterans have been trained to have good posture, this person may interpret this posture as reflecting a cocky attitude and feel intimidated when around veterans.

Communication Skill

Veterans tend to express themselves clearly or avoid speaking. Veterans normally speak directly, in a succinct manner and maintain eye-to-eye contact. Veterans have been taught not to speak in a timid manner. Thus they tend to talk in a somewhat loud manner and with a lower pitch. In addition, because of their maturity, confidence, and more assertive communication skills, most veterans are not intimidated by contact with professors, as are some non-veteran students who come to college right out of high school. If a person does not take account of the fact that veterans have been trained to talk in a confident, mature, and assertive manner, this person may interpret a veteran's speech as indicating an arrogant attitude.

Veterans Social Skills

Because veterans have had some unusually challenging experiences, they sometimes reflect worldliness that is unexpected from someone of their apparent youth. Additionally, most veterans have experience as leaders, even at their young age. As a result, they are not easily intimidated by college authority figures. Sometimes professors conclude that veterans who are not intimidated by a their status are being disrespectful. Also some veterans are not prepared on how to behave with professors, administrators, and most students who originate in the middle or upper classes (Allen, Herrmann, & Giles, 1995; Apply, 1992; Roth-Bouquet & Schaeffer, 2006a,b).

Behaviors and Self-presentation of Professors, Administrators, and Students

Although infrequent, poor treatment of veterans still occurs on college campuses (Campus Antiwar Network, 2003, 2004; Hall, & Schweizer 2005; Herrmann, 2007a,b; Herrmann, Raybeck, & Wilson, 2008; Magruder, 2005a,b, c; Mears, 2005; Petrovic, 2006; Students for a Democratic Society, 2008; Wilkes-Edrington, 2007 and other popular press sources about poor treatment of veterans while in college, reviewed in Chapter 2). "As college students hit campuses across the nation this week, a new generation of young veterans will step off the battlefields of Iraq and Afghanistan onto the ideological battlefield of our university campuses. For those on the front line in the war on terror, the antiwar hostility of liberal professors and campus activists will assuredly prove unsettling," (Hall, & Schweizer, 2005; see also Magruder, 2005a,b, c).

Practices of Some Professors Interfere with the Academic Performance of Veterans

It is true that today's veterans do not encounter as much hateful speech as veterans did during the Vietnam era. However, as noted above, some professors and administrators have been reported to say things inside or outside of class that upset and interfere with the academic progress of veterans (Magruder, 2005b). Comments inside of class tend to differ from what is said outside of class.

Comments in Class. Some professors make negative comments about the military and defense policy in order to stimulate debate or simply want to convey to younger people their own political views. Anti-military comments are made most often by older professors who began teaching during the Vietnam War era (Mason, 1990; Burkett, 1998). Regardless of the origin of these comments, most veterans are not eager to get into debates in support of, or against, the military. Most veterans just want to study and obtain a college degree.

In some cases, professors criticize the military in class because the course has something to do with the military, such as in history or political science courses. Such criticism is acceptable for these courses except when the criticism becomes insulting of the military. Some professors and administrators treat veterans poorly because they believe that the first amendment permits them to say anything they want in the classroom, including statements that are anti-military. For example, the military has been criticized in classes involving biology, English, and sociology, despite pedagogical rules that professors should use lecture time to talk about their discipline only.

However, the first amendment does not extend to slander or libel just because a professor believes in what he or she says. Such comments are not justified under the first amendment. In sum, some professors incorrectly believe that academic freedom means they are exempt from the laws governing slander or libel. Professors, and administrators who are anti-veteran should know that they cannot express slanderous anti-veteran views without fear of punishment or negative exposure.

Comments Outside of class. What professors say outside of class tends to differ from what they say inside of class. If a professor insults a veteran, it is usually done outside of class and usually when no other students are present. For example, a professor said to one veteran after class "veterans are stupid." Another veteran was told by a professor outside of class, "you military guys are kind of slow." Another professor told a veteran that he was a "baby killer" (Hall & Schweizer, 2005; Mason, 1990).

In contrast to anti-veteran comments, professors today do not say sexist, racist, homophobic things to students because their institutions have instructed them in diversity training sessions that they could get themselves and their employer sued. Yet, among the minorities specified in such training, veterans are usually absent. When veterans encounter such insults, these comments discourage them, as other minorities are discouraged by prejudicial insults. For example, after a professor made explicit insults, one veteran avoided attending the classes of the professor and another veteran dropped out of college entirely, destroying his opportunity for an education.

Discourteous Behavior. Some professors never overtly make antimilitary or anti-veteran comments. Instead, they simply treat veterans impolitely. For example, some professors treat a student in a curt, stiff manner, once they discover the student is a veteran. Also, some veterans report that a professor ignores their questions and gives priority to the questions of non-veterans. In contrast, this professor gives an answer in polite and informative responses when responding to questions from non-veterans.

Insensitive Speech When Talking to Combat Veterans. After learning that a certain student is a veteran, some professors ask the veteran about his or her military experience. Those who do ask veterans about their experiences should be aware that there is etiquette about what is proper vocabulary to show respect for military experience. Generally, veterans do not like non-veterans, including professors, to joke about a veteran's military background. For example, veterans might accept it if another veteran questioned his marksmanship, but veterans will not like professors saying something like "I bet you were a good shot." Also other topics are out-of-bounds. For example, a professor should not ask a veteran if he or she ever received non-judicial punishment, was ever court-martialed, or ever demoted in rank. A veteran can ask another veteran these questions but a non-veteran should not address these topics.

Veterans sometimes report that some professors initially treated them in a friendly manner but subsequently asked inappropriate personal questions about the veteran's war experiences. For example, the professors appeared at first to be sincerely interested in what war is like and in a veteran's combat experience, such as about hazardous duty or combat experiences. Then they asked invasive questions that make the veteran feel uncomfortable. For example, some veterans reported that they have been asked, "What does it feel like when you kill someone?" or "How does it feel to know you killed babies?" However, etiquette dictates that ghoulish questions should not be asked.

If war is discussed, etiquette also dictates that certain terms should be used. Casualty is a term used for military men and women who are wounded or even die in combat. It is commonly said that service men and women who lose their lives in war have made the "ultimate sacrifice." Pacifists and protesters are those who oppose war; protesters seek to prevent or stop a war. Ironically, pacifists and protesters often think they are opposed to war more than anyone. The irony is that no one is repulsed by war more than those who have participated in one.

Size of School. For unknown reasons, the negative treatment of veterans by professors appears to occur mostly at four-year institutions rather than at two-year institutions. This difference in treatment of veterans at two and four year colleges can also be observed on the web. A search on the Web for sites that mention veterans and education results in much fewer hits for four-year than for two-year colleges and universities.

Practices of Some Administrators Interfere with the Academic Performance of Veterans

The vast majority of administrators treat veterans positively. Nevertheless, some administrators insult veterans. For example, an administrator at a school repeatedly and severely criticized a veteran for typos the veteran made in a handout designed to help veterans. Some administrators may perform a routine task for veterans at a much slower rate than for non-veterans. In some cases, administrators require veterans to follow a procedure that is contrary to their best interests. For example, administrators at some schools have been known to direct the GI Bill payments of veterans to someone at their school other than the veterans.

Practices of Students that Interfere with the Academic Performance of Veterans

Students are influenced by different pressures than are professors or administrators. Some students disrespect and insult veterans out of a strange sense of competition (Clark, 1998). Veterans bring academic and social competition to campus that makes them not welcome by some students. Accordingly, some non-veteran students may say things to undermine the confidence of veterans just to try and get a step ahead of them.

Some students make comments in class that support the anti-military comments of their professor during a lecture. When students say insulting and slanderous things about the military in imitation of professors, then they do not say these things because of their beliefs. In such cases the responsibility for the students' actions lies, not only with them, but also with the administration and the professors.

Outside of class these students also insult the veterans in a social setting, usually when other students are present. Like some professors, students may ask veterans questions pertaining to a veteran's war experiences. These questions may be asked out of naive ignorance, but sometimes these questions appear to be asked so that the non-veteran students may subsequently air their personal opinions about a past or current war.

Pre-conceptions of Professors

Some professors know to be courteous to members of different groups and to take account of their background when communicating with them. Professors know that they communicate differently when talking with foreign students than with native students. They know what is proper when talking with women or men, nontraditional or traditional students, and when talking with members of different races, different religions and different sexual preferences. However, some professors can possess one or more of several preconceptions that interfere with their communication with veterans.

Academic Pre-conceptions

Some professors have certain academic prejudices about veterans that need to be corrected. These prejudices may be conscious or unconscious (Davidio, Kamahi, & Gartner, 2002). Because many veterans did not go directly to college after high school, some professors and administrators assume that veterans are not intelligent and talk down to veterans. Collectively, veterans are as smart as non-veterans. In addition, equality in aptitude of veterans and non-veterans is the case at the college or university in which they both have been admitted and attend (Sailer, 2004).

Educators are wise to assume that veterans should be educated in college in the same way as any other group. However, veterans are not the same as anyone else. Although veterans are not yet afforded the same protection against discrimination as many groups such as women, minority races, minority sexual preferences, and particular religions, veterans are protected by a variety of laws. The Vietnam Era Readjustment Assistance Act of 1974 (38 U.S.C. Sect. 2021, et seq.) protects veterans from employment discrimination. Veterans who are employed in any manner by a college or university are entitled to such protection.

Many colleges extend the protection of the Vietnam Era Readjustment Assistance Act against discriminatory actions regarding employment of veterans to educational programs and activities such as admission, majors, scholarships, athletics, and other college-administered program. In addition, professors and administrators at institutions that receive federal funds above $10,000 for research and other programs can have the payment of these funds terminated for discriminatory activities, according to Executive Order 11246 and the Geiser Consent Decree. Discovery of discriminatory actions of any kind toward veterans in college obviously can result in negative consequences for the school, professors, and college administrators.

Some educators treat veterans poorly if the veterans perform poorly academically. These educators mistakenly attribute the poor academic performance to laziness or low intelligence when the poor academic performance is most likely due to the veterans having received a poor academic education earlier in life or needing more time to catch up with other students. For example, some professors hold the same view expressed by Senator John Kerry in 2006—that service men and women end up in the military because of poor academic potential (Fields, 2006; see also Roth-Douquet & Schaeffer, 2006a,b). Once a professor regards veteran students as unintelligent, the professor is inclined to regard the performance of these students as poor and to consider the veterans as below average in intelligence.

Socio-economic Pre-conceptions

Academic performance is affected by sociological variables, such as class, income, and socio-economic status (Allen, Herrmann, & Giles, 1995; Appy, 1992; Langbert & Wells, 1982; Klein, 1989; Roth-Douquet & Schaeffer, 2006a, b). Such performance is also affected by gender, age, and cultural variables, such as ethnicity and other factors that pertain to the group to which a student belongs. Sociological variables and cultural variables affect academic performance for two reasons. Students from different sociological and cultural backgrounds vary in the quality of their preparation for college and in the effort they expend in studying in college. In addition, the adjustment of students to a college or a university will be dependent on the attitudes of professors, administrators, and students toward veterans in the classroom.

Preconceptions based on Anti-veteran Prejudices

Veterans do not feel welcome in some colleges and universities for the same reason why some minorities do not feel welcomed there, i.e., because of prejudicial kinds of behavior (Brown, 1998) that may be expressed consciously or unconsciously (Dovidio, Kamkami, & Gaertner, 2002). Like all prejudices, those about veterans are based on false beliefs (Brown, 1998; Stangor, 2000). In this case, the false beliefs pertain to veterans' educational benefits, the socio-economic lower class from which most veterans originate, and about the military (Mason, 1990; Znakov, 1990).

Higher education has done more to eradicate certain prejudices than have other sectors of society. Research has investigated the nature of prejudice by anthropology, psychology, and sociology. The results and conclusions about research done on prejudice has helped in the process of eliminating sexism, racism, prejudice against members of a different sexual preference. Unfortunately, very little research on the prejudice against veterans has been conducted in higher education. Nevertheless, different disciplines in higher education have the tools to better understand and eliminate such prejudice. When veterans learn that a professor or administrator holds these prejudices, veterans are discouraged and fear that the prejudices will cause them academic or administrative difficulty. The nature of the five mentioned prejudices against veterans is discussed next.

The first prejudice: the belief that the GI Bill makes veterans wealthy. Several studies have shown that generally non-veterans are wealthier than veterans. The belief that the GI Bill makes veterans wealthy can be shown to be prejudicial by careful consideration of the origins of this prejudice. It is true that if a veteran attends a public college or university, the GI Bill may be enough to cover tuition and fees. However, the GI Bill very rarely helps much in attending a private college or university.

Even with the new GI Bill at a state school, a veteran still has to pay for meals, transportation and other costs of living. To pay for these extra costs veterans usually have to take on a part-time or full-time job or they have to take out a loan. The parents of veterans typically do not help veterans because the parents regard their veteran offspring as financially independent, and veterans want to live on their own with their spouse and children. Also for various reasons, veterans never receive as much financial aid from their school or other sources as non-veterans.

The second prejudice: the belief that veterans have an advantage over non-veterans in their careers. Some people assume that veterans acquire an educational benefit that gives them an advantage in their careers over their non-veteran peers. However, many veterans do not catch up with their peers in high school who did not serve in the military. Veterans who obtain a college degree earn less money in their life than non-veterans with such a degree (Angrist, 1993; Cohen, Segal, & Temme, 1992; Langbert, & Wells,

1982; Pedan, 1987). Even if the pay earned while in the military is added to the wages earned in a civilian career this total is less than the career earnings of a non-veteran because military pay is inevitably less than the initial pay earned by non-veterans.

Service in the military whether for a short time or a career seems to lead veterans to less lucrative careers than their non-veteran peers. The veteran starts out in his or her career behind in experience and education when entering the work force after discharge (MacLean, 2005). To add insult to injury, because veterans start their careers later than their non-veteran peers, veterans sometimes end up working for classmates or at least non-veterans of the same age or younger than them (Angrist, 1993; Cohen, Segal, & Temme, 1992; Langbert, & Wells, 1982; Pedan, 1987). Thus, even those veterans who use the GI Bill often do not catch up with their non-veteran peers.

The third prejudice: the belief that, in general, the intelligence of a veteran is lower than the intelligence of non-veterans. Some people believe that veterans are not as intelligent as non-veterans. These people justify this belief, first, because more veterans proportionately than non-veterans choose to not attend college after high school. Second, veterans are presumed to not be very intelligent because they do not take college prep courses while in high school and some may not put as much effort into their studies as they should. Third, the decision to enter the service is interpreted by some people as indicating that the veteran was not smart enough to attend college. In any event, the distributions of scores on military aptitude tests are comparable to the distributions of scores on intelligence tests (Cronbach, 1984; McIntire & Miller, 2007; Sailer, 2004).

Alternatively, it has been argued that military service and combat makes some people wiser than they would have been otherwise (Jennings, Aldwin, Levenson, Spiro, & Mroczek, 2006). Several U.S. Presidents have been veterans (e.g., Washington, Jackson, Grant, Teddy Roosevelt, Eisenhower, Ford, Kennedy, the elder George Bush, and George W. Bush). There are many more presidents who were veterans than would be predicted from the proportion of veterans in the American population (a little more than nearly 3% of Americans have served in the military).

The fourth prejudice: the belief that veterans enjoy war. Those who prepare for war or served in a war are keenly aware of the horrors of killing another human, and of having good friends and fellow servicemen killed or mutilated. The experience of war permanently changes a person and the change does not involve liking war more than non-veterans like war (LeShan, 1992). Anyone who has seen war up close is even less inclined to want to go to war than those who have not experienced it (Kingston, 2006).

Some anti-veterans will point out that veterans who have returned from war have been known to commit murder. War scars some veterans so extremely that they lose their balance and sometimes are violent. Such cases are extremely sad (such as Timothy McVey who blew up the Federal Building in Oklahoma City). But it is also true that many non-veterans become psychopathic killers without having been in combat. Consider Lucy Borden, Charles Manson, Ted Bundy, Jeffrey Dahlmer, and Hannibal Lector.

The fifth prejudice: the belief that the military is a dangerous part of society that does not belong in higher education. Some professors and administrators treat veterans poorly because they see veterans as representatives of the military that they hold in low regard. It has been alleged that many, if not most, American higher educators holds anti-military beliefs. A valid example of these beliefs being widespread may be found in the lack of membership of the Servicemembers Opportunity Colleges (SOC, 2004, 2007a,b). The number of colleges and universities that belong to SOC is more than 1800. To belong to SOC, a higher educational institution must promise to provide active-duty personnel and veterans the services necessary to pursue a college degree. However, because there are over 3000 colleges and universities in the United States, approximately 1200 or more higher educational institutions have chosen to not affiliate with SOC. Institutions that choose to not belong to SOC must judge that they cannot, or prefer not to, provide services needed to help veterans further their education. Therefore, approximately 30% of colleges and universities prefer not to help veterans while they attend their school. At least three reasons exist that explain why academia in general does not perceive the military favorably and why it does not treat veterans in a friendly and respectful manner.

To begin with, academia is opposed to the military because of the destruction that war brings. Academia has the responsibility of developing and maintaining the knowledge on which society depends. Wars are destructive to the products of that knowledge and sometimes destroy higher educational institutions. Many in academia are opposed to the military because they believe that they must protect a person who refuses to participate in a war because that killing a human being is wrong. Additionally, academia conducts much of the ongoing discussion about the appropriateness of war and the conditions of a just war—or whether a just war is possible to conduct. Those who morally oppose war, called conscientious objectors, generally assert their opposition to war while they teach or study in a college or university, although some do so at religious institutions.

Apparently because of the prejudice that the military does not belong in higher education, some colleges cultivate a reputation for not welcoming veterans (Mason, 1992; North, 2005). Some of these schools are very well known (including some from the distinguished Ivy League), setting an example for lesser-known schools (Lewin, 1990).

Ignorance of the Positive Characteristics of Veterans

Most veterans possess positive characteristics that make them good students, and good employees as well. Faculty who taught World War II veterans discovered that veterans have certain strengths as a result of military training and experience that non-veterans usually did not have because they have not had such training and experience (Lipsett, & Smith, 1949). However, many more recent professors are unaware of these positive characteristics. The strengths of veterans regarding the demands of college are as follows.

Veterans are older than non-veteran students (the average age of most younger veterans is 24 years old but retired veterans are 38 years old or older). Being older, veterans are usually more mature, more experienced, and more focused than students who enter college right after high school (average age of 19 years old). Veterans are more likely to be married and to have started families than their non-veteran peers who are typically not married and do not have families. Having to support a family is generally sobering for a person at any age, but especially while attending school.

Veterans are well prepared for shouldering the responsibilities expected of students. Also, veterans who were in college before serving in a war, do better academically after the war than they did before the war (Love & Hutchison, 1946). Indeed, those veterans who have been exposed to danger while in the military may possess a kind of wisdom that non-veteran students do not have (Jennings, Aldwin, Levenson, Spiro, & Mroczek, 2006). Veterans in general are also much more accustomed to austere circumstances and adverse conditions than same-age peers or students who enter college right after high school (Melymuka, 1999).

As a group, veterans tend: to be more highly dedicated to their academic work; to set a good example; to require minimum supervision; to keep good records; to meet deadlines; to maintain good self-care; to be drug free; to set a good example for other students; and to work in teams. Veterans are good problem solvers, even under pressure. They are taught to believe that failure for them is not an option, that every difficult problem has a solution. Veterans can follow directions and do not "rattle easily" (Jennings et al., 2006.

Most veterans have been to more places in the United States than young non-veterans. Many veterans are more likely to have been overseas and traveled to several countries than young non-veterans. Veterans have certain strengths as a result of military training and experience that non-veterans usually do not have because they have not experienced such training and experience. For example, veterans' knowledge of places that non-veterans have not visited enables the veterans to comment usefully in some courses. Also most veterans are more aware of what is going on in the world because they have participated in American presence overseas and because they never knew quite where the military would send them. This awareness of global politics enables veterans to contribute to class discussion in ways that non-veterans cannot do.

The Effects of Poor Treatment of Veterans On Their Academic Performance

Direct Interference with Academic Performance

Lost Study Time. Many veterans report that anti-veteran advisors, professors, and administrators erected time-consuming obstacles such as having to exhaust considerable time in applying for transfer credit or in trying to find financial aid suitable for veterans. These obstacles take the time that a veteran needs for studying. The time and effort consumed in fruitless activities is discouraging to veterans. Obviously, a substantial reduction in real study time will lead to lower grades and poorer performance in class.

Lower Grades. Some professors appear to grade veterans lower than they grade non-veterans. Veterans have reported being certain that they received lower grades in a course just because they were veterans. Of course, no professor would openly admit this, as to do so would be contrary to the ethics of teaching and could lead to their dismissal. Nevertheless, some veterans know this to be the case.

Even if a professor does not grade a veteran correctly, the belief that a professor might do so robs a veteran of his or her motivation to succeed academically. Veterans learn that they might avoid being graded unfairly if they simply do not self-identify in college, that is, they do not tell their professors and fellow students about their veteran status (McDaniel, 2006).

Veterans Try to Finish School as Quickly as Possible. Because they are older, many veterans are eager to get a degree and get a job appropriate to their degrees. Accordingly, many veterans report doing whatever they can to get their degree completed quickly so that they can leave academia as soon as possible. The competition that veterans bring to campus, both academically and socially make them feel not welcomed by some non-veteran students. Additionally, by accelerating the rate at which they complete their program, they unfortunately give up opportunities for participation in extracurricular and cultural campus activities.

Indirect Interference with Academic Performance

Problems can interfere with a veteran's motivation to study and thus, lead this student to fail academically. When professors, administrators, or students treat veterans in a negative manner, veterans are likely to feel that they do not belong at that school and if treated negatively, veterans are less motivated to work as hard in their studies. In addition, indirect interference also becomes direct interference to the extent that they take up veterans' time, time that is needed for study.

Veterans sometimes discover that there is no way to get their grievances evaluated properly at many schools. They are reluctant to use a college or university's grievance system to complain about unfair grades because they fear that those who conduct the grievance systems may be anti-military and will not process the grievance appropriately.

What Colleges and Universities Can Do About College Culture Problems of Veterans

Higher education is the key to solving so many problems of this world so it will not come as a surprise that we, the authors, believe that education is the key to solving the campus culture problems of veterans. We believe that most professors, administrators, and staff do not intend to deter veterans from pursuing their college education. Even poor treatment of veterans that is a consciously aimed at the government is not really directed at the veterans themselves. A college or university can for the most part eliminate the campus-culture problems of veterans by conducting an educational program for professors, administrators, and students.

Similar to sexual harassment training, specific examples of inappropriate speech should be pointed out to members of an academic community. Education about how to treat veterans should also address what is considered polite conversation when talking with veterans. Professors and administrators should be instructed on the appropriate way to ask veterans questions about hazardous duty or combat experiences.

Professors and administrators should be instructed on the common misconceptions about veterans. This instruction should acquaint members of the academic community about beliefs pertaining to veterans that are prejudicial, such as: veterans are less intelligent than non-veterans; that veterans like wars; that the GI Bill makes veterans wealthy and more educated than non-veteran peers.

Part of such an education should explain how members of the academic community could protest military and other actions of the government. This explanation should provide appropriate addresses, phone numbers, and email addresses of relevant people in government so that members of the academic community can register any protest they have as quickly and as effectively as possible. Once professors and administrators are able to register their protests promptly, there will be no temptation to treat veterans poorly. The grievance system at most schools, while suitable for non-veteran students, usually needs modification in order that it is rendered sensitive to the concerns of veterans. Unless an institution makes a clear effort to help veterans with the campus-culture problems they encounter while seeking a degree, veterans are inclined to become discouraged and may stop studying for a degree.

College Instruction of Non-veteran Students About Interactions with Veterans

All students should be instructed about appropriate speech on protected classes, i.e., gender, race, religion, and sexual preference, and that their speech to veterans should be as respectful as is their speech to members of protected classes. Students might be encouraged to help veterans who appear to be hassled by campus climate problems. Once it is apparent that professors and administrators want to help veterans with climate problems, veterans will work more and more efficiently on their academic challenges.

College Instruction for Veterans

Veterans also are a group in academia that may benefit by instruction on how to interact with other members of the campus culture. Many colleges have courses on typical vocabulary, grammar habits, and body language of people in different groups. By knowing this information about another group it is possible to better interpret what others try to communicate. One of the groups that veterans could learn about is college professors and administrators. If veterans were provided with such instruction early in their first year, they will be more able to adjust their bearing and apparent confidence so that professors will not misread them as impudent or disrespectful. Also, if the professors and staff received the same training, they would understand the same characteristics and traits the veterans have, leading to a better atmosphere on campus.

Summary

This chapter has reviewed how veterans sometimes encounter a variety of problems on many college campuses that make them feel unwelcome in the college culture. Many professors and administrators do not realize that they misunderstand the behavior of veterans. Professors need to recognize that veterans are like other special groups on campus who possess different characteristics that need to be taken into account when teaching members of a group.

Professors and administrators may treat veterans in a less than positive manner because they are unaware of the positive characteristics of veterans. Veterans are surprised and disappointed when they discover that their faculty members do not respect what veterans bring to the classroom. Professors may treat veterans in less than a positive manner because the professors feel that veterans are not intelligent and have a poor educational background when considering how to teach him or her. These professors need to overcome the belief that veterans should be taught in the same manner as non-veteran students. They must learn that veterans are not lazy or stupid, and that veterans actually have good work habits. Some professors may treat veterans in a less than positive manner because they misread the manner by which veterans carry themselves as indication of a veteran's disrespect. Professors need to learn how to recognize that a student may be a veteran because of her or his military bearing and by communication skills.

Veterans should not be regarded as inferior by professors because of academic prejudices of the professor. Similarly, non-veteran students need instruction on appropriate interaction with veterans. Conversely, veterans should also be instructed on their characteristics that professors might sometimes misread.

Chapter 8

Educational Programs Tailored to Veterans: Capitalizing on Veteran Backgrounds

In the past few decades, college teaching has moved from being an art to a science (McKeachie, 1999; Moore, 1989; Smilkstein, 1991). A great deal of research has focused on improving the best way to teach in college (D'Avanzo, 2003; Slavin, 1995; Smilkstein, 2002). A theoretical perspective that has influenced the development of educational programs is to focus programs on particular groups of students by assisting the students from a group with problems that impede academic performance. However, regardless of the considerable advances in educational theory and procedures that focus on particular groups, veterans have been overlooked.

The ability of students to succeed in college depends not only on educational backgrounds, but also on employment histories, financial capabilities, concurrent responsibilities, health status and societal pressures (Pedan, 1987). The result is that modern higher education routinely seeks to specify and remedy the educational needs specific to students in various groups (Golden, 2006). For example, although not inclusive, institutions have special programs for first-generation students (individuals who are first in their family to attend college), for students with distinguished high school records, for athletes, for academically weak students, for women, for international students, for minority groups, and for the financially challenged.

Educators who are familiar with veterans recognize that veterans constitute another specific set of needs of veterans in that has yet to be developed fully anywhere within the United States. Some schools have faculty or staff who direct veterans to the offices they need to contact within the college or university. A relatively small number of two-year institutions and a smaller number of four-year institutions have an office to assist veterans. However, many of these offices exist just to register veterans for the exclusive purpose of receiving their GI Bill and to route those funds—usually directly to the institution's bursar.

Like all students, veterans will need to participate in educational programs that function outside the classroom. However, veterans will also need help with problems that most students do not encounter. Some other educational programs that veterans need are directed entirely toward non-veterans. The rest of this chapter is devoted to explaining how certain educational programs currently fail to help veterans as much as they help non-veterans. The chapter explains also how these programs can be presented in a way that is beneficial to veterans. This chapter proposes that at least eight educational programs conducted at most colleges and universities are crucial to a student getting through college.

These programs pertain to aspects of a student's formal education, but also to the practicalities of getting through college. All of these programs are directed to serve non-veterans simply because about 97% of the students are non-veterans at most colleges and universities, and veterans are not considered a "targeted audience" at most colleges and universities. As a result, these programs are administered in ways that do not serve the special needs of veterans.

Four of these educational programs are sufficiently complex that an entire chapter is needed to address them. These programs are concerned with financial aid (Chapter 9); transfer programs (Chapter 10); college health service (Chapter 11); and the employment search program (Chapter 12). Four other standard programs that are not as complex, but, nevertheless, impact negatively on veterans are contained in this chapter. These programs include: the orientation program for new students, the academic programs pursued by students, the advising program, and the education provided for study skills. This chapter explains how these programs typically place veterans at a disadvantage and what might be done to transform these into suitable programs for veterans.

Readers who are professors or college administrators will find that they are familiar with much of the content of this chapter as it applies to non-veteran students. Nevertheless, regardless of background, all readers will learn here some specifics about the difficulties that veterans encounter in certain standard programs that are conducted at schools across our nation serving primarily non-veterans.

Orientation

As noted in chapter 3, most colleges and universities hold orientation sessions for new students. These sessions are useful for all students, veterans and non-veterans. Students are forewarned that college requires discipline and hard work. They are told that they should study for at least two hours outside of class for each hour in class. They are briefed on academic standards, such as that cheating may lead to punishments they would want to avoid, such as: being given a failure in the course; being given not only a failure but have a disciplinary note put on their transcript; and in some cases being suspended or dismissed. The students are told that plagiarism is a form of cheating that will not be tolerated and that a college student needs to know how to avoid plagiarizing anyone else's work.

They are informed that an advising system exists that allows the students to consult with academic advisors prior to registering for courses. They are told that advisors are available to advise them on what courses are appropriate for the major or minor they seek. The students should be aware of the deadline for dropping or adding courses. They are told that their school's administration performs a variety of services for them. Students have professionals who might teach them study skills in general. The students are told that if they find a high level of difficulty in a course that they should seek help to improve her or his skill in studying the content of this course. Their enrollment office can transfer credits obtained at any other college or university into the academic credits offered at their school. The school's health service is available for the students in the event that they are injured or become ill. As the students near the end of their academic programs, the school has a career center that can help them search for and obtain employment.

However, veterans need an orientation that includes additional instruction and counsel that takes into account military background when given an orientation session. Invariably, these sessions nearly everywhere say little or nothing about veterans. Obviously non-veterans do not need to learn about

92

the information that veterans need. However, veterans do need orientation that explains to them how their needs, like the needs of all students, will be met. Veterans should be told about those aspects of their course of study that is unique to them. The veterans also should be told about the practicalities of college life as they specifically apply to veterans. Additionally, veterans need further orientation sessions that apply specifically to their unique academic needs. Table 8.1 lists a variety of information that could be included in an orientation program for veterans.

Table 8.1
The Needs of Veterans that Should be
Included in their College Orientation

Making the transition from military to civilian/college life
Transferring military experience into college credits and credit for
    courses taken in colleges, in universities, in the military
    services, and elsewhere before the veterans came to their
    present school
Applying for all of the financial aid available to veterans through
    the GI Education Benefits, FAFSA, scholarships and grants,
    and any program that provides funds specifically to veterans,
    e.g., Anheuser-Busch, Coors and Miller have programs, which
    provide some educational funding for veterans and their
    children
Finding appropriate housing
Locating financial and social support for a family, e.g., day care,
Places of worship, physicians, dentists, places for social contact
    among peers and age-mates
Selection of an academic major and minor
Being advised on academic courses of study
Obtaining instruction in study skills as needed
Obtaining assistance for disabled veterans with their disabilities
Choosing a civilian career
Sharing common concerns with other veterans
Finding suitable employment upon graduation

The Principal Offices of the College or University

Most orientation programs explain the organization of the college and university. Essentially this means that students are told where the offices are and their mission in a sentence or so. When orienting veterans, the explanation of the organization should also emphasize how certain offices serve the needs of veterans (as shown in Table 8.2).

Table 8.2
College or University Administrative Offices that Assist Veterans

Admissions. The admission offices at many schools lists new students who identify themselves as veterans. Being on that list makes veterans more likely of notification of events, pertinent to veterans.

Reserve Officer Training Corps Program (ROTC). The Army, Air Force and Navy ROTC programs educate students to be officer/leaders in the military, and sometimes coordinate activities for veterans.

Career Center. The Career Center provides veterans with Information and advice about careers that they might pursue after graduation.

Enrollment Services. This office is responsible for ensuring that veterans receive college credits for military training and experience and for credit from other colleges that veterans have attended.

Financial Aid. The Financial Aid office has the same responsibility to veterans as for all other students. This office directs veterans to fill out the FAFSA by dates set by states..

Library. The college library provides a system of education for students who are veterans to prepare them to make best use of the library.

Registrar. The Registrar verifies for/to the Federal Department of Veterans Affairs whether a student qualifies to receive GI Bill benefits and distributes VA information to veterans.

Student Academic Services. This office provides numerous programs for students to improve their reading and study skills. This office should train staff to teach veterans about study skills.

Dean's Office. Each student veteran should be told the location of the office for the "college" or "division" responsible for veterans.

President's Office. All students should be informed of the location of the President's office, even if most students will never need to find this office. All appeals ultimately come to the President if the matter is not resolved at another academic level.

Orientation Programs Target Non-veterans Almost Exclusively

As noted above, non-veterans currently receive a relevant, complete, informative orientation prior to the first year of college. Non-veterans get more appropriate information about academic programs than veterans get. The non-veterans are permitted to major in areas of interest whereas veterans do not have the opportunity to major in an area of interest if that is an area specialty they acquired in the military service. Non-veterans receive fuller advisement than veterans simply because the 97% of advisors do not have a military background and, therefore, are insensitive to the full academic needs of veterans. Non-veterans receive better counseling because the staffs of study skills centers are usually unaware of the academic dedication of veterans. Also non-veterans have worked to improve their study skills as part of a college preparatory program.

Moreover, non-veteran students receive some orientation to college prior to the first year of college. Most veterans do not take a college preparatory program in high school and so are not aware of the pre-college orientation to college that non-veterans receive. Many students in college preparatory programs, and sometimes parents, have been briefed by high school guidance counselors how to obtain financial aid. Non-veterans have worked to improve their study skills as part of a college preparatory program. Non-veterans often have knowledge about what majors and minors are available to them in college from parents who were secondary students or at least know the system.

Clearly, the orientation for first-year students who are veterans, should inform them how to do things that are unique to them that they must do.

Course of Study

In order to receive a degree, all students must learn the knowledge for a major and minor, as well as the content of courses that they freely elect to take. In addition, most schools now require students to take a collection of courses intended to give them as well rounded background. This collection is often called "general education" courses.

All courses are assigned credit hours that correspond to the number of hours of lecture for a course in a week. Typically, most courses are assigned three credit hours. Some courses count for one credit or two credits; these courses are usually, for perfunctory requirements such as a state's history, required by some state universities or physical education. In addition, some courses carry more than three credit hours. At some institutions credit hours are also assigned to laboratory activities that a course involves. Similarly, credit hours are sometimes assigned to internships.

To graduate, a student must complete enough courses (and also laboratories and internships at some schools) up to 124 credit hours. Some schools require more than 124 credit hours and some schools require less. In the final analysis a student must take the equivalent of approximately 42 to 43 courses at most schools to graduate. This total consists of credit hours for a major, minor, general education, and electives. The number of hours varies somewhat across different kinds of majors. Typically the credit hours for a major range from 32 to 52, involving 11 to 18 courses. A minor usually consists of 15 to 18 credit hours. General education credits total about 47 to 70 credit hours. The electives vary in credit hours. The total of 124 credit hours is, therefore, the sum of the credit hours for a student's major, minor, general education credits and electives.

To graduate, a student's grades for all of the 124 credit hours must average at least a C grade. Courses with an F do not count toward the 124 credit hours. Also, every course with a D must also be counter-balanced with a B or an A with the same number of credit hours. Courses in a student's major must be C or higher.

Transfer Credits

A better transfer-credit system for veterans is needed. A considerable number of students arrive at school with credit hours that they obtained in high school, from other colleges near their home, and from college level exams. Veterans can receive these credits and also credits from military schooling, training and experience. However, veterans often do not receive the number of military credits for which they are eligible and entitled to. Non-veteran students, of course, do not receive military credits. Alternatively, because most veterans did not take a college preparatory program in high school, they usually did not take advance placement courses. Thus, veterans start out somewhat behind those students who are awarded advance placement credits. Chapter 10 discusses the topic of transfer credits and proposes ways that the system for awarding these credits can be improved.

Course Selection

It might appear that course selection involves the same process for both veteran students and non-veteran students. While the course load is the same for veteran and non-veteran students, the course selection is more challenging for the veteran student than the non-veteran student. Course selection is more challenging for veteran students because they come to college with a broader background of knowledge than non- veteran students. This broader background makes it necessary that a veteran study course descriptions more carefully in order to decide whether his or her background makes the course necessary or not. If veterans do not spend enough time and thought in course selection, they might inadvertently select courses that overlap with their prior knowledge.

Academic Load

The typical load of most students in most schools ranges from four to six three-hour courses, usually not less than four courses (12 credit hours). While the assigned load is the same for veteran students and non-veteran students, it could be argued that the load invariably is greater for veterans who have to go through additional challenges and burdens (applying for financial aid; seeking transfer credits; coping with problematic relationships with professors, administrators, and students; resolving issues in the family, child-care, part-time employment) that most traditional-age non-veterans do not have (American Council on Education, 2007b; Defense Activity for Non-Traditional Education Support Agency, 2004; Flint, 2000; Shuckra, 2006).

Nature of Major and minors

A major is intended to prepare a student for a particular career or a field of related careers. Selection of a major should reflect a student's career goals. Career selection, and therefore selection of a major, is based on a student's background and interests. Some non-veteran students have had internships and jobs in high school that influence what they want to study. Like non-veterans, selection of a major is based on a veteran's background and interests. However, because veterans bring rich backgrounds of knowledge to college, their choices of a major are normally much more complicated and difficult than this choice is for a non-veteran.

Some schools offer majors that are related to veterans' military occupational specialties (MOS). If veterans want to continue with a course of study similar to their MOS, they will find unfortunately that it is normally not possible at many schools. Some schools will permit taking courses relevant to a veteran's prior MOS from other colleges, on line, as a co-op student. Of course, many veterans may want to study something different from their prior MOS, which makes the process of selecting a major somewhat less complicated, but still not easy.

Majors and Minors that Build on Military Occupational Specialties

In principle, colleges and universities create majors and minors in various specialties to meet the needs of their region and the nation overall. Sometimes higher education already produces enough graduates in a certain specialty. Other times it produces too many or too few of the graduates needed by society. In the past, the determination of the need for various specialties has been made in higher education without regard to the number of new veterans who rejoin society with military specialties that could be adapted to meet the needs of civilian society. Plans on how many educated persons are needed for a certain specialty should also take account of how many veterans should be educated to meet these needs.

All service members acquire at least one specialty, if not many, while in the service. Most veterans leave their specialized skills behind them when they leave the service (Cornelius, 1993). Veterans do not discuss their specialized experience because our society assumes that months and years of military training to be generally irrelevant to civilian careers. However, this assumption is false. Nearly every military specialty area has its equivalent in everyday life. In addition to the knowledge of specialties and leadership, the vast majority of veterans bring with them knowledge about computers. Approximately 40% of veterans have military careers that translate directly into a particular field (Melymuka, 2006).

Nearly every military occupational specialty has a civilian counterpart. By ignoring what veterans have learned in the military, our society essentially throws away the funds spent on military training and military experience that could be applied to vocations in the civilian world. If society examined what veterans have to offer, it would recognize that the technological expertise and the managerial- leadership abilities of veterans could add substantially to the pool of technical experts and leaders in our society. A comprehensive national plan is needed to enable colleges and universities to offer programs that allow veterans to pursue a civilian form of their military occupational specialties. Many colleges and universities are unaware that they could offer programs that would let veterans continue to study their military-occupational specialty.

Specialties/Managerial Skills. Besides being trained in one or more specialties, many veterans are given extensive managerial and leadership training and experience as noncommissioned or commissioned officers. However, most of these same veterans leave their managerial experience behind them when they leave the service because our society assumes that training and experience in military leadership is generally irrelevant to civilian careers. However, this assumption is also false. Many members of the military have had challenging leadership experiences much earlier in their lives than their civilian counterparts. For example, noncommissioned and commissioned officers acquire ample experience in resolving disputes in pay, responsibilities of command, sexual harassment and personnel disputes. All of this experience can be applied to civilian management positions.

Independent Study of How to Apply Military-Specialty Knowledge to Civilian Contexts. Besides awarding ACE credits for military background, veteran-friendly colleges and universities should enable veterans to integrate their military training and experience into their course of study. For example, professors in such an institution may provide veterans who have specialties in aviation mechanics to do an independent study to demonstrate how knowledge of military airplane mechanics applies to civilian aircraft. Such independent studies can be represented on veterans' transcripts, that later may facilitate the veterans finding a career their background in mechanics.

Consider veterans who were noncommissioned officers and who want to integrate their knowledge and experience about management into their academic program. Again, veterans may ask professors to do independent study in this case about how to apply their management knowledge and experience to non-military management positions. Educational programs in management could be provided by specialty departments (such as in aviation, athletics, or psychology) or by schools on campus that focus on management training (such as the College of Business for those universities that offer a business degree).

Class Attendance

A problem arises sometimes in college because a student's employment conflicts with class attendance. Students know that they must do the work required for the class and that they must learn what is covered in the class. Additionally, if an exam is held, a student who has a second commitment that cannot be changed knows that he or she must arrange to take the exam at some other time. Many professors make class attendance mandatory and subtract points from a student's performance when the student misses class.

Unfortunately, this procedure is sometimes used to discourage members of the National Guard or Reserves from missing class. These students have no option in this situation. If students miss military duty to attend class, they will face disciplinary action that may lead to a loss of rank or pay or worse. These students should be given a way to make up the work that they miss because of having to attend to military duties.

Advisement

All students at virtually all institutions are assigned an academic advisor. Some schools make it optional for students to see their advisors prior to registering for courses for the next semester. The advisors are usually professors. In the first two years of college, the advisors have the responsibility of guiding students to take general education courses and other foundation courses while the students prepare to take particular majors. When a student declares a major (typically at the end of a student's second year), an advisor who teaches courses in the department of the student's major will be assigned.

Veterans have the same academic needs for advising, as do non-veteran students. However, veterans have additional practical and academic needs that non-veterans do not have. An advisor could help veterans with special needs. An advisor of veterans should know something about military occupational specialties, as well as about military training and experience, and how to obtain academic credit for a veteran's military background. An advisor of veterans should be prepared to familiarize veterans with collegiate terms, jargon, idioms and concepts that non-veterans are familiar with but veterans have yet to learn. Ideally veterans should be assigned advisors who are veterans. If advisors are familiar with some of the common terms in a service member's language, advisors and students can communicate more effectively. Advisors should know something about a veteran's training and experience in his or her specialty so that the advisor may give veterans solid consistent advice about the avenues to earn college-level credit. A major duty for an advisor is to bridge the gap of how "to learn to learn" from one setting (the military) to another setting (the college). Veterans have in the most part learned by using skill development techniques. "Skill development in all domains (cognitive, affective, and psychomotor), but more especially in the psychomotor domain, must be evaluated in terms of what a student can do" (Hopkins & Antes, 1990). Learning in college is directed more to the cognitive domain. This difference should be made clear to veterans early in their college tenure. Basic understanding will become a bigger part of learning in college than it was in the service.

Education in Specific Study-skills

As mentioned in the previous chapter, non-veteran students arrive on campus with their high school study skills sharp, possibly at least as sharp as they were a few months earlier when they graduated. Both veteran and non-veteran students need to have good study skills, test-taking skills, reading skills, writing skills, and note-taking skills (Diyanni, 1997; Mayer, 1999). However, these skills will initially be dull or non-existent for veterans because they have been out of high school for one or more years. Veterans are wise to take study skills courses before or after entering college. In the final analysis, veterans find their courses more difficult than non-veterans find them until the veteran is able to acquire the academic skills that are comparable to the skills possessed by non-veterans.

The Modus Operandi of Many College Study-Skills Centers

Most colleges and universities have a center where students can go and learn more about learning in college. These centers offer students non-credit courses in study skills. The skill training that they offer is almost always that which would be given to a non-veteran who enters college after high school. These courses are usually intended for students who were conditionally admitted or admitted under "open access" or at least for students who did poorly in high school and have a poor learning skills background.

Thus, the staff members at a study skills center need to work with individuals who are less than fully prepared in academic skills for college. These students are regarded as being less mature than the good students and, as a result, they are expected to approach their studies in a less than fully responsible manner. They are also expected to do poorly academically.

Unfortunately, the staff of study skills centers is generally not familiar with veterans. As a result, the staff members who work in these study-skill centers tend to treat veterans like the marginal students who have just emerged from high school. They treat veterans as if they too are immature, irresponsible, and unmotivated for college. Surprisingly, most veterans (who are usually 21 or older) dislike being treated in this manner and, consequently, they cease attending their school's study skill center unless the staff makes allowance for this difference in age, skills, motivation and experience.

Few college programs begin with the assumption that veterans possess good learning skills acquired from their military training. Programs to impart college-learning skills to veterans should begin by explaining the difference between learning from training and learning in college. Administrators who work in improving the learning skills of students in general should recognize that their programs have not been tailored to help veterans. Nevertheless, an appropriate program could easily be developed in light of recent advances in procedures for improving memory and study skills (Herrmann, 2009; Herrmann, Raybeck, & Gruneberg, 2002; Herrmann, Raybeck, & Gutman, 1993; Mayer, 1999).

The teaching of good study-skills needs to be done by professionals who know how to communicate with veterans. Staff of college study-skill centers should be taught to treat veterans as mature, responsible adults (not as students who have just finished high school). Also the staff should be taught that veterans are very experienced with learning through training and will respond well to training given to them. The staff should, as well, understand the sensitivities that come along with being veterans, especially those with disabilities. Veterans have much experience at learning while in the military. All veterans have had months and even years of job training; and everyone in the military has built on occupational skills from experience on the job after training.

Instruction in Vocational Training versus Learning in College

Study-skills centers staff members need to be able to teach veterans the differences between instruction in vocational training and in college. Traditionally, the staff of a study skills center teaches study techniques that apply to conceptual learning but do little about techniques that apply to training. It is commonly held that learning in college is conceptual and does not involve training. It is true that many courses in college are abstract and require a learning style that is different from that used in training. However, several majors involve a good deal of training. For example, training is required for programs in nursing,

Traditionally, the staff of a study skills center teaches study techniques that apply to conceptual learning and not to training. The staff at a center that helps veterans to improve their learning skills should familiarize veterans with the difference between learning by training and learning by instruction. Because veterans are very familiar with vocational training, they are accustomed to training where course content is concrete. They are accustomed to training that leads to breaking a job description into specific pieces and steps at each piece. Learning in vocational training is considerably different from the abstract learning in college. The learning obtained while in training requires listening, understanding, and absorbing the hands-on instruction. Notes are rarely taken and learning usually does not involve studying as it is done in college.

Moreover, the testing in vocational training is different from the testing provided in college. Testing usually is done right after training. Typically, testing requires the student or trainee to perform the task in a skillful manner addressed in training. When multiple-choice tests are used, the choices are not abstract; they are concrete. The choices mainly check whether the trainee obtained the right terms and learned the referents of the terms.

The staff members of a study skill center need to teach veterans how the nature of learning skills in college differs from the learning process in training. In college, the content is usually abstract and rarely lends itself to being broken into steps. In college, learning requires listening and usually note taking (Diyanni, 1997; Herrmann, Gutman, & Raybeck, 1999; Herrmann, Raybeck, & Gruneberg, 2002; Mayer, 1999). In college, understanding often comes over a period of time and examinations are given later. With training, the trainee absorbs the content (unintentional learning) whereas in college most learning comes from note taking and studying (intentional learning).

In college, most testing occurs well after initial presentation of content in contrast to the immediate testing in training. Also testing in typical college courses is generally abstract. Examinations for measuring what is learned in most college classes are designed to assess understanding. Exams often require a student to answer multiple-choice items designed to challenge retention and comprehension of course concepts. Exams may involve some short and long essays, either totally or in addition to multiple-choice questions. Sometimes spot quizzes are required of students but again these quizzes are usually intended to determine whether students have understood a recent reading assignment or lecture.

Given the considerable experience of veterans with training, any instruction in college for skill development should begin by showing the veteran the difference between learning in vocational training and learning in college. If veterans are introduced to the instruction in college learning skills as given to non-veterans in either conditional admission or open access, the instruction will be confusing to veterans. They already know that they are good at learning. If the veteran is introduced to the differences between learning in training and learning in college, it will be much easier for the veteran to understand what aspects of his or her learning has to change to succeed in college.

College Preparation for Veterans who Take the Upward-Bound Program

A relatively small number of veterans are given extensive preparation for college through the Upward Bound program. This educational program, developed by the U.S. Department of Education, prepares veterans who are the first generation in their family to attend college and who have financial need. Participants in this program usually have not acquired a robust education in high school. In other words, they may be considered educationally disadvantaged.

This program offers refresher courses In English, mathematics, biology, and computer literacy to help prepare for college. Follow-up courses are provided for vocational/technical school training. Veterans who participate receive one-on-one tutoring, as well as career, enrollment, and financial aid counseling. Students in this program usually succeed in college.

What Colleges and Universities Can Do
About How their Educational Programs should Help Veterans

Colleges and universities can facilitate the adjustment of veterans to college if they integrate information needed by veterans into certain standard education programs. The integration of appropriate information into the standard programs discussed in this chapter (the orientation program, selection of course of study, the advisement program, and the tutoring program for improving study skills) may be achieved by having faculty members and students who are both veterans advise on the content of these programs. By creating programs in this manner, a school will be regarded as "veteran-friendly." First, schools can create an orientation program specifically for veterans when they begin college. Second, schools can design majors and minors that allow those veterans who so desire to concentrate their studies in their occupational specialty. Third, schools can provide veterans with advisors from the veterans' major department who have the knowledge to advise veterans about (1) whether courses they might take are redundant with knowledge acquired in the military and (2) whether courses would be consistent with a major or a minor that pertains to their military occupational specialties. Fourth, schools can provide study skills programs to veterans that teach these skills in a way that accounts for their unique backgrounds of knowledge and skills.

Summary

In recent years, higher education has focused on the problems that interfere with the academic performance of certain groups. Veterans, although they constitute a very small group on most campuses, deserve to be recognized as a group that has special educational needs, The educational problems of veterans discussed in this chapter occur simply because 97% of professors and administrators at most schools are not veterans and, consequently, do not recognize the problems covered here.

Presently veterans need to receive an orientation program at the beginning of the first year of college where this orientation will tell veterans about the things that they must do in college that are unique to them. It would also help veterans considerably if the college catalog would present information that veterans need to consider as they select a major or a minor. Veterans need to be able to major in areas of interest, including being able to major in a specialty they acquired in service when they want to. Veterans need to be given better advisement that takes account of veterans' military backgrounds. Finally, most veterans need some instruction in study skills. This instruction, however, needs to teach veterans the difference between training (which is common in the military) and learning in college

Chapter 9

Financial Problems of Veterans in College

American society has long assumed that the Department of Veterans Affairs (VA) takes care of all of the financial needs for all veterans in higher education. However, this assumption is not true. This false assumption is based on the belief that the GI Bill was designed by Congress to cover all of a veteran's expenses while earning a college degree. Instead, the GI Bill was designed to cover a substantial amount of the costs of a higher educational degree but not all of these costs. Moreover, due to inflation, the cost of a college education is continually increasing (Sparks & Caddi, 2002). The new Post 9/11 GI Bill substantially increases the financial support to veterans in college but it does not eliminate the costs of their education.

America cannot fully delegate the education of veterans to the VA or any other agency. Changing times and societal expectations make it necessary to give serious consideration of what the costs of education are for veterans currently. The budget of the Department of Veterans Affairs is devoted largely to helping disabled veterans with their medical treatment, prescriptions, modified housing, education, and employment, and even these expenses are not budgeted sufficiently by congress each year. As a result, the amount of GI Bill awarded veterans varies considerably across time and across veterans due to legislative problems not anticipated by Congress (CQ Researcher, 2007; Dickson & Allan, 2004; Gaines, 1945/2004; Mettler, 2005). Full support of education programs for veterans is beyond the limited support of the GI bill and simply is not reasonable.

The amount of the GI bill is not corrected for inflation. Consequently, as time marches on, the amount paid by the GI Bill covers less and less of a college education. The new GI Bill (post 9/11) increases the amount of support for tuition and fees in an amount that covers these costs for any state school including the most expensive school in a veteran's state. Unfortunately, the new GI Bill does not support the full tuition and fees of private colleges, precluding most veterans from attending these schools. The new GI Bill covers the costs of housing. However, the costs of subsistence and travel are not covered.

Financial Burdens of Veterans

There are some excellent books that address the financial aid provided by the government (Caudell, 2005; Hunter & Tankovich, 2007). However, these books do not get at the full ranges of veterans' financial issues. They do not do so partly because they do not yet cover the support of the new 9/11 GI Bill, but also because veterans have more financial burdens than non-veteran students straight out of high school. There are at least three reasons for the difference between veteran's and non-veterans ability to pay for the costs of college. First, veterans have less money than non-veterans (Allen, Herrmann, & Giles, 1995; Appy, 1992; Klein, 1985; Langbert & Wells, 1982; Roth-Douquet & Schaeffer, 2006a, b). Second, veterans also are much less likely to have the financial support of their parents than are traditional students. Their parents do not have the financial resources that the middle and upper strata have available to pay for the education that their children need. Third, many veterans with disabilities are poorer than veterans without disabilities because they tend to originate in lower economic strata than the veterans who do not acquire disabilities (Clark, 2004).

The Role of Colleges in Helping Veterans with their Financial Burdens

Some colleges and universities employ one or more incorrect financial procedures that lead veterans to have less financial support than they need and fairly deserve. These incorrect procedures occur because financial aid officers are unaware of the full financial picture for veterans and incorrect assumptions are made. Most financial aid officers who employ these procedures believe that they are treating veterans fairly and simply have not been informed of the consequences of employing financial practices that are inappropriate for veterans.

There are five kinds of financial procedures that have interfered with the education of many veterans. Some institutions may have engaged in only one of these five practices. Other institutions have engaged in as many as all five of these procedures simultaneously. These five procedures are as follows.

First, financial aid provided to veterans is lower at many schools because the administrators of some colleges and universities require veterans to use their GI Bill to pay for tuition and fees in a manner that is incorrect. Second, some colleges and universities do not try to find scholarships for veterans from their institutions or from other organizations. Third, incorrect curricular advice about what courses to take increases the cost of an education at some colleges and universities because the advice leads veterans to take courses that they do not need to take. Fourth, colleges and universities generally do not help veterans with financial support of spouses and children that accompany them to school. Fifth, GI Bill programs, as formulated by Congress allocate funds in an inequitable manner across veterans who are either still on active duty or who have been discharged. The new 9/11 GI Bill goes a long way to correct these inequities, although some inequities remain.

Purpose of this Chapter

Most veterans receive virtually no guidance when financing a college education. There are no professionals available to guide veterans as they seek to fund their college education. This chapter addresses the five kinds of college financial aid procedures that process the funds that veterans should have. In the process, it becomes obvious that more veterans would be likely to attend and complete college if their financial burdens were eliminated.

Incorrect Estimation of Financial Aid

As is well known, the GI Bill enabled veterans who would not have done so otherwise (Adams, 2000; Bound & Turner, 2002; Greenberg, 2004; Harris, 2005; Serow, 2004; Snyder, 2002; Stanley, 2003, 2000). After World War II, Korea, and Vietnam, veterans received GI Bill assistance if they applied for it. In 1985, the Montgomery GI Bill (MGI Bill), was passed which pays benefits "only to those veterans who have contributed" to their GI Bill account in their first year of service (Department of Veterans Affairs, 1994, Marklein, 2007; 2004; Schram, 2008; Snyder, 2002; Stiglitz & Bilmes, 2008). Service members no longer have to contribute to the account that pays their GI Bill check.

The new Post 9/11 GI Bill was designed to avoid the problems of prior GI Bills. This new GI Bill pays schools directly for tuition and fees. The amount paid is that required by state colleges or universities. If a veteran attends a private school, the amount paid is equal to the highest tuition and fees paid to a public school in the veteran's state. The administration of the Post 9/11 GI Bill will be worked out in the future, so this chapter will not address the details of this administration. Nevertheless, there are several procedures for calculating the financial aid of veterans that causes them to lose aid for which they are entitled.

Incorrect Financial-Aid Calculation Practices

Financial aid offices have significant latitude in the amount and type of aid that they give to students. Some people assume that veterans are able to receive more financial aid than non-veteran students (Schlachter, 1998), but the supposed financial advantage of veterans is simply not the case. The amount of aid provided depends on what funds the schools' have allocated for financial aid over all applicants who apply for such aid.

The amount of aid given to any student, and the factors that determine this amount are generally kept confidential at most schools. The confidentiality presumably exists to provide privacy to a student's status and/or parents' financial status and at times to shield the practices of the institutions from outside sources. The director of financial aid at a college or university is free to use judgment in determining the need of any particular student and in maintaining the confidentiality of funds provided a student. Unfortunately, this practice of confidentiality prevents those outside of the financial aid office from challenging the fairness of certain financial aid practices. Considerable investigation has shown that some schools employ one or more of three financial aid procedures that decrease the possible amount of financial aid of veterans.

Procedure # 1: Subtracting GI Bill benefits From Possible Financial Aid of Veterans. The GI Bill payments of veterans are not supposed to be regarded as wages that veterans receive for military service. Nevertheless, it is legal for financial aid officers to employ this procedure because the rules of Department of Education hold that it is an institution's discretion to include a veteran's GI Bill in determining financial aid (Ashby, 2002). Thus, discretion allows financial aid officers to attempt to determine whether students have the "means" to pay for their interaction.

The subtracting custom is not fair for three reasons. First, this "means test" treats veterans' GI Bill as wages, which is contrary to the Bill. Second, the discretionary element of this procedure results in an inconsistent administration of financial aid across American colleges and universities. Many schools subtract some or all of veterans' GI Bill funds from the total possible financial aid while other schools do not employ this practice. The procedure leads many veterans to receive no financial aid consideration, but other veterans to receive some or full consideration. Third, the administration of GI Bill is inconsistent across different generations of veterans. No veteran who received GI Bill funds after World War II, Korea, and Vietnam had their financial aid reduced by subtracting the GI Bill from the amount of possible financial aid.

Consider the **unfair calculation of need**. To appreciate the inequity caused by the subtraction practice, consider how schools compute financial aid for students in general. Financial aid is awarded to help students with their financial needs: the greater the need, the greater the amount of financial aid. Need is computed by subtracting a student's Expected Family Contribution (EFC) from the total costs of attending a school.

Need = Cost of Attending an Institution—EFC The costs of attending an institution include tuition and fees, books, lodging, meals, laundry, and any necessary medicines. The EFC is based on the assets (home, savings, and investments) and earnings of a student or the parents of the student (see <http://studentaid.ed.gov/students/attachments/siteresources/EFC_Formula_Guide0304.pdf>).

The computation of the EFC is done on the assumption that parents are not expected to liquidate their assets or give up all of their salaries to pay for the costs of college. Some families are sufficiently well off that they can pay all of the costs of college on the basis of assets and salaries. Many families are expected to take out loans to cover some of the costs that cannot fairly be drawn from assets and salaries. As mentioned earlier, the parents of veterans rarely support them, unlike most non-veteran students, while they are in college.

Financial aid practices are contrary to the best interest of veterans at those colleges or universities that subtract GI Bill from the total of college costs. At these institutions, the need of a non-veteran is Need = College Costs—EFC. The need for a veteran at these colleges is Need = College Costs-

EFC—GI Bill. Accordingly, the need indicated for any veteran with the same assets and salary as a non-veteran will be less than the non-veteran.

Most financial aid officers are familiar with the subtraction procedure and that it is counter to the best interest of veterans. Professors and other administrators at a school that engages in this procedure **are often unaware** that their financial aid office puts veterans at a disadvantage in this way. Most non-veteran students are also unaware of the practice.

Many veterans are aware of this practice but feel helpless when they complain about it because these financial aid offices do not admit that this practice is inappropriate. Financial Aid offices that employ the GI Bill reduction may follow this procedure partly because so few people in their institution know that the reduction is taking place. The subtraction practice results in veterans appearing to have lower need than non-veterans with similar assets and salary. As a result veterans become ineligible for loans or eligible for smaller loans and grants than non-veterans. This subtraction procedure is not appropriate for different reasons.

Many sources that discuss the financial aid of veterans note that GI Bill cannot be regarded as the "expected family contribution," but state it can be considered as a factor in determining a veteran's financial aid (Ashby, 2002; Carpenter, 1992; Rye, 2001). Nevertheless, federal rules do not prohibit financial aid officers from treating GI Bill as a relevant factor in meeting college costs. In effect, current practice at some institutions allows GI Bill benefits to be subtracted from Costs in determining need in the same manner as the EFC is subtracted from costs in determining need. In the final analysis, GI Bill is treated mathematically the same as the Expected Family Contribution at these institutions.

The procedure of treating GI Bill benefits as the Expected Family Contribution is not fair to veterans because no comparable procedure is applied to assessing the needs of non-veterans. For example, many non-veteran students receive an allowance from their parents while in college. Nevertheless, allowances are not subtracted from college costs in determining the need for non-veterans.

The procedure of treating GI Bill benefits as the Expected Family Contribution is also contrary to personnel requirements of our military. When service members enlisted with the promise of GI Bill, they were not told that the use of GI Bill could reduce their Expected Family Contribution. Any procedure that leads GI Bill to reduce a veteran's opportunity for loans and grants is a violation of the promise that led a person to enlist (Asch, Kilburn., & Klerman, 1999; Farrell, 2005).

Prior to the new Post 9/11 GI Bill, veterans invariably received less financial aid than non-veterans because many college and universities subtracted the GI Bill funds from the total allotment. By reducing the potential financial aid in this manner, veterans have much less of a chance to receive other financial aid than non-veteran students. The post 9/11 GI Bill may decrease the need for veterans to seek employment to help them pay their bills, but it remains to be seen whether some financial aid office will subtract both the tuition and fees, as well as the costs of lodging, from the costs of education. If they do, they will estimate financial aid in a manner that is contrary to the intentions of Congress when it passed the Post 9/11 GI Bill.

Procedure # 2: Ignoring the Costs of Living From Financial Aid Needed by Veterans. Prior to the new GI Bill, some colleges did not include the costs of food for those veterans who do not live on campus. Veterans rarely live on campus whereas many non-veterans often do live on campus. This procedure reduces the total amount of financial aid for which veterans can apply (Ashby, 2002;). In contrast, these schools do include the cost of board for students living on campus (that usually includes non-veteran students, but rarely includes veterans due to their social status of being married or having a family). The rationale offered by these schools for not including subsistence costs in the estimate of veterans' cost of education is that it is impossible to estimate the cost of eating for veterans who do not live on campus. This rationale is invalid because it implies that veterans who live off campus do not have to pay for meals while they are in college.

By making the total costs of an education lower, the procedure of ignoring meals expenses when estimating total college costs decreases the amount of financial aid for which veterans can apply (Ashby, 2002; Carpenter, 1992; Rye, 2001). Because most non-veteran students reside in a college dorm and use the food plans available on campus, these colleges include the costs of meals for these students. This procedure allows non-veteran students to apply for a much larger amount of financial aid than veterans can apply for (Ashby, 2002; Carpenter, 1992; Rye, 2001). Again, this financial aid procedure suggests to active duty personnel and veterans that higher education institutions may not truly want to help them get a degree.

Procedure # 3: Counting a Veteran's Previous Year's Salary as Part of Expected Family Contribution for A Veteran. When service men and women retire their yearly income drops at least 70%. When they apply for school, some financial aid offices want to use their income prior to discharge as the Expected Family Contribution, which artificially raises their income too high and takes them out of the range to be able to have or apply for Pell Grants and other grants and loans. This is done even though these veterans do not have this income any longer.

Scholarships for Veterans

In higher education, scholarships are traditionally designed to reward young motivated students who excelled academically in high school. In other words, most scholarships currently are designed to reward non-veteran students who intend to go to college after high school and who worked hard in a college prep high school program. In contrast, almost all of the scholarships that exist for veterans are mostly defined according to need. In addition, scholarships designated for veterans are very rare in comparison to those designated for non-veterans. The details of this inequity are as follows.

Veterans Have Little Probability of Being Awarded Scholarships

Professors who have tried to find scholarship support for veterans have discovered the difficult situation that exists with respect to scholarships for veterans. Financial aid officers report that almost no scholarships exist for which veterans might qualify. Most veterans knew in high school that they were going to serve, so they did not aggressively pursue a college preparatory program. Most non-veteran students knew that they were going to college and that their parents wanted them to try to get a scholarship. Thus, many non-veteran students made high grades in the college preparatory courses that qualify them for some kind(s) of scholarship. Because veterans obviously did not pursue an academic program, their high school record made them ineligible for the scholarships designed for non-veteran high school students.

Many veterans seek scholarships for college after having done some military service. However, veterans generally do not know how to seek out and apply for financial aid (Gilroy, 2007). When veterans seek scholarships they discover that they are disqualified for certain types of financial aid due to age and other factors such as not being directly out of high school. College catalogs and various books on how to compete successfully for scholarships give the impression that veterans have as great a probability of winning a scholarship as a non-veteran (American Legion, 2005; Army National Guard, 2004). These publications do not point out that veterans have little chance at getting a scholarship.

A part of the non-veteran culture is given incentives to study in high school and possibly get scholarships. Another part of the American culture, the military service culture, is not given that incentive. Some professors and students feel that this arrangement is fair because the college preparatory route is recommended to those who are most interested in higher education. However, veterans also deserve rewards for their achievements in military training, military experience and the years of their lives they have given up in protection of freedom. There are few school grants and or scholarships awarded to those who have give much to the "protection of freedom."

Scholarships Available Provide Little Help to Only a Few Veterans

Veterans' service organizations (VSO) offer a small number of "scholar-ships" for veterans. To begin with, these so-called "scholarships" are actually grants largely awarded for need. In addition, there are just a small handful of these VSO scholarships/grants, so the vast majority of veterans are not helped by the VSO. Grants are also offered usually by some states. Typically, these grants provide a fixed amount that covers only part of college costs. The paucity of appropriate scholarships for veterans is a situation that should be corrected.

Some scholarships for veterans exist for other purposes (Caudell, 2005; Hunter & Tankovich, 2007). For example, some of these scholarships are for the children of veterans. Many states offer such scholarships, especially for the children of disabled veterans. It is gratifying that some state legislatures valued veterans' service enough to help their children. However, these schol-arships do not help veterans who want to seek a college degree presently.

A Need for Scholarships Designed for Veterans

A campaign should be developed to create genuine scholarships for vet-erans. Because existing scholarships are largely for non-veterans who followed a pre-college program in high school, these scholarships are not based on accomplishments that veterans might have in their background. To counterbalance the inequities in existing scholarships that are biased toward students with a college preparatory program in high school, some scholarships might be based on being a veteran who has honorably served, excellence in military training or in exemplary service experience.

Unfortunately, the small number of efforts to get colleges and universities to develop programs for veterans has been ignored. If scholarships for veterans are to be developed, it probably will require considerable effort from the veteran and active military communities.

Most colleges and universities hire students in a work-study arrangement to perform clerical duties. The VA also offers a Work-Study program in which veterans can be employed to perform clerical duties concerning VA benefits. Unfortunately, many colleges and universities make no effort to provide jobs for veterans, assistantships targeted to veterans, or a VA work-study program for the veterans on campus.

Costly Curricular Advice

Most advisors do not appreciate the relationship between military knowledge and the knowledge that traditionally is taught in college. Consequently, students make the best use of their dollars when they take the courses that are just right for them. Colleges and universities typically assign advisors to students. These advisors must be contacted or can be optionally contacted to get the best advice on courses to take and when to take them. Unfortunately, almost no college or university (other than the military academies) has counselors who are familiar with a student/veteran's military background and how that background can meld into the courses a student may take. Consequently, it is not unusual for a student/veteran to discover that he or she has taken a course or courses that was/were unnecessary.

Financial Support for Families of Veterans

Colleges and universities cost more for many veterans than for nonveterans because some veterans do not get help with the costs of supporting a family. Many veterans come to college with a wife, and many of the married veterans have children to support. They must provide lodging, board, and medical care for the members of his or her family. Although most administrators know that many veterans have family responsibilities, apparently no college has a program in place to specifically help finance veterans with a family. Some kind of financial counseling program is needed for veterans while they are in college and more financial help for veterans with families is needed while they are in college (Berry, 1977).

Because they are deficient in funds due to supporting a family, they must take on more employment than non-veteran peers outside. To begin with, if the veterans have been discharged recently, they have to adjust to the sudden decrease in incomes. Veterans with families will need to pay for the food, transportation, clothing, health care, childcare, and education, as well as the purchase of miscellaneous goods and services. The average cost of raising a child to the age of 18 was estimated in 2006 to be approximately $171,000. Add the normal costs of college to the normal family costs of living and it is apparent that veterans have huge financial problems while also coping with classes and all the college challenges for non-traditional students. Even with the help of the new GI Bill, veterans with families will experience substantial financial burden.

Whether veterans have a family to support or not, they have greater financial needs than most non-veteran students (Anderson, 2004; Dyhouse. 2004; Kime, 2006, 2007a,b; Klein, 1981; Trewyn, 1994; Schram, 2008; Young, 2005;). Veterans get much less financial help from their parents than do non-veteran students. The parents of many veterans, especially the parents of veterans with disabilities, simply do not have the money to give to their veteran offspring to go to college. Additionally, while the parents of traditional students often give substantial financial support, the parents of veterans typically believe that the cost of college belongs to their adult veterans and those expenses will be borne by the VA. Both veteran and non-veteran students can ask their parents for financial help with the costs of college; but most veterans do not receive the financial support from parents that non-veterans receive.

Unequal GI Bill for Veterans Who Rendered Comparable Military Service

The fifth financial aid problem is that colleges and universities administer a GI Bill program that does not fairly allocate funds over veterans.

However, this problem is not due to the practices of colleges or universities. Instead this financial problem is due to legislative mistakes in the formulation of GI Bill programs. In brief, the amount of GI Bill provided a veteran is not the same for all veterans who have served in a comparable manner. Instead, the amount of GI Bill awarded differs across veterans who (1) served in either the active duty or reserve branches of the service, and (2) who served in the military at different times.

The GI Bill also differs among veterans who served in either the active duty or reserve branches of the service. In some cases, veterans who serve on active duty and in combat for the same amount of time are entitled to different education benefits depending on whether they served in a regular branch of the military or in the Guard or Reserves. The real purchase value of GI Bill dollars is affected seriously by inflation. For example, it is much more difficult to finance a college education with GI Bill if a veteran was discharged right after a new financial arrangement by congress or much later (Adams, 2000; Anonymous, 2001; Chapman, 2007; Donnelly, 2006; House Committee on Veterans Affairs, 2001; Kime, 2006, 2007a,b; Partnership for a Total Force GI Bill 2006; see also American Association of Collegiate Registrars and Admissions Officers, (AACRAO), 2006; Mettler, 2005; and Miami Times, 2005; Nelson, 2006; Walters, 2006; Stiglitz. & Bilmes, 2008; Webb, 2007; Wisconsin Department of Veterans Affairs, 2007; Young, 2005, and many more).

The financial support that a person might receive to go to college is a substantial incentive to join the service. Take that support away and some people will decide not to enlist after all.

What Colleges and Universities Can Do
To Help Veterans Finance their College Education

As described in this chapter, colleges and universities can greatly improve the financial situation of veterans by paying attention to one or more of the following problems that pertain to them. First, schools can ensure that fair and correct procedures are used to estimate the financial aid a veteran should be awarded. Second, some schools should try to find scholarships for veterans. Third, college can cost more than necessary for a veteran because the veteran is given incorrect curricular advice about courses to take. Fourth, financial aid offices can try to help veterans who have a family to support while in college. Fifth, GI Bill programs can be administered in a way to allocate funds to veterans in an inequitable manner.

Summary

Most veterans begin college with more financial demands than most non-veterans. Many people in American society assume that the financial burden of the education of veterans belongs to the VA when in fact this burden is on society and, more specifically, on the financial aid offices of the schools that veterans attend. This chapter explained several reasons why veterans are not in as good financial shape as are non-veterans. The staffs at financial-aid offices at colleges and universities everywhere are supposed to be dedicated to helping "all students" who come seeking financial help. If these staffs examine why veterans have financial problems, staff members can develop ways to solve the financial aid problems of veterans.

Chapter 10
Transfer of College Credits for Veterans

Veterans arrive at their college with credits that they have earned in many ways while in the military. The colleges and universities are familiar with how non-veterans at their school acquired credits prior to enrolling. Unfortunately, most colleges and universities are not fully aware of how veterans have earned their college credits. Sometimes, schools' transfer staffs provide veterans with few or no academic credit for the credits earned in the military. At other times, the schools lead veterans through bureaucratic procedures that are tedious and discouraging. As a result, veterans sometimes give up on the transfer process.

It is not clear why those responsible for awarding school academic credits to veterans deny them some or all of their credits. The staff may disapprove of the credits for which veterans apply. The staff may be reluctant to give transfer credits to veterans because they want veterans to take more courses offered by their school and earn the school more money. The general education department along with the department where a veteran has a major may try to force veterans to take extra courses.

Because the transfer staffs at most colleges and universities do not include veterans, and veterans are such a small percentage of students, these staffs do not have insight into the manner and situations by which veterans acquire credits prior to enrollment. Most transfer staffs of colleges and universities do not willfully create hassles for veterans who apply for transfer credits. However, many of the transfer staffs employ procedures that slow or stop the transfer procedure because the possible transfer credits of veterans are affected by factors for which staff members do not understand. The manner and situations by which veterans acquire credits prior to enrolling in a particular school is different from the manner and situations by which transfer non-veterans acquire credits prior to beginning college. The veterans are required to apply and reapply for credits that non-veterans are not required to do (e.g., Penn Foster, 2007).

The Purpose of this Chapter. This chapter examines the manner and situations by which veterans acquire credits while serving their country. Much of what is discussed in this chapter will be familiar to college administrators and professors. However, most college administrators and professors will not know the sources of difficulty in fairly awarding transfer. Once they come to understand where the potential transfer credits of veterans come from, they will understand how transfer credits may be incorrectly denied to veterans.

This chapter explains the transfer problems encountered by veterans in the following manner. First, the chapter describes the logic by which the transfer process is supposed to occur for all students, veteran and non-veteran. Second, the chapter describes the four kinds of transfer credits available to all students, veteran and non-veteran. These kinds include knowledge demonstrated: through advance placement exams; through courses taken at other colleges and universities; through military training and military experience; and through performance on college level entrance exams.

Third, the chapter discusses how veterans are denied one or more of the four kinds of credits. At some schools, veterans tend to be awarded with certain kinds of credits more than other kinds. They almost never get advance placement credit and get less credit for courses taken at other colleges. Veterans often get less or no transfer of military earned credits because aspects of the system for transferring these credits are fundamentally flawed. Furthermore veterans sometimes have difficulty receiving credit for passing college level exams.

Fourth, the crucial role of advisers in seeing that veterans do or do not get the transfer credit that they should receive is explained. Fifth, the differences in customs of transfer for veterans are reviewed as a function of institution size. Finally, it was concluded that the problems that veterans encounter with the transfer of credits constitute an injustice in light of the contributions veterans have made for our country.

The Logic For Transfer Credits

Knowledge is equivalent wherever it is learned. Accordingly, higher education everywhere recognizes that genuine knowledge taught at one accredited school is comparable to the same knowledge taught or learned somewhere else. For example, a course concerning a certain kind of knowledge at one school is in principle transferable to another school. If a student has learned about knowledge "xyz" in a course taught by another college, and if this college is accredited, the student will also be awarded credit for this "xyz" course at the student's current college. When the current college records that a student has taken a course in "xyz," it is said that the student has transferred the credit from a previous school to the current school.

Credits versus Grades

Generally, only the number of credit hours is transferred. The student's grade in a course is not transferred. Thus, the grades for transferred credits do not affect a student's overall cumulative average at the present college. Nevertheless, the number of transferred credit hours contributes to the total number of credits required for a degree and major.

Commonality across the Curricula of Schools

A critical part in the logic for transfer credits is whether or not the college where the student is currently enrolled teaches the course that the student took elsewhere in the past. For example, a student may transfer course "xyz" to his or her current college only if the current college does teach or might teach this course when there is a professor with this specialty on the college's faculty. If a course is not in the current college's curriculum, the current college could refuse to give a student transfer credit for this course.

However, many schools choose to give transfer credits to students for a course not in the school's curriculum if that course could be taught and if the school had a professor qualified to teach the course. They may also choose to give credit for the course if a "like" or similar course is or could be taught at their school. Alternatively, a school also may choose to conclude that it would never teach that certain course, whereupon transfer credit is never awarded for this course. The right of refusal of acceptance of transfer credit is an important issue in the transfer process.

Transfer As a Function of Course in a Student's Education

Academic credit earned elsewhere can be awarded for one or more of three educational purposes. Awarding academic credit for knowledge learned elsewhere previously might be granted at the college or university level, but denied to serve as a course in a student's major or minor. Academic credit earned elsewhere may be approved at the college or university level, denied at the department level, but considered acceptable as credit for the general education program. Finally, academic credit earned elsewhere may be approved at the college or university level, denied at the department level, denied to be used in meeting requirements for the general education program, but acceptable to serve as a free elective.

Fundamental Nature and Logic behind Transfer Credits

If you are a college educator, all of what has been said above is very familiar. However, regardless of whether you are an educator or not, the application of this logic becomes complicated when applied to different sources of transfer credit for veterans (Wenger, Rufflo, & Bertalan, 2006). The source of transfer credits include knowledge demonstrated: through advance placement exams for any student; through courses taken at other colleges and universities for any student; through military training and military experience for veterans only; and through performance on college level entrance exams for any student. The ways in which veterans are denied transfer of credits and the differences in customs of transfer for veterans as a function of institutional size are discussed below.

Legitimate Kinds of Transfer Credit

Advance Placement Credit

Advanced placement programs were briefly described in Chapter 6, which was concerned with educational programs in college. Veterans (due to their time in service) usually do not take this kind of test for advance placement credits, which generally apply to introductory college courses. Typically, the students who take advance placement exams do so after taking an advance placement course in their high school.

Knowledge Acquired at Other Colleges and Universities

On entering a particular college or university, the veterans, like other students, submit their transcript(s) from other schools to the transfer office of their institution. The transfer office then determines what credits will be given.

Military Credits

Knowledge acquired through military training and experience, as mentioned earlier, may also receive academic credits that correspond to that college or university. The majority of credits recommended for military service experience, training and education is done according to the American Council on Education (ACE) system. Since 1945, ACE has provided a collaborative link between the U. S. Department of Defense and higher education through its biennial publication, the Guide to the Evaluation of Educational Experiences in the Armed Services, used by registrars, admissions officers, academic advisers, career counselors, and Department of Defense (DOD) Voluntary-Education professionals. The Army/ACE Registry Transcript Service (AARTS), sailors and marines by the ACE Registry Transcript (SMART), and members of the Air Force through the Community College of the Air Force provide transcripts. Many colleges and universities claim to recognize these ACE- endorsed transcripts as official documentation of military experiences and accurate records.

The ACE accreditation system can also be used to help veterans who may want to pursue a major or minor similar to their military specialization. For example, a veteran may receive ACE credits for having been trained as a mechanic for certain airplanes or as an electronics technician for electrical systems on ships. The ACE accreditation system awards college transfer credits for military training, schooling and experience and can also be used to help guide veterans who want to pursue a major or minor similar to their military specialization (Anonymous, 1993).

Military-Credit System: Before Discharge. When a serviceman or woman is reaching discharge, he or she should go to the education officer to apply for the branch of service's transfer transcripts. In most cases, military schools attended by service members are listed on an ACE registry transcript according to the branch of service or on a DD-214, which is the certificate of discharge for veterans. Members of the army, navy, and Marine Corps are eligible to receive an ACE registry transcript directly from ACE. The air force does not use an ACE registry, but instead uses the Community College of the Air Force that is a regionally accredited degree-granting Community College. The coast guard uses a transcript-issuing service through the Coast Guard Institute, which issues transcripts to colleges for the awarding of college-level credit for members of the Coast Guard. The army National Guard uses a transcript-providing agency known as the National Guard Education Support Center, also based on ACE- evaluated military experiences.

Military-Credit System: On Enrolling in College. When entering one's chosen college or university, the veteran submits the military transcripts to the transfer office of the selected institution. Someone designated as qualified to award transfer credits examines the military credits and determines whether these credits correspond to courses in the schools curriculum. Every veteran who has served for six months or more is entitled to some or all of a school's General Education Credits, if the veteran's school will transfer military credits into academic credits. In addition, depending on how much training has been received, the military occupational specialty (MOS), duty assignments and military schools attended, a veteran most likely will qualify for upper-level courses in the veterans major or minor.

Transfer of ACE credits follows the same process as the transfer of credits from other colleges and universities. A veteran-student reports which kinds of discipline knowledge the ACE system indicates should be transferable. A professor in the college or university then evaluates the discipline knowledge that corresponds to ACE credits and decides whether or not this knowledge corresponds to the knowledge provided by a course in the curriculum of this professor's college or university.

Military Credit: Applied to Majors and Minors. A veteran-friendly college or university should enable veterans to integrate their military training and experience into their course of study if a veteran decides to pursue a degree similar to what they were doing when they were in the service.

Knowledge Demonstrated on College Level Entrance Exams

Available for both veterans and non-veterans are exams to assess whether or not a person has the knowledge for a particular college course. If a person passes the exam, this person is eligible to receive college credits. These examinations are similar to college-level end-of-course examinations and are widely accepted by colleges and universities. Nevertheless, the awarding of credits for passing exams is up to the colleges or universities. The "qualifying" scores vary among colleges and universities; some are more lenient than others.

For veterans, the exams are administered at military sites (Defense Activity for Non-Traditional Education Support Agency, 2004), with credit recommendations appearing on AARTS and SMART transcripts. Some of the types of tests available on various bases for free to active duty, guard and reserve members of our military are: DSST also known as DANTES tests consisting of 37 types of examinations, 3 semester hours each; and College Level Examination Program (CLEP) consisting of 34 types of examinations, 3 semester hours each. The American Council on Education recommends college credit for successfully completed exams listed above with credit recommendations appearing on AARTS and SMART. For more complete information on these examinations, visit ACE website at < http://www.collegeboard.com/testing/>. Also see: <http://www.acenet.edu/AM/Template.cfm?Section=Military_Programs>.

Erroneous Denial of Transfer Credits to Veterans

Veterans may have some lower-level credits transferred, but almost never qualify for advance placement credits. Sometimes their military credits, for which veterans are eligible because of military schools, training and military experience, are not transferred as well. This problem is widespread at little known, non-accredited colleges. Why veterans do not receive transfer credits in the ways just mentioned will now be explained.

Failure to Give Access to, and Approval of, Advance Placement Credits
Veterans rarely get advance placement credits because they often do not take the courses in high school that would prepare them to take the exams. As discussed earlier, they do not take these courses because they usually do not follow a college preparatory program in high school.

Guidance counselors in secondary schools should encourage all students, including students who plan to join the military to take advance placement courses. Students who might later join the military should be told that the credits for these courses would be beneficial, and that this may help them with pursing an education in the military.

Veterans who have advance placement credits are sometimes denied having these credits accepted by their school. Schools may deny credits because several years have elapsed since the veterans completed high school and when they were discharged from service. Schools may also deny credits because the courses for which veterans passed for advance placement were not appropriate for its programs. For example, advance placement for a course in

American History may be seen as irrelevant for a school concentrating on a degree in the fine arts.

Failure to Give Credit for Courses Taken at Other Colleges and Universities

If a non-veteran student attends a two-year or four-year college while in high school, these credits are often accepted by the college or university that they attend after high school. When students, both non-veterans and veterans choose a college to attend, they often chose a higher educational institution that is in the state or region in which the students grew up. Transfer staff or professors at any institution usually know the reputation and quality of other schools in the state or region and are more inclined to approve transfer applications of non-veteran students because they are familiar with the schools that a non-veteran attended previously. Consequently, because the institutions from which non-veterans obtained credits while in high school are near to the institution where the non-veteran seeks a degree, many non-veterans have the credits they obtained while in high school easily transferred.

Veterans, like many non-veteran students, often seek a college degree at an institution in the state or region where they grew up. However, the schools where veterans may take college courses are often far away from the institution where they seek their associate or bachelor degree. Veterans most likely take college courses at institutions far from their state or region because these courses were at the base they were stationed. Unfortunately, the transfer staffs are usually not inclined to give credits for courses taken at schools unfamiliar to them. Due to the current school of non-veteran students being more familiar than the school of veterans, non-veteran students are much more likely to receive more transfer credits .

Failure to Give Academic Credits for Military Schooling, Training and Experience that is Equivalent with Knowledge Acquired in College

Many veterans who have spent four or more years in the service may be qualified for as many as 50 lower and upper college credits, or even more. If a college or university accepts these credits, veterans may be able to finish a degree a year or two sooner than normal. Unfortunately, veterans encounter difficulty at many institutions in obtaining academic credits for their military schooling, training, education and experience credits.

It appears that the failure to transfer any or enough military credits is arbitrary. Sometimes different members of the transfer staff will award different amounts of academic credits for the same military credits. Instead of awarding credits on the basis of the knowledge taught, the credits awarded to veterans are often the result of a negotiation between the veterans and the transfer staff, if done at all.

The transfer process is also not consistent across different schools that have essentially the same mission and courses. For example, the courses offered at liberal arts institutions are similar to each other. Yet, different liberal arts institutions may award different kinds and amounts of transfer for military credits.

Timing of Application for ACE Credits. When applying for admission to a higher educational institution, veterans should bring a copy of their discharge form (DD214) and any additional documents that describe military schooling to the admission office, or if possible make arrangements and send them to the school prior to attending, and ask them to evaluate their military career for credits. Active-duty military and veterans should seek to have their credits transferred before they enroll in a college or university when possible. Promises by some institutions to transfer military credits sometimes cannot be trusted. Even schools that belong to the Servicemembers Opportunity Colleges (SOC), that have promised to provide transfer credits for military schooling, training, education and experience, sometimes do not live up to this promise. Therefore, the transfer agreement should be made in writing. Once an institution has established the transfer credits to be awarded, veterans should schedule meetings with the director of general education and with the chair for the department major to determine how the evaluation at the institution level applies to their general education or the major.

An Example of Refusal to Transfer Military Credits: Physical Ed. Some higher educational institutions do not give veterans academic credits, even for the physical education they received in the military. While on active duty, service members receive a considerable amount of physical training. This is true for every branch of service, although some branches and some military occupational specialties involve more physical training than other branches and specialties. In most cases, service members will have had much more physical education than physical education teachers at colleges and universities.

Nevertheless, a large number of physical education departments demand that veterans take elementary physical education courses. Various reasons are offered for insisting that veterans take these courses. For example, it has been claimed that their courses include recent theory of physical training that would not have been covered in the military. However, the nature of such theory is never explained and the absence of such theory in the military's physical training is never demonstrated. Some professors from other departments and some administrators believe that the requirement for veterans to receive such training exists to increase enrollment in the elementary physical education courses or to increase income at the schools. Regardless, service members receive the latest technique and drills in physical education, and also a great deal of training in nutrition and first aid. This requirement should be eliminated.

Failure to Give Credit for Passing College Level Exams

Generally, if veterans pass examinations at college levels, they will receive credit if there is a course in their college that corresponds to the knowledge pertinent to the exam (Defense Activity for Non-Traditional Education Support Agency, 2004). Some administrators and professors may believe that veterans are never denied credit for passing college level exams; however, such transfer is unfortunately not guaranteed.

Sometimes schools will claim that they do not have courses that correspond to the exam. This claim is sometimes made regarding transfer of credit to serve as electives. Such decisions are up to an administrator or professor in the college or university that veterans attend; therefore the transfer of a college level exam may also be negotiated. Also a school may deny credit for an exam if a lot of time has elapsed between taking the exam and when veterans begin college, at which time they apply for transfer credits.

A Serious Flaw in the Transfer Credit System As It Applies to Veterans

The Nature of the Flaw

Denial of transfer credit to veterans for prior credit experience (advance placement, courses from other colleges and universities, military credits, and college level exams) is rooted in a fundamental flaw in the way colleges and universities conduct the transfer process with veterans. This flaw is that each and every school is currently allowed to apply whatever criteria to the transfer decisions that are assumed to be unique to that school without a set or standard criterion. This is evident when many veterans have reported obtaining transfer of certain credits at one school that other veterans discover is denied for the same at another school. This discrepancy is somewhat understandable when the schools involved have very different missions (for example where one school is a liberal arts institution and the other is an engineering school). This discrepancy is not understandable when the two schools have essentially the same mission.

A Correction of the Flaw

The criteria for transfer decisions should be universal, regardless of school, regardless of course and regardless of veteran. The criteria that permit approval of the knowledge content for some prior credit experience should be the same everywhere. For example, the criteria that lead to transfer of the following courses should be the same at virtually all colleges: physical education, English composition, and college mathematics. The number of credits awarded for those courses may vary from time to time because different schools employ different schemes for allowing for credit hours, but most of the time should not.

Legislative Attempts to Eliminate the Flaw

Congress has created laws that were intended to render the awarding of transfer credit fair and equitable. One rule was that prior credit experience would be acceptable for transfer if it were from an accredited school or an accredited body. However, this rule did not preclude schools from rejecting transfer credit for prior credit experience from an accredited school or body on the basis that the prior credit experience did not meet the criteria of the school for such experience. Recently Congress passed a law that they thought would take care of the veterans transfer problem. In 2006, the House passed the Reauthorization of Higher Education Act that requires institutions to publicly disclose their transfer policies and specifically state whether the institution denies transfer credit based solely on the accreditation of the institution from which veterans are seeking transfer. However, Congress failed to realize that this Act still does not prevent an institution from deciding to not award credit arbitrarily. For example, a school may refuse credit because it has formulated new policies since they previously disclosed transfer policies. They may also refuse credit on the basis of accreditation of the source of the prior credit experience. Additionally, it may still deny transfer on the basis of the claim that their school's mission is unique.

The Proper Way to Eliminate the Flaw

The only resolution of the veterans transfer problem is to establish a system that requires universal criteria for transfer. The prior credit experience that is transferable at one school should be transferable at another school. Denial of transfer credit would require a school to explain how it does not offer any course relevant to the prior credit experience or that some or none of the prior credit experience would be acceptable for transfer anywhere. In order for Congress to establish a universal system, it will be necessary for Congress to establish a means for evaluating decisions about denial of some or all of a prior credit experience. One way this could be done would be to assign the major accrediting bodies the responsibility of evaluating appeals of transfer decisions. Another way would be to ask state approving agencies to establish panels of experts (such as are used by accrediting bodies) to evaluate the appeals of veterans regarding problematic transfer decisions. If not the state government or the federal government might similarly establish panels of experts (such as are used in evaluating grant proposals) to evaluate transfer appeals.

There is no formal evaluation of how prior credit experiences meet or do not meet the criteria of higher educational institutions. There is no attempt to determine whether the transfer decisions are consistent with academic standards in general. Veterans also are not told the specific knowledge from the prior credit experiences that are not relevant to the schools. The veterans are also told what criteria are unique to schools that provide the basis for rejecting transfer of prior credit experiences.

Presently, administrators or professors on transfer staff may reject courses for transfer and not truly disclose why transfers are denied. Custom has it that only the administrators and professors of schools can judge whether knowledge is within the scope of their school's mission. Consequently, they can deny credits for any transfer, regardless of whether the denial is legitimate. Under the current custom, no one can overturn the decision except some higher-level administrator or professor. However, as noted above, the vast majority of schools do not have fair transfer appeal processes where higher level administrators or professors are free to overturn decisions of lower level administrators or professors. As a result, the transfer decisions are capricious between schools and across transfer decisions at the same school.

The Crucial Role of Advisers in the Transfer Process

Veterans can earn college credit in various ways. Understanding that each service branch has its own resources is essential to provide good academic advising for both service members and veterans. Each branch has trained professionals in place to guide service members through a complex network of tuition assistance, the transferability of credits, and military documentation but often service members are not given the necessary training. Having trained staff capable of understanding the service member's unique situation helps to facilitate a positive learning community (Berry, 1977).

The members of the Servicemembers Opportunity Colleges (SOC) colleges and universities promise to provide transfer credit to veterans (SOC, 2004). However, SOC does not police its membership to determine whether their member schools are fairly providing the transfer credits. There are some SOC schools that are not providing the transfer credit as promised.

The good news is that some schools have veterans' advisors. Also some schools have certifying officials who play the role of veterans' advisors (Association of Veterans Education, 2006; National Association of Veterans Programs Administrators; NAVPA (2006). No doubt, these advisors help veterans obtain their transfer credits. However, these schools are the exception and not the rule in our educational system. The veterans' advisor should be the rule and not the exception for all schools.

Transfer Customs Differ Between
Students who are Veterans and Who are Non-veterans

In essence, veterans are denied transfer of prior-credit experience, or have to go through more bureaucratic procedures to obtain such transfer than do non-veteran students. As previously stated above, non-veteran students receive advance-placement credits whereas veterans rarely do. Non-veteran students have a greater proportion of their transfer applications for college courses taken elsewhere approved than do veterans. Military credits transferred are less often accepted for transfer than they should be. Veterans may receive credit for passing college level exams, but non-veteran students rarely have the need to take such exams.

It is incongruous that higher education, the bastions of unbiased thinking, will often not give veterans credit for what they have learned while they were in the military. It is also inappropriate that America has established the GI Bill program and other programs to help veterans finance their college education (Caudell, 2005; Department of Veteran Affairs, 2005; Hunter & Tankovich, 2007; Peterson's College Planner, 2007a,b; Veterans Administration, 1991), and at the same time, deny credits to veterans and, thereby, force them to take more time to get a degree than should be necessary. Furthermore, to the extent that veterans are aware of the unfairness of the transfer process at many schools, individuals will be less likely to enlist in order to obtain a college education (Asch, Kilburn, & Klerman, 1999; Colloquy, 2006; Farrell, 2005).

What Colleges and Universities Can Do About
The Transfer Problems of Veterans

Transfer problems for veterans are easy for schools to eliminate. First, in the case of advance placement credits, veterans should be given academic credit for them regardless of how long ago the exam was taken. Had they attended college for a year right after high school, they would have received transfer credits that would usually have remained on a transcript until they returned to school.

Second, credits obtained for courses take at other schools should be transferred even if the schools are not well known as long as a school was accredited. Third, military credits (based on military schooling, training, education and military experience) should be transferred. Fourth, transfer credits should be awarded to veterans who achieve passing scores on college level exams.

Transfer of credits for veterans is a problem that occurs in higher education in general. American higher education should develop a transfer system that is consistent across the United States. Until such a system is developed, a college or university that wants to be fair to veterans should communicate with other schools to ensure that all that can be done is done.

Summary

Veterans, like non-veteran students, can apply for transfer credits. This chapter described four different kinds of transfer credits available to students and veterans. These kinds include knowledge demonstrated: through advance placement exams; through courses taken at other colleges and universities; through military schooling, training, education and military experience; and through performance on college level entrance exams. Second, the chapter discussed how veterans are denied credits. Veterans almost never get advance placement credits and get fewer credits for courses taken at other colleges. Veterans often get less or no transfer for military credits because the system is fundamentally flawed or deliberately not followed. Also veterans many times have difficulty receiving credit for passing college level exams. Third, the chapter examined the crucial role of advisers in seeing that veterans receive the transfer credits that they deserve. Finally, it was concluded that the problems that veterans encounter with the transfer of credits is wrong and must be corrected.

Chapter 11

The Health Problems of Veterans and their Academic Performance

The United States tries to do a lot medically to help veterans, more so than most nations around the world. Despite sensational reports in the national news, medical care given to most veterans is good. Given that veterans constitute somewhat less than three percent of the US population, the medical help that the United States gives its veterans is quite impressive. Veterans who have been wounded, became ill, or acquired a disorder as a result of military service are given the best medical care possible under most circumstances. Even if the best medical care is given, nothing can truly compensate for a wound, illness, or disorder. No one would want to have such a debilitating problem.

The Purpose of this Chapter. Physiological and emotional problems of veterans can impact their capability to obtain a college education. This chapter reviews the effects of wounds, illnesses and disorders on learning. Some of the content of this chapter will be new to readers who may not be familiar with the military. Somewhat less of the content will be new to veterans who did not develop a medical problem themselves while in the service or did not report or recognize it while in the military or to the VA after leaving the service.

Much of what is said in this chapter will be very familiar to some readers from the veteran community. However, all readers will discover something in this chapter about how wounds, illnesses and other disorders may limit veteran's educational opportunities, and how colleges, universities, the Department of Veterans Affairs (VA) and society may treat veterans' medical problems.

The chapter begins, first, by reviewing information about the disabilities that veterans may have. Second, the chapter examines how colleges and universities should provide treatment for the medical problems of veterans. Third, there is a need to educate veterans about health care. Fourth, because disabilities can lessen veterans' ability to learn, it is proposed that society should provide more support for veterans' health problems when they attend college.

Health and Academic Performance

Recent theories in educational psychology indicate that academic performance is the product of a variety of psychological processes. Central to academic performance are cognitive processes and skills, such as reading, writing, and note taking (Mayer, 1999). However, many researchers have recently agreed, that in addition to the cognitive processes, a person's physical and emotional states also are involved in academic performance (Herrmann, Raybeck, & Gruneberg, 2002). The physical and social environments, as well as a person's ability to respond to the physical and social environments also affect the cognitive processes. Thus, it will not come as a surprise to any reader that any wound, illness, or disorder experienced by service members can make the educational process more difficult.

Medical problems of veterans may constitute temporary or permanent educational disabilities. Medical problems may involve a disabling of the senses (visual, auditory, kinesthetic), making it difficult for veterans to perceive educational presentations, either by an instructor or by media. Damage in certain areas of the brain can make cognitive understanding of lectures and instructions by veterans difficult. As with other non-traditional students, evaluating what veterans have learned can be hampered by damage to one or more of veterans' modes of communication, both receptive and expressive (speech; use of fingers for sign language; brain control of a computer). Any medical condition that involves pain will interfere with both learning and the capability to express what has been learned. Additionally, all disabilities interfere with the educational process to the extent that they interfere with daily life, decreasing the time and energy veterans have to devote to their studies.

Disabilities interfere with the educational process to varying degrees, from negligible interference with this process to preventing a veteran from receiving any education at all. Thus, understanding the disabilities of veterans may help professors, administrators, and students appreciate the problems of veterans with who they interact. This chapter has the goal of conveying the many ramifications of veterans' disabilities that may interfere with their opportunities to obtain a college education. The chapter first reviews information about the nature of veterans' disabilities. Second, the chapter examines how colleges and universities do, or should, treat the medical problems of veterans. Third, the need of veterans to be given continual education about health care is considered. Finally, it is proposed that there is now and always will be a need for society to provide veterans with more support for their health problems than in the past and a need to treat the medical problems of veterans that impact their education.

Disabilities

Determining that veterans are disabled in some manner is obvious in some cases, but not obvious in other cases. This chapter begins with a description of how veterans may be classified as having certain disabilities and a discussion of the nature of wounds, illnesses, and other disorders that veterans may acquire through military service. The chapter looks at the classification of medical problems with educational disabilities. Next, the VA system for assessing whether veterans have disabilities is explained, along with those disabilities that are not recognized by the VA. Finally, the process of determining whether a medical problem constitutes a service-connected disability is explained.

The Nature of Wounds, Illnesses, and Disorders of Veterans Acquired Through Military Service

The vast majority of service members experience hazardous duty sometime during their tour of duty. Such duty sometimes leads to their death; such duty sometimes leads to serious injury or illness. A substantial number of those who serve in peacetime, experience a serious injury or illness of a temporary, or even permanent, nature.

For those who go to war, many of them experience injury or illness of a temporary or permanent nature. Some estimates hold that about 10% of those who go to war also make the ultimate sacrifice. However, it is very difficult to accurately assess this due to the many veterans who die later in life of injuries they received in combat when they were young. Regardless, an individual who loses his or her life also loses all of the good that may come from life, such as enjoying the families they left behind and the families they may have wanted to start. They also lose the opportunity to enjoy a career and participate as a citizen in the affairs of a community, state, and our nation.

The number of service members who survive a war, but who are wounded, is approximately three times as many as those who die in a war. This estimate is based on the number of wounded service members who have declared their injury. Due to the advancements of modern medicine, the survival rate is growing each year our nation is at war. Wounds from war can be short-term or last a lifetime.

Of those medical problems that last a lifetime, some will permit somewhat of a normal lifestyle. Yet, many medical problems limit the conduct of life to some degree. Regardless of the limitations, both mild and severe, all of them will require intermittent medical care. Other limitations are so severe that it is impossible for the individual to have a normal life at all. Some veterans spend the remainder of their lives in VA medical or psychiatric hospitals, nursing homes or other care facilities due to the severity of their medical problems.

Disabilities Resulting from Wounds, Illnesses, and Disorders

Medical problems that are superficial or brief are usually first treated by the military medical staff. These problems do not always result in physical disabilities, but can either immediately or later in life. Medical problems that last somewhat longer are usually treated sooner or later in a VA medical facility (Leisner, 1995). Programs must attend to the wounds and their effects in a comprehensive manner (Kingsbury, 2007). These problems, and those that last longer, are regarded as disabling for at least a while.

Some disabilities limit veterans from carrying out some aspects of life that they would have had no difficulty doing prior to acquiring the disabilities. Some disabilities may not be considered permanent by certain medical standards, VA regulations or doctors. Those disabilities that last a lifetime are normally considered permanently disabling.

Medical problems that are permanently disabling do so to varying degrees. A permanent disability does not necessarily disable veterans from doing everything. Blindness, paralysis, loss of limbs, some illnesses and some disorders limit many things veterans do. However, most disabilities acquired through military service are only partly disabling. Although permanent in nature, the veterans with some partial disabilities can still function to some extent. For example, a limp involves a disability when walking but does not disable the person when sitting down. Some disabilities are not apparent to people other than afflicted veterans. For example, a veteran with an injured back limiting a full range of motion, a recurring illness such as malaria, or a post-traumatic stress disorder (PTSD) are often not recognized by others as having a disability, unless the veteran has shared with others the nature of his or her disability or others have observed the specific effect it has on the veteran.

The VA System for Assessing Whether Medical Problems Qualify as a Disability

The VA Medical system has the responsibility for treating all temporary and permanent disabilities that are recognized as having resulted from or worsened due to military service. Medical problems that result from military service are called "service-connected" by the VA. A veteran who disables a foot by tripping over toys off-duty cannot be said to have a service-connected disability. However, a servicemember who breaks a foot during maneuvers, organized physical training such as running or actual combat will be said to have a service connected disability if the break limits the veteran from carrying out some aspects of life.

Because disabilities can disappear or become worse over time, the VA assesses and reassesses the disabilities of veterans periodically as needed, based on the disability and a set of criteria. The assessment of disabilities requires a rating of the degree to which the disability limits daily life. This rating expresses the degree of limitation by percentages, ranging from zero (recognized, but not compensable) to 100% (total disability and compensable). Thus, a decrease in a rating, such as 30% to 0%, indicates that the disability has decreased in severity. Disabilities that are temporary may not need medical care after the medical condition that caused the disability is corrected. An increase in a rating, such as from 30% to 50% indicates that the disability has worsened or has become more limiting, indicating that additional medical care may also be needed.

The Validity of the Assessment Process. The VA provides medical care for disabilities for as long as a veteran has the disabilities. Medical assistance for medical problems that do not appear until after discharge or become worse after discharge require that the veteran so affected submit a claim for the need for assistance (Maze, 2007a; Roche, 2000).

The VA also provides assistance with daily living in proportion to the percentage of the disabilities. Complementing medical assistance with treatment are such adjuncts as medications, prosthetics and other means of treatment. The VA also provides monetary assistance to compensate veterans earning power and to enable them to confront difficulties caused by the disability that the VA medical staff cannot treat. The amount of monetary assistance is based on the percentage rating of veterans' disabilities. For a detailed look at how the VA rates veterans see Department of Veterans Affairs (2007;VBA 3800, <http://www.warms.vba.va.gov/bookc.html>). The disability assessment process ensures that veterans who have the greatest need for medical and financial support get it.

Overview of the VA Assessment Process. Veterans with medical problems when discharged from service normally have a "discharge physical." This physical helps identify medical problems and determine if or how a problem may have occurred or may have been exacerbated by military service. Problems found during this discharge physical are then looked at in more detail by specialists as time permits. The reports of these physicals are given to case managers who work with the VA during the discharge process. Those veterans who are judged to have problems that are service related are said to have a "service-connected" disability. This disability then receives a disability rating as discussed above. Unfortunately, not all service members who are discharged receive the same detailed physical as others and therefore, many possible disabilities are overlooked.

Medical Problems Due to Military Service that Arise After Discharge

Some veterans have physiological and emotional disabilities that are service- connected, but not known until after discharge. Sometimes these medical problems arise in college. In many cases, the VA does not know about certain disabilities prior to veterans enrolling in college. Sometimes, veterans do not recognize their own medical problems until they become severe.

In some cases, the VA has reason to suspect that veterans may have certain disabilities as a result of service. However, a suspicion is not enough to require the VA to inform veterans that they have medical problems that qualify as disabilities. Even if the VA suspects that certain medical problems of veterans are due to military service, the VA is not obligated to inform veterans about potential disabilities until science has established that the illness or disorder is service-connected.

Determining that a New Medical Problem is a Service-Connected Disability

The process by which a medical problem comes to be regarded by the VA as service-connected is illustrated by the history of this process for veterans of the Vietnam War (1964-1975) who were exposed to Agent Orange (Dockery, 1997). The US sprayed Agent Orange on foliage in the Vietnam jungles to cause trees, bushes and ground plants to loose their leaves and die. The compound was called Agent Orange because the sky appeared orange when it was sprayed in the air. The containers of this chemical were encircled by orange bands, in contrast to Agent Blue whose containers were encircled by blue bands. Once trees lost their leaves, it was much easier for American forces, fighter planes and ground troops, to see North Vietnamese and Viet Cong troops who were aggressing on the American posts and troops. The use of Agent Orange is held to have saved American lives.

Unfortunately, the medical problems caused by Agent Orange were not recognized until years later when. Vietnam veterans began reporting various illnesses after returning from the war. and suggested that these illnesses were linked to exposure to Agent Orange. At first, the VA denied that any illnesses were due to Agent Orange. Nevertheless, the VA sponsored much research into the role of Agent Orange in the development of various medical conditions. Today, thanks to the VA research, at least a dozen illnesses and disorders are recognized as originating with Agent Orange exposure. Research continues into the possibility that this chemical has other disabling effects on Vietnam veterans.

The evolution of service-connected status for veterans is also illustrated by the medical problems of veterans of the Desert Storm Conflict (1991). Sadam Hussein's troops used toxic gasses and possibly biological gasses as weapons in some battles against American forces (Tucker, 2006). However, it was unclear whether the amount of these gases or their composition injured American combatants of that war. Again medical problems due to these gases were not recognized for many years. Initially, veterans of the war with Iraq did not receive compensation for any disabilities that they claimed arose from the gas warfare to which they were exposed. The VA again engaged in research to determine whether or not the gas exposure actually resulted in both physiological and psychological illness (Storzbach, Campbell, Binder, McCauley, Anger, Rohlmann, Kovera, 2000). As a result, many illnesses are recognized today as having originated in the gas warfare of Desert Storm. Currently research is being conducted into the negative long-term effects that the anthrax vaccinations may have had on our service members.

Because the VA's procedures for evaluating a claim are protracted, a veteran is not entitled to full medical treatment without cost for a substantial amount of time and, sometimes, not at all. In any war, the VA system is stretched to the limit, and many claims do not get the immediate attention that they deserve. The deficiencies of the VA's claims system are well known and deserve legislative revision (Stiglitz & Bilmes, 2008)

College Health Care and Veterans

Colleges and universities invariably have a health center or a health-care professional to serve students with health problems. The purpose of a college health service is to treat all students for minor illness or disorders and to refer more serious problems to the appropriate health centers staffed by professionals. Virtually all college health services encourage students to sign up for health insurance that the health service recommends. Veterans sometimes make the mistake of assuming that the VA will take care of all their serious medical problems and do not sign up for this insurance. Failure to sign up is unwise if medical problems develop.

Medical Problems of Veterans That College Health Services Might Encounter

Veterans sometimes bring service-connected wounds, illnesses or disorders to campus that college health services are just not prepared to treat (Storzbach, Campbell, Binder, McCauley, Anger, Rohlmann, & Kovera, 2000; Sullivan, Krengel, Proctor, Devine, Heeren, & White, 2003). The staffs of these health centers generally have not had the appropriate training to treat many service-connected medical problems. Even if college doctors or nurses have experience relevant to particular disabilities of veterans, the health services usually will not have had on hand medical equipment and medicines needed to treat the disabilities.

Service-connected Medical Problems that Veterans May Bring to Campus. Each conflict brings health risks to some participants in each war. Veterans of WWII and Korea may experience exposure to nuclear weapons and chemical agent experiments. Some participants in the cold war also experienced exposure to nuclear testing. As described above, Vietnam veterans experienced Agent Orange, hepatitis C, and PTSD. Gulf war veterans suffer from exposures to smoke, chemical agents, biological agents, and depleted uranium. Veterans from the war on terror experience penetrating injuries, blunt trauma, burn injuries, traumatic brain and spinal cord injury, vision loss, amputation, and inappropriate medications (Office of Academic Affiliations, 2005).

Consider some of the many health challenges that veterans may bring to college and university health services and may impair a veteran's ability to complete college tasks. Some veterans return to campus with wounds, diseases, and disorders that make it harder for them to complete a degree. Some veterans have head injuries (Herrmann, Schooler, et al., 2001; Leisner, 1995) that may be manageable in college (Parente & Herrmann, 2003). Some veterans have spinal cord injuries (Lavela, Weaver, Smith. & Chen, 2006; Leisner, 1995). Chemical exposures interfere with the adjustment of some veterans (Carney, Sampson, Voelker, 2003; Spaulding, Eddy, & Chandras, 1997; Storzbach, Campbell, Binder, McCauley, Anger, Rohlmann, & Kovera, 2000; Sullivan, Krengel, Proctor, Devine, Heeren, & White, 2003). Some veterans are troubled by sleep apnea (Likar, Panciera, Erickson, & Rounds, 1997). Some may have arthritis (Callahan & Pincus, 1988) but surprisingly they may be less susceptible to age-related problems of cognition (McLay & Lyketsos, 2000).

While in the military, veterans often experience danger and sometimes risk their lives (Armstrong, Best & Domenici, 2005; Brady & Rappoport, 1973; Egandorf, 1985; Figley, 1978a,b, 1988; Geraerts, Kozaric-Kovacic, Merckelbach, Peraica, Jelicic, & Candel, 2007; Keane, 1998; Kubaany, Leisen, & Kaplan, 2000; Mindy & Lester, 1994). The experience of hazardous duty or combat can be expected to create psychological problems for many veterans (American Psychiatric Association, 1994; Armstrong, Best & Domenici, 2005; Geraerts, Kozaric-Kovacic, Merckelbach, Peraica, Jelicic, & Candel, 2007). Danger can have lingering effects, such as pervasive anxiety, that may influence the college performance of veterans (Armstrong, Best, & Domenci, 2006; Black, Westwood, Sorsdal & Michael. 2007; Burriss, 2007; Enzie, Sawyer, & Montgomery, 1973; Indianapolis Healing Arts Program, 2006; Joanning, 1975; Hyer & Boudewyns, 1988; Zahn, 2007).

Some veterans experience anxiety problems or Post Traumatic Stress Disorder (PTSD; Manguno-Mire, Sautter, Lyons, Myers, Perry, Sherman, Glynn, & Sullivan, 2007). As a result, it is necessary for professionals in the VA Psychiatric Service, Veterans Centers, and in private practice to counsel students who are veterans (Berry, 1977; Black, Westwood, Sorsdal & Michael. 2007). PTSD is a common outcome of combat and hazardous duty that may not appear until after a year or more in college (Boscarino, 2006; Figley, 1978a,b; Keane, 1998; Kubany, Leisen, & Kaplan, 2000; Kubany, Haynes & Abueg, 1996; Lanham, 2005; Muran, & Motta, 1993; Powell & Doan, 1992; Roca & Freeman, 2001; Yehuda, Keene, Harvey, Levengood, et al., 1995; Williams, 1987; see also Schnurr, Rosenberg, & Friedman, 1993; Shepard, 2003; Strange, 1974; Tick, 2005).

The psychological difficulties of some veterans may constitute disabilities, as defined by the American Psychiatric Association (1994). Some service men and women develop alcohol dependency and substance abuse (Bensen, 1989; Cook, Walser, Kane, Ruzek, & Woody, 2006) when they try to deal with their disabilities. Some veterans have engaged in sexual abuse (Coyle, Wolan, & Van Horn, 1996; see also Dobbs, Hopper & Jurkovic, 1990). Suicide is a danger for some veterans, requiring that they be watched when the signs of suicide suggest it may be impending (Nursing Standard, 2007; Tiet, Finney, & Moos, 2006). Some may need of some form of counseling (Berry, 1977; Black, Westwood, Sorsdal, & Michael. 2007).

In addition, hazardous duty and combat can have an impact not only on veterans, but also on their families and loved ones. A wife may find her spouse to be withdrawn, hostile, aggressive and even sometimes violent. In recent years, women have increasingly served in the military (Creveld, 2001). Women who have served in combat or are wives or significant others of veterans may acquire psychological distress caused by veterans with PTSD

(Gimbel & Booth, 1994; Manguno-Mire, Sautter, Lyons, Myers, Perry, Sherman, Glynn, & Sullivan, 2007; Minnesota National Guard, 2007a,b; Sherman, Zanotti, & Jones 2005). Husbands or wives who have been in combat experience the same problems. Members of the families in general, including children, may encounter the violence of a veteran (Rentz, Martin, Gibbs, Clinton-Sherrod, Harrison, & Marshall, 2006). Consequently, treatment of veterans who are in college for PTSD and related disorders will often require treatment of members of the family for the distress they experience because of veteran behavioral problems (Lanham, 2005; Minnesota National Guard, 2007a,b; Stoll, 20067).

College Health Services and Service-Connected Disabilities

Some veterans know how to take care of their disabilities and know where the nearest VA hospital or clinic is in case they need care. If their disability has been treated, they usually know the routine care that they will need for their service-connected disability.

Sometimes veterans may have a medical emergency. Most colleges and universities are supposed to, and sometimes-even claim to, be able to cope with emergencies. Nevertheless, the medical personnel of college health services are generally not trained or equipped to deal with many of the emergencies that veterans may have.

Higher educational institutions are not prepared to address emergency care for veterans for two reasons. There is no requirement for the health centers of colleges and universities to obtain information about disabilities from the VA. Consequently, colleges and universities may not seek information about the disabilities of veterans on their campuses to avoid financial liability for treating these disabilities. If a college or university were aware that veterans had certain disabilities and that this school's health service failed to provide emergency care for veterans' disabilities, it is possible that veterans could sue the school for the poor care.

Alternatively, there also is no requirement for the VA to inform a school about the disabilities of veterans who are on a school's campus. Consequently, the VA—in particular, the staff of rehabilitation units—does not voluntarily provide information about veterans' disabilities. It might be argued that the VA does not inform a school about the disabilities of veterans who attend the school because the VA is required to keep the confidentiality of disabilities of veterans. However, veterans can waive this confidentiality if asked.

Some veterans would not mind if the VA informed their school of their disabilities. However, there is no routine procedure of the VA or colleges to ask veterans if they would waive this confidentiality. Even if some or all of the veterans on campus were to keep their disability confidential, it would still be possible for the VA to tell colleges the nature of disabilities on campus while not providing the names of the disabled veterans. The knowledge of the veterans' disabilities on campus would enable a health center director to prepare the center's staff for emergencies associated with the disabilities reported to the school. For example, currently it is known that some returning veterans of all wars have a Post Traumatic Stress Disorder (PTSD) or other mental health illnesses. The VA and some other organizations can provide veterans with help with PTSD (Eagle, 2007; Egendorf, 1985). However, almost no college health service has a contingency plan for treating the PTSD or mental health problem of the veterans attending their institutions despite knowing that they should be sensitive to the possibility of the emergence of medical problems of veterans and others (Spaulding, Eddy, & Chandras, 1997).

College Health Services and Non Service-Connected Disabilities

As described above, new disabilities and new causes of disabilities occur all the time. A period of time elapses before research may establish a scientific basis for determining that a certain disability is service-connected. Sometimes that period involves many years; the approval of some disabilities may be delayed indefinitely. As a result, institutions cannot be expected to have insight into how to treat veterans' illnesses or conditions that the VA has yet to regard as service-connected. Most colleges or universities obviously cannot have a contingency plan to help veterans with problems that have yet to be understood or recognized by the VA.

Some college health officials feel that such treatment is the responsibility of the VA. However, until a medical problem is classified as service-connected, the problem is the responsibility of the entire health-care system (including the National Institutes of Health, the Center for Disease Control, local hospitals, and clinics) . Some agency in the Federal Government should be assigned the responsibility of informing college health services that veterans may return with medical problems that are currently not designated as service-connected, but with which the veterans need care, treatment, information, medication, and support for selves and family members. In the meantime, college health officials have the same responsibility to treat veterans with medical problems unrecognized by the VA, as they would have to treat non-veterans with medical problems with similar symptoms.

The Need of Veterans for Continual Education about Health Care

Both veterans and non-veteran students must take care of their physiological and emotional health. Some veterans and non-veteran students will have physiological and emotional disabilities. However, veterans are in a greater need of periodic exposure to health care information because of their military experience.

Veterans need information about self-care of health issues for several reasons. As described above, veterans who have served abroad or in combat may have medical problems that may emerge long after they have left the service. Also, many veterans do not know what care is offered by health services, VA hospitals and clinics. They should be advised that service organizations such as the American Legion, Veterans of Foreign Wars, and Disabled American Veterans, as well as state-operated Veterans Affairs offices could assist them with information on where to go for medical treatment, and to help them with their VA claims.

Veterans should be informed on admission that their school will not provide much or any treatment of students who do not have health insurance. Thus, veterans should be advised routinely by the VA to purchase a college's health insurance for medical problems that are not currently recognized as service-connected.

College and universities presumably do not discriminate against disabled veterans who study at their institution. No clear case has been reported in which a student veteran has been excluded from some educational activity because of his or her disability. However, there is a case recently in which a professor who was a disabled veteran charged his university with discrimination against him because of his disabilities (R. Wilson, 2006).

Societal Support for Treatment of Veterans' Health Problems

For various reasons, the President's budget never provides sufficient support for the VA's medical program. As a result, many veterans wait for months for the health care that they need (Stiglitz, & Bilmes, 2008). Because the process for establishing a certain disability as service-connected requires considerable investigation, considerable time must pass before the claims of veterans for treatment of certain conditions are approved. America's veterans are normally treated well, but the immediacy of care can be improved. Recently considerable effort has been made to improve the timeliness of care for veterans with disabilities (Anonymous, VFW, 2007a).

What Colleges and Universities Can Do About The Treatment of Veterans Health Problems

The health-care problems of veterans in college arise because there are no government regulations to ensure that colleges and universities are given information about disabled veterans enrolled at their school. Without such information, college/university health systems cannot know what veterans might need medical attention. Nevertheless, any college or university that wants to address the health problems of veterans can do so. Hopefully, the government will establish such a system that will provide colleges and universities with the medical information that they need about veterans.

Presently, in order for a college health service to treat veterans, a school should first contact the rehabilitation office of the nearest VA regional office and ask the Rehabilitation Office for the names of all disabled veterans who are at their school. The VA office will probably reply that it cannot provide the names because of confidentiality. Then the college or university should ask the VA office to ask the disabled veterans who attend their school to permit giving their names and kind of disabilities to their school. If the VA says that it cannot ask disabled veterans about this matter, persist and they will eventually give the names of veterans who do not want to maintain confidentiality.

If the VA will not provide any or all of the names of disabled veterans, the school should ask for the nature of disabilities on their campus in order to prepare for treatment of a disability in an emergency. The VA rehabilitation office will not be able to provide this information if there are just a few veterans on campus because knowledge of disabilities may still identify the disabled veterans. However, the VA rehabilitation office will be able to provide this information when there are more than a few veterans at a school.

Second, the college health service should ask the VA Rehabilitation Office for the nature of diseases or disorders that currently are not classified as service-connected but may be so classified in the future. Explain that this information is requested so the college health service may be able to treat such problems should they emerge while the veteran is a student at their school. The VA rehabilitation office should be able to provide this information.

Third, once the college health service has identified the nature of some or all of the major disabilities or potential disabilities on campus, the school should prepare a contingency plan for the treatment of these medical conditions. A contingency plan should include at a minimum, name and location of the nearest VA hospital or clinic for veterans, should the college health service not be able to treat them. In certain cases, professors and administrators should be sensitized to certain symptoms that may indicate to them medical emergencies.

Fourth, college health services should contact veterans on campus via campus mail or email and provide them with health information. In particular, veterans should be advised that the college health service is not obligated to treat veterans for service connected, or potentially service-connected, disabilities unless he or she has the college's health insurance. In addition, college health services should be able to forward to veterans any information about the treatment of a wound, illness, or disorder that may pertain to them because of their military service.

Summary

This chapter reviewed many ways that wounds, illnesses, and disorders could become a disability and could affect veterans' ability to learn. This knowledge reviewed may help professors and administrators appreciate the medical problems that challenge veterans while in school. An understanding of these disabilities may also help non-veteran students appreciate the disabilities that some veterans may have to deal with.

Chapter 12
Employment for Veterans When They Graduate

Veterans seek a college degree to obtain better employment than they would have without a degree (Cooper, 2007). Veterans who have most of their college programs completed, usually in the middle of their senior year, begin to search for positions to take after graduation. The process of finding a position requires time and effort. This is a stressful time for most students who are about to leave the semi-protected cocoon of college.

Ideally, a graduate would like to choose from several offers that occur at about the same time. Graduates also want to find an opportunity in a location that is best for them. In addition, the graduate definitely wants full-time employment instead of temporary or part-time employment. However, for some careers, an internship is required before attaining full-time employment. In addition, a typical graduate wants to accept a position that pays well. All of these considerations place a great deal of pressure on the soon-to-be, or new, college graduate. The current economy may prolong the time a graduate needs to find a job.

The Purpose of this Chapter. Because our country invests considerable funds into veterans' education, it would be expected that veterans who are about to obtain a college degree would be provided with a system to easily find employment. Unfortunately, there is no system to ensure that veterans who graduate get the good positions for which they qualify. Such a system has yet to be developed because the government has not mandated one be established. An appropriate employment-search system has not been developed for veterans who are college graduates because the VA primarily deals with the employment of veterans who do not have a college degree.

This chapter first explains how search programs at nearly all colleges and universities are currently conducted at their career centers. Second, it explains how these programs work well for non-veteran graduates, but poorly for veteran graduates. Third, search programs conducted by the Department of Veterans Affairs (VA) and by the Department of Labor on behalf of the VA are discussed, and it is explained why these search programs do not meet the needs of veterans who are college graduates. Fourth, consideration is given to the characteristics of an ideal search program for veterans who have graduated from college. Finally, the chapter looks at the costs to American society by not providing a veteran with an employment search program appropriate to their college degree and military background.

Typical Career Search Programs of Colleges and Universities

The College Career Center

A college or university's career search program is conducted usually by a career center that assists students and graduates as they develop career plans. A variety of services are provided for students to help them get started on their career. In order to understand the problem with veterans finding jobs at graduation, we must also look at how available positions are found, how graduates learn to find a position related to the individuals skills, and the procedures career centers use to guide graduates toward appropriate employment.

Search Procedures of Career Centers

Career center staff personnel focus on finding employment that is appropriate for any student's major, interests, attitudes, aptitudes and experience. The staff instructs the soon-to-be graduate on how to seek employment through a variety of sources: the school's alumni association, job fairs and, professional organizations that are relevant to a set of particular attributes of the individual searcher. The career center will circulate a student's resume where opportunities exist. At many schools, students are directed to talk with alumni who have volunteered to help new graduates find employment.

Providing Preparation for Searching Tasks

Career centers typically offer courses in resume writing, role-playing interviews to develop skills and comfort, and how to find available positions in print and on-line sources. The staff of a career center will help students to identify skills, such as those in communication, computer, foreign languages, and others. Many career centers maintain files of application letters so that sample letters will be readily available when students are searching for jobs.

Finding the Opportunities Available

Staffs of the typical career centers are trained and/or experienced in finding positions for college graduates. The staff members are aware of the various sources that list job opportunities that are currently available. They are familiar with job banks, now commonly found on-line. These staff members are also normally associated with the businesses in the immediate area. They forge relationships with employers and other sources for information about jobs.

The staff members of career centers are also aware of the major employment agencies and how to find employment specialists who seek people (as "head hunters") to fill certain positions that industry or government need to be filled. If necessary, career center staffs will administer various vocational interest or aptitude surveys (e.g., Strong Interest Inventory and Myers-Briggs Type Inventory) and counsel students who, in the senior year, are not sure of what would be best for them.

College Career Search Programs for Veterans

Career centers provide all of the above services to veterans just as they provide them for non-veteran students. Nevertheless, most colleges and universities are unable to give veterans the help they need because these centers search for positions for veterans in the same manner as they search for jobs for non-veteran students. These staff members seek employment that may be appropriate for veterans' majors but often overlook the training and experience that the veterans have had in the military. Most colleges and universities are not aware of how to market graduates with military experience when seeking employment for them. The career center staffs at many institutions of higher education are unaware of the strengths that a veteran offers to employers as they market veterans who graduate (Buyer, 2004; Melymuka, 1999).

The Alumni Network

Career centers in many colleges and universities assist non-veteran students with finding jobs by connecting students to alumni with similar backgrounds, that is, who are usually non-veteran. The alumni network of non-veteran alumni provide non-veteran graduates with invaluable help in finding a job. However, career centers currently do not provide the same service for veterans by providing them with alumni who have military background or experience. Each center needs a pool of alumni who are also veterans to advise the new veteran graduates. The need for a pool of veteran alumni is discussed later in this chapter.

Government Career Search Programs for Veterans

This section of the chapter discusses VA job placement programs and explains why these programs are not totally helpful for veterans with college degrees. Then it is explained why it is unreasonable to expect the VA to develop a program to job search for veteran graduates.

VA Job-Finding Systems

Unemployment among veterans, especially both younger and minority veterans is usually higher than the national average (Crawley, 2006; Department of Veterans Affairs, 2006; Griffith, 2006; House Committee on Veterans' Affairs, 2004). Many veterans will return home from war and even become homeless (Eric. 2007; Howell, 2007; Leverenz, 2005; Maze, 2007b; National Coalition for Homeless Veterans, 2007; Paige, 2007). Consequently, both the VA and the Department of Labor have developed several programs to help veterans find jobs. Clearly, some employers are discriminating against veterans (Fogg-Davis, 2007).

Nevertheless, legal action may be taken against employers who discriminate against veterans in the hiring process (Columbian, 2007; Jowers & Kauffman, 2007; Hemingway, 2007; see also Chavez, 2006). Certain employment programs that make it possible for veterans to avoid discrimination include the Veterans Employment and Training Service (VETS, 2006), e-vets, Realifelines, National Veterans Training Institute (1994), and others (see Nielsen, 2001). Disabled veterans receive additional help by the federal employment centers for veterans.

However, the federal programs intended to help veterans find employment, focus on veterans who are not college graduates (Nilsen, 2001). Most veterans do not have college degrees and do not seek to use their educational benefits to obtain a degree; rather they seek vocational, technical and apprentice training programs of shorter duration or a more manual focus. The VA's first responsibility is to find vocations for them.

Some web sites, such as VeteranEmployment.com, Military Connection, Military Exits, and Military Job Zone, have been developed that will help veterans who have had some college find a job appropriate to them. These web sites provide veterans with assistance that they need. Nevertheless, these sites do not take advantage of the knowledge that a veteran's college or university career center have or what a network of alumni who are veterans from their school could achieve.

The Belief that the VA is Responsible for Finding Jobs for all Vets

Some professors and college administrators believe that both the national VA and the states VA have the capability to help veterans who have difficulty finding employment (Klein, 1981; Pedan, 1987; Trewyn, 1994). However, it is unreasonable to expect the VA to take the responsibility of finding positions for college graduates. The VA cannot be expected to create a job search program for college graduates for at least two reasons.

First, the creation of a VA job search program would require the development of a new and large bureaucracy. A large staff of professionals would have to be trained on how to find jobs for college-educated veterans. Also, this college career search program would need to develop a network of veterans and employers to help new veterans find employment. Second, the creation of such a program would be costly and the VA budget now is already replete with many other costly programs.

To attempt to establish such a bureaucracy makes little sense because colleges and universities have career centers that are well equipped to assume the mission of finding jobs for veterans who graduate from their institutions. These centers have staff members who are already trained in employment search. These staff members could be oriented to assist veterans find appropriate positions. In addition, college career centers have networks of alumni who could easily be enlarged to include connections with alumni who are veterans ready to assist younger veterans.

Ideal Career Center Search Program for Veterans

The same principles of a job search for non-veterans can be applied for veterans. The systems in place for searching for the opportunities for non-veterans can be applied to veterans after being properly modified and developed for veterans. Each career center should have at least one staff member as the "resident expert" for veterans in helping them to find career opportunities. These staff members could learn about how the different kinds of military backgrounds of veterans are useful to civilian careers (Cornelius, 1993; Drier, 1995; Farley, 2005). Additionally, career centers should determine who among alumni are veterans or have experience dealing with veterans, and create pools of alumni who could then assist graduating veterans find employment. When such pools are established, career centers can be especially helpful to veterans by directing them to alumni who can not only assist them in finding employment, but also providing additional advice as they get ready to graduate.

The Basis for a Job Search

Knowledge and Skills. Ideal positions for veterans would focus on the veteran's major and minor if possible, as well on other achievements that can be displayed and discovered by becoming acquainted with veterans and their attitudes and aptitudes through interviews. In addition, ideal positions for many veterans would also make use of each veteran's military training and experience, if he or she wanted to continue to use that experience. Consequently, the search would be most useful for many veterans if that search would take into account not only the veteran's major and minor but also his or her military background. Career center employment counselors, with appropriate training, could learn to find ideal jobs for veterans based on the veterans' interviews, backgrounds and desires.

Personal Characteristics. The ideal job for veterans would also be one that makes use of both their extrinsic and intrinsic characteristics that they have. Thus, employment counselors in college career centers might direct veterans to jobs that not only take account of the major, minor, and military background, but also the intrinsic characteristics that they have.

The valuable characteristics of veterans were discussed in some detail in Chapter 4. The characteristics were described as useful when veterans leave the service and make the transition to civilian life and college life. Nevertheless, these characteristics are also useful when considering the properties of an ideal job for veterans. Veterans have excellent work habits. As a group, they tend to be more highly dedicated to their work than non-veteran graduates. They set good examples for the non-veteran graduates to do their work well and on time. Employers who are veterans, or who have had veterans work for them, know the strengths those veterans brought to the work place.

As discussed in Chapter 4, veterans are known to be mature, stable and respectful of authority. Employers should also be familiar with the general abilities veterans have due to military experience, e.g. problem-solving ability, interpersonal skills, communication skills, and leadership ability. In general, veterans have better habits of self-care than non-veterans of the same age. They also have good personal appearance and bearing. All of these characteristics should be pointed out to potential employers by those helping a veteran find employment and by the veteran himself or herself.

Veteran-Friendly Employer Networks

Networks should be assembled of employers who are veterans or appreciate veterans. Such an employer will be disposed to seriously consider veterans as employees. Such networks should be developed by career centers of schools. Veterans service organizations should collaborate on veteran-employer networks in general.

However, in that the number of living veterans consists of less than 3 million individuals, the likelihood of encountering by chance an employer who is a veteran is low. Consequently, networks of employers friendly to veterans need to be developed largely of non-veterans who appreciate what veterans have to offer as employees by giving veterans a chance.

Non-veteran employers may have a positive attitude about veterans for various reasons. Some employers recognize the strengths of veterans in the workplace. Some employers are grateful to servicemen and servicewomen for their service to their country. Some non-veteran employers recognize the strengths of veterans because they have relatives who have conveyed the benefits of military service. If a veteran employer is involved in hiring, the strengths of the veteran applicant will be considered as seriously as a non-veteran applicant.

Costs to American Society Due to the
Inadequate Employment Search for Graduates who are Veterans

By ignoring what veterans have learned in the military, career centers may guide them to employment opportunities that are not ideal. In addition, such placement is not ideal for our society because it essentially throws away the money spent on military training and experience that could be applied to work in the civilian world (Todd, 1949). In doing so, valuable resources of talent are discarded and not used to strengthen work in civilian life and society. However, if society does not ignore what educated veterans have to offer, the nation's pool of individuals with technological expertise and/or the managerial-leadership would grow (Jones, 2005).

In general, veterans with college degrees tend to have jobs that pay less than non-veterans, even with comparable education (Angrist, 1993; Anonymous.VFW, 2007b; Cohen, Segal, & Temme, 1992; Langbert, & Wells, 1982; Pedan, 1987). It is sadly ironic that America invests enormous amounts of money in educating veterans, in their health care, and other aspects of life, and then fails to help them find employment based on the education that America has given them. Educators who truly care for our country and the young men and women who have served, will not want to see this happen. Improving the employment search process for veterans with college degrees is in the best interest of not only veterans but also all other citizens.

What Colleges and Universities Can Do About
The Employment of Veterans on Graduation

The Career Centers of colleges and universities can easily make the changes needed to ensure that veterans have the best possible chances to get a job. These colleges and universities will benefit if graduates who are veterans obtain the best job by having more veterans attend in the future, and later the sons and daughter of veterans attend. Legislation may be needed to help fund the development of a veterans' employment search system for veterans with college education. However, because the creation of legislation is a slow process, schools will most likely need to be creative for the benefit of both the veterans and education institutions.

Such a program would need the following innovations in college career centers. Career center staff members will need to learn something about the military background of veterans who are about to graduate to be effective. The American Council on Education has a website that helps describe the background that career center staff can use to learn about particular specialties or jobs in the military. A career center should also connect with the job search programs for veterans conducted by the VA and by the Department of Labor. It is in the best interests of schools to get their graduates the best possible employment. Successful graduates are the best advertisements for a school (and happy alumni often donate).

Summary

This chapter examined the job search process for veterans who are soon to graduate or have graduated from college. Four points were addressed. The chapter first explained how job search programs at most colleges and universities focus on a new graduate's majors and minors. Second, it was explained how these programs work for non-veterans but not for veterans. The job search process of college career centers partially, or totally, ignores the military training and experience of veterans. Additionally, while non-veteran graduates are directed to alumni for advice about job opportunities and other matters, graduates who are veterans do not have this advice. Third, the job search programs conducted by the VA and by the Department of Labor on behalf of the VA are not adequate to assist graduating veterans. It was explained that these job search programs function for veterans who choose job training other than college. Colleges and universities can easily take into consideration veterans' major or minor in combination with a military background. Finally, it was proposed that the an employment search program for veterans either government funded, or created by the schools will be a win-win situation as it will not only provide the right jobs for the veterans, but bring in future students and donations to the colleges and universities.

Section III:

What More Might be Done to Improve the College Education of Veterans

Chapter 13
Consequences of Not Eliminating the Problems

This book has been written to address the **Veterans Higher-Education Problem.** Statistics demonstrate a greater percentage of non-veterans than veterans attend and complete college. Thus, higher education in America does a better job of educating non-veterans than it does veterans. That is the essence of the veterans' higher-education problem.

If the current problems that veterans face in college or that discourage them from going to college were corrected, then the same or similar percentage of veterans as non-veterans could receive a college education. If the percentage of those receiving a college degree were the same and a fair job-search system was established, veterans would finally have the same opportunity to achieve career success in spite of the span of time the veterans have spent outside of the academic realm while in the military.

The Need for Change. The chapters of this book show that one important reason that veterans are not educated at an acceptable rate is that American higher education is not equipped, administratively, academically or attitudinally to help veterans get the education that they could receive. Academia, no doubt, is as patriotic as any other sector of American society, so the authors of this book believe that once higher education understands the difficulties that many American veterans encounter in college, higher education will make changes to ensure that veterans can choose any collegiate institution in which to get a college education and obtain the degree that they want. Chapters 3 through 12 documented a considerable number of problems that veterans encounter in higher education and discourage them from getting a college education. Each of these chapters made recommendations about what colleges and universities could do in order to eliminate the problems of veterans discussed in the chapter. Table 13.1 summarizes the recommendations of the previous chapters.

Table 13.1
Support for More Veterans Entering Higher Education

To increase the likelihood that veterans will seek a degree, a
college or university should:

1. Promote a public image of higher education as holding
   generally positive attitudes toward American veterans.
2. Direct faculty to not openly advocate anti-military
   attitudes and anti-veteran attitudes in class.
3. Teach faculty how to read the countenance of veterans
   and to distinguish them from non-veterans similar in age.
4. Encourage students to not say rude and disrespectful things
   about veterans to veterans.
5. Provide assistance to veterans with their transition from
   military to civilian and college life.
7. Calculate veterans' financial aid without subtracting GI Bill
   benefits from the financial aid that veterans could receive.
8. Guide veterans to apply for scholarships.
9. Establish scholarships that are tailored to student veterans.
10. Help veterans with families financially.
11. Make education programs helpful to veterans and
    non-veterans.
12. Provide programs designed specifically to help veterans
    shift from the learning style appropriate for military
    training to a learning style required by college.
13. Help veterans major in their military occupational specialty.
14. Transfer military training/experience into academic credits.
15. Address the service connected health concerns of veterans
    including the care necessary for disabilities.
16. Help veterans who are to graduate with their job search as
    much as non-veteran graduates are helped.

The Purpose of this Chapter. This chapter addresses consequences if colleges and universities do not follow the recommendations presented in the previous chapters and listed in Table 13.1. These consequences include from those affecting the veterans themselves to other sectors of society. This chapter will review the consequences of the treatment of veterans for: veterans, academia, our society and our country.

The Consequences of Good Treatment of Veterans

The Consequences for Veterans

Good and fair treatment of veterans will yield positive outcomes. More veterans will apply for and enroll in college. Fewer veterans will drop out and more veterans will obtain one or more degrees.

The Consequences for Academia

Americans who value veterans will come to respect higher education more than before. Lectures will not involve anti-veteran discussion in courses unrelated to such discussion. Higher education will experience an increase in enrollments due to the attendance of veterans.

The Consequences for American Society

It is in the best interests of our nation and society if veterans obtain college degrees and achieve more productive and fuller lives (Kirsch, Braun, Yamamoto & Sum, 2007). Our nation will benefit from the training and experience that veterans have in the military. Veterans would be able to contribute more to America's prosperity as they become employed in civilian occupations that take advantage of this military training and experience. Society itself might function better because academia would not be so isolated from its other components: business, medicine, law, and religion. Also, other nations will respect us for helping our own veterans. Should our nation need to become involved in warfare, our service men and women will perform better and more safely because they are confident of their future.

What Colleges and Universities Can Do About Possible Consequences of Their Treatment of Veterans

Colleges and universities can avoid the possible negative consequences of failing to educate veterans. College presidents can resolve some of these consequences by changing policies that give rise to the problems of veterans, such as those involving how veterans finance their education. College administrators can make changes also such as altering the ways that veterans get college credits for military credits. Faculty governance can change policies as well, such as by creating grievance procedures for veterans that are comparable to those for non-veterans. Professors can adopt the practices discussed in this book about how to treat students who are veterans.

Summary

The manner by which a nation educates or does not educate its veterans has consequences that extend well beyond veterans themselves. Good treatment of veterans will obviously yield positive results. More veterans will apply for and enroll in college and fewer veterans will drop out, and many more veterans will obtain one or more degrees.

How veterans are treated by higher education may result in consequences for academia itself, our society, and even the perception of our nation in the world. Americans who value veterans will respect higher education more than in the past. Our nation has invested significant amounts of its annual budgets in the training and maintaining of our military troops and their support. Treating veterans better in higher education will help ensure that our nation profits from such training.

Chapter 14
Helping Veterans Feel Comfortable in Higher Education

This chapter and the next chapter propose general programs that American higher education might implement to help veterans with their overall education. An individual college or university that wants to ensure that it helps veterans as much as possible may want to implement some of these programs or create others not yet identified. In addition to programs that might be adopted by a particular school, the American higher education community might establish broad collective, universal programs that may be shared by all schools across the United States.

Helping Veterans Feel Comfortable
In a Particular College or University

The Boards of Trustees, Presidents, and faculty governance of a college or a university can render their institution veterans-friendly in several ways. The leaders can appoint a task force to investigate the degree to which their higher educational institution is successful in addressing the recommendations made in Chapters 3 through 13. The changes that particular colleges or universities may make are for the most part easily identified. First, schools may provide professors and college administrators with instruction about how to best educate veterans. Second, the administration of a college or a university may be rendered more effective by revising its grievance procedures for dealing with complaints raised by veterans.

Instruction of Members of a Particular Institution about How to Treat Veterans

As discussed earlier in this book, administrators and professors may be instructed that protest of a government policy to government leaders or policy makers is different from protest of government policy to those who are duty bound to carry out such a policy. Administrators, professors, and students should be instructed that veterans are required to follow many rules and regulations. Thus, they deserve privileged treatment and so—like the two sexes, different races, different sexual preferences, and different religions—veterans will be given the college education desired for them.

Coordinated Management of Offices that Serve or Help Veterans.

The decisions about veterans at schools are distributed over a variety of different offices, such as the Admissions Office, the Financial Aid Office, the Enrollment Office, and others offices. When numerous administrators and professors are responsible for components of decisions, the decision-makers may lose awareness of each other, the entire issue, and the veterans on whose shoulders the issue falls. Veterans, in general, have to do more business with administrators and professors than non-veteran students. If the decision-makers do not work in a coordinated manner, veterans find themselves directed to the wrong office to get administrative help or being turned away. Veterans should be provided when enrolled with an organizational chart that identifies which offices are responsible for specific functions pertaining to them.

Establish Grievance Procedures Tailored to Veterans

In that veterans are a small minority at most schools, they may have few friends or supporters among the faculty and administration. As a result, veterans are reluctant to raise complaints, fearing that the professors and administrators who had treated them poorly and are the targets of complaints will punish them. Also, as a result, matters pertaining to veterans sometimes are sometimes not decided fairly or in their favor. The best grievance system for veterans is one where confidentiality is maintained until, if, and when, a hearing is held about a grievance. The grievance rules should clearly specify that retaliation in any form would result in punishment.

Provide Veterans with Advisors who are Veterans

Besides academic advisors, veterans will be made more comfortable if they have an advisor, such as a professor, administrator, or staff member, who is a veteran. An advisor should be assigned to just a few veterans as advisees. Most colleges and universities employ very few veterans. If it is not possible to find veteran advisors on a campus, a school can contact a local veteran's service organization (VSO) and ask if one or more members could serve as veteran advisors.

Make Clear to Academia How Veteran-Unfriendly Practices Appear Unpatriotic and Unethical to Most Members of Society

Many members of society see the protests and anti-military bias in academia as inappropriate. Protest of a government policy to government leaders who conceive of a policy must be distinguished from protest to those who are duty bound to carry out such a policy. The former is legitimate, but the latter is both unpatriotic and unethical. It is unpatriotic to treat poorly those who are commissioned to carry out the orders of our government.

It is unethical to abuse employees because of objections to the policy of employers. There are several analogies of why the latter is unethical. It would be unethical to punish the children of parents who are lawbreakers. It would be unethical to punish members of a union for going out on strike when union leaders are responsible for initiating a strike. It is likely that most professors and administrators would agree that it is illogical to not help veterans when it is the government that the professors and administrators disapprove.

A Program to Encourage Veterans to Attend College

Veterans could be provided with vocational tests that guide them to a major in college and a career. Veterans should also be provided with information that enables them to pick out the schools that are most appropriate. The program should provide a procedure for estimating the costs of college and include scholarships beyond the GI Bill benefits that are most appropriate for veterans and takes into account their unique needs

Develop Programs that Help Veterans Select the School and Program that They Need

When a veteran decides to go to college, that person must decide on the college to attend. There are programs that could help veterans with this selection process. A system of rating schools based on how they treat veterans should be established. For those veterans who want to attend college only with other veterans in an environment conducive to them, a veterans university should be established.

Provide Veterans with a System for Rating Colleges and Universities Based on Treatment

Currently, veterans enter college having no idea of whether the school they select will present them with one or more of the many problems discussed in this book. The veterans do not know the climate toward them until they are on campus for at least a short while. Furthermore, on enrollment, veterans do not know if their school will help veterans with a variety of other transition and health issues discussed earlier in this book.

The development, implementation and continuation of an institutional rating system of receptivity to veterans would require regular administration of veterans college-surveys by any school that veterans attend and can be justified due to the receipt of federal funds. One kind of survey might be a rating scale on how veterans report the degree to which a school engages in the veteran-friendly procedures. An example of such a survey is provided in Appendix 14-A. A summary of a survey's results might be provided in an index that would indicate the degree of veteran friendliness or unfriendliness. An example of such an index is provided in Appendix 14-B.

Provide Veterans with Advice Prior to Attending College

Veterans should be encouraged to attend college and pursue the careers they want. To begin, veterans may be encouraged to attend if they were provided information about a possible career, possibly by a comprehensive website that includes career and educational information, diagnostic, skill and ability tests and attitudinal surveys, and information about apprentice programs, technical skills development, and career in the vocational realm as well as links to other websites with professional, vocational and educational information.

Establish a Veterans Website about the Benefits of having a College Degree

The VA Website provides a great deal of information that is useful to all manner of veterans. However, the VA website currently fails to meet its standards for information quality when it comes to those veterans who want to seek a college degree. As explained below, the VA website gives little information for veterans who want to go to college. Veterans who are interested in going to college receive little information to critical questions. A detailed account of the shortcomings of the VA Website for veterans who want to, or do, attend college is presented in Appendix 14-C.

A website needs to be sponsored by a not-for-profit organization that is independent of the VA and other organizations, and is therefore autonomous of outside influence. It should present the results of a rating system to alert veterans whether a particular college or university presents problems. It should identify all the good and bad financial points about each college and any other tuition issue discussed in this book. Such a website should seek to help administer scholarships that may be developed for veterans. It should also say something about how veterans with families can get support for their spouse and children while in college.

A veteran's education website should discuss all the credit transfer issues detailed in this book and explain how to get maximum credit transfer, along with matters dealing with ACE evaluations. The veteran's education website should explain how a school's educational program fails to give information about/for veterans.

The veterans' education website should provide a ratings of schools based on treatment of veterans. This website should also describe whether vocational rehabilitation is available to veterans at each school. Also it should describe state-by-state benefits that are provided by state's veterans agencies for the assistance of those with needs for vocational rehabilitation and financial assistance veterans can expect to receive.

Encourage Academia to Adopt Positive Procedures Regarding Veterans

Academia in America involves many faculty members, administrators, and support staff who respect veterans. In addition to increasing the diversity desirable in any student body, the veteran population brings a rich and unique set of experiences to the classroom. The veteran-friendly campus views this as an asset and seeks to include it in the range of perspectives brought to serious intellectual inquiry. This standard sometimes, in the heat of academic argument when politico-military matters are discussed, requires attention to maintain. Table 14.1 summarizes the good practices that higher education might adopt.

Table 14.1

A list of Good Practices that May Help
Veterans Obtain a College Degree.

1. Student counseling is sensitive to the veterans' unfamiliarity with academia and its processes. Absence from this environment may necessitate attention to matters such as study skills, brush-up work, detailed academic programs, communication styles, and sometimes advice about how to account for what veterans learned while in the military.

2. Their service backgrounds are not seen as necessarily indicative of their views of civil or military matters. Like other students, adverse comments by others about the veterans' service are not tolerated. Academic freedom is modified in no way to accommodate veterans, but merely extended to veterans on the same open-minded and objective basis as to anyone else.

3. In financial aid matters, veterans are not penalized. It is incorrect to base calculation of financial means on a military salary veterans earned a year ago, but no longer receives. Calculation of financial means also does not presume parental help, in that veterans have been independent of parental help for years. It is also incorrect to base calculation of financial means on educational benefits received for military service. Special needs of veterans, who are generally older than traditional students and may have more family responsibilities, are recognized. Wherever possible, veterans are assisted in finding sources of funding for their special education needs.

4. Colleges are attentive to any medical, physical or psychological needs veterans may have. College services are coordinated with those available to veterans from the government.

5. Academic learning of veterans while in the military is properly recognized. College-level credits earned while on active duty receive a comprehensive and correct hearing for transferability. The academic creditworthiness of military training and experience, determined by the American Council on Education, is evaluated in terms of veterans' academic program and applied whenever possible. College placement or employment search is based on both veterans' degrees and military backgrounds where possible.

If veterans are recalled to active duty, the institution with good practices ensures that the veterans' academic program does not suffer. Provisions are made to return lost tuition and expenses or to apply them on return, readmit the veterans after service without delay or penalty, and allow academic work already begun to be completed when possible. In cases of injury or death on active duty, appropriate provisions are made to manage tuition reimbursements, assignment of grades, and related issues, so that the veterans or their families are not penalized.

What Else Colleges and Universities Can Make Veterans Feel Comfortable as They Study for a Degree

As said several times previously in this book, veterans will feel comfortable as they seek a degree if a college's professors and college administrators implement the recommended practices in the nine categories as discussed in Chapters 3 through 12. Additionally, veterans will feel comfortable if colleges and universities stand up for the rights of veterans in not only higher education but in society overall.

Summary

This chapter advanced proposals for improving the higher education of veterans beyond correcting the earlier problems reviewed in chapters 1 to 12. Changes were proposed that would make veterans feel more comfortable while they study for a degree. Additionally, changes were proposed that colleges and universities in general could make. Finally, programs were proposed that might help veterans choose the right school for them, including the selection of an education appropriate for their career choices.

Chapter 15

Improving the Higher Educations System for Educating America's Veterans

Purpose. This chapter presents proposals for systemic changes in higher education. First, there is a need to develop a discipline that will indicate the best way to educate veterans. In other words, higher education needs a pedagogy designed for veterans. Second, higher education may designate certain educational institutions as having a mission to educate veterans. Third, higher education may establish programs that would educate veterans to become professors and college administrators in order that more veterans would participate in higher education and be able to encourage better treatment of veterans who are students. Fourth, higher education may develop better treatment of veterans if other sectors of society called for such treatment.

Establishment of Pedagogy for Veterans

Research is needed to develop a program that explains how veterans are best educated. A discipline about the theory and practice of teaching any special group such as veterans needs to determine two things. First, research should determine the characteristics of the members of the group and how these characteristics affect how the members learn in college. Second, research should determine the pedagogy appropriate for teaching the members of the group effectively. The following section addresses the characteristics of veterans that may affect their learning in a way that differs from other students. After these characteristics are addressed, the issue of developing pedagogy for veterans is considered.

Educational Characteristics of Veterans

Veterans differ from each other in their potential for college because they vary in how well prepared they are for the challenges that college poses to students (Herrmann, Raybeck, & Gruneberg, 2003; Mayer, 1999). In particular, these challenges include the following: carrying out academic tasks; learning how to execute cognitive tasks; maintaining health (Figley, 1978); adjusting to cultural change (Appy, 1992; Card, 1983; Helmer, 1974; and choosing a career and planning a career path. Chapter 5 (that was concerned with transitions veterans must make) lists various kinds of challenges encountered by veterans in college and what veterans bring to these challenges. Overall, this book demonstrates that veterans have considerably more challenges in college than their non-veteran student peers.

The characteristics of veterans affect their potential to learn in college. Recent theories of learning and memory (Herrmann, Plude, Yoder, & Mullin, 1999) indicate that academic performance originates from different sources or modes. Central to academic performance are cognitive processes and skills. Cognitive psychologists have recently agreed that the cognitive processes involved in academic performance are affected by a person's physical and emotional state (Herrmann, Plude, Yoder, & Mullin, 1999; Herrmann, Yoder, Gruneberg, & Payne, 2006). The physical and social environment and a person's ability to respond to the physical and social environment also affect these processes. In addition, academic performance is affected by sociological variables, such as class (Allen, Herrmann, & Giles, 1995; Appy, 1992), income (Langbert & Wells, 1982; Klein, 1989), and socio-economic status (Herrmann & Guadagno, 1997).

Development of new Methods of Teaching Veterans

Educators recognize that veterans constitute a special group that possesses special knowledge, skills and specific needs that should be considered when providing the members of this group a college education. Methods need to be developed that take account of a veteran's age, high school background, military training, military experience, and the cultural background due to socio-economic status along with the major and minor goals of veterans. Currently, educational psychology does not have research findings that would enable the development of the veterans-education methods that may be taught to college professors who might specialize in the educational psychology of veterans.

Historically, research into the educational matters of veterans, conducted largely by the federal Department of Veterans Affairs, has focused almost exclusively on how cognition may vary with various disabilities (see National Association of Veterans Research and Education Foundation, NAVREF, 2006). Some research has focused on remedial training for a minority of veterans who were educationally disadvantaged prior to entering the service to enable them to become capable of succeeding in college (the Upward Bound program). Nevertheless, the number of veterans in the Upward Bound program is just a small fraction of the veterans who attend college. Thus, only a small amount of research has examined how the vast majority of veterans who are not disabled or educationally disadvantaged survive in the college environment (Cornelius, 1993).

Development of pedagogy for teaching veterans presumably would be based on research into differences between the educational performance of veterans and such performance of non-veterans. Unfortunately, research that has compared veterans with non-veterans has evolved very slowly, as shown in citations of articles about such research. There are not many of these articles (note, these citations are in chronological order: Love & Hutchison, 1946; Todd, 1949; Enzi, Sawyer, & Montgomery, 1973; Joanning, 1975; Peter, 1975; Berry, 1977; Henderson, 1977; Thorn & Payne, 1977; Figley, 1978a,b; Price, 1980; Klein, 1985; Callahan & Pincus, 1988; Dobbs, Hopper, & Jurkovic, 1990; Schnurr, Rosenberg, & Friedman, 1993; Leisner, 1995; Spaulding, Eddy, Chandras, 1997; Sailer, 2004; MacLean, 2005). In the absence of research, informed decisions about the veterans' higher-education problem are rarely possible.

Identify Educational Institutions Whose Mission is to Educate Veterans

Designate some Existing Colleges as Veterans-friendly. Some colleges may want to do much more for veterans such as establishing a division dedicated to helping veterans with their veteran-specific issues while they seek a degree. This division might be analogous to the divisions that have programs for students of other minorities. The staff of the veterans unit might be composed of professors and administrators who are veterans and would help them with any and all problems associated with school, many covered in this book.

After World War II, some colleges and universities identified units within them as responsible for educating veterans. Unfortunately, some of these colleges became unfriendly to veterans during the Vietnam era. Recently some higher educational institutions have established programs to help veterans obtain a degree (Heller, 2006; Harmeyer, 2007; Lanigan, 2007). However, as noted earlier in this book, the number of schools who have veterans-friendly programs is still relatively small. The Servicemembers Opportunity Colleges (SOC, 2004, 2007a,b) do require their members to promise to help veterans in certain ways, such as providing transfer credits for military training and experience. However, SOC promises do not cover many of the problems of veterans discussed in this book and SOC does not have a system in place to ensure that schools live up to the promises they make when joining SOC.

To be given a regional designation by the VA or the Department of Education (DoE) as a "Veterans-friendly Higher Educational Institution," colleges and universities should be required to have certain characteristics. For example, these institutions might be expected to demonstrate their capability to help veterans with an administrative, curricular and co-curricular issue in at least one or several academic divisions. Also, smaller colleges might be the entry point of such an accreditation program of veteran-friendly institutions due to the less complex systems in place in the smaller institutions.

Establish a "Veterans' University." Although regional veteran-friendly institutions may usually have the capacity to provide the education needed by veterans, times might arise when these institutions may not be able to help all discharged or retired veterans. For example, when our nation is engaged in an unpopular war, there may be too many anti-war, anti-military people on a campus of a regional veteran-friendly university for veterans to feel comfortable. Also, some veterans would feel more comfortable studying at an "all veterans campus." Therefore, our nation may want to also establish an independent "Veterans University" with students who only are veterans. Such an institution would employ only faculty and administrators who treat veterans properly.

This independent "Veterans' University" would strive to ensure that veterans receive the highest quality education in an efficient manner. A veterans' university should hire faculty members who are veterans themselves whenever possible (at least 80% of faculty). Veterans on the faculty could better help student veterans because such faculty do not harbor anti-veteran attitudes and are aware of how to best assist veterans in their educational progress.

Educate Veterans on how to Pursue Careers in Higher Education

With appropriate education and training, veterans could assume important roles in academia and could contribute to the education of younger veterans. Veterans could be educated to become counselors of students who are veterans, i.e., veterans student-counselors.

Veterans-Student Counselors

In the 1970's the VA created a program for veterans-student counselors. Schools were free to apply for grants that would support this program. However, funding for these grants disappeared after a few years. Some schools decided to keep this program and pay for such a counselor as part of their regular administration. If a veterans student-counselor program were not established at the college or university level, the VA might assign these counselors at the State VA Departments or the regional VA office. These counselors should be trained to advise veterans on the legal implications of a school's failure to provide certain services. The VA's regulations have become so complex that veterans who are students cannot be expected to know what they should do regarding educational benefits and claims about medical care.

Veterans as Professors

A program should be established to attract veterans to become professors. Currently very few veterans become professors. Thus, veterans have few allies in the faculty to help them cope with their burdens. If more veterans were professors, veterans would feel more comfortable in the academic community that is largely staffed by non-veterans.

Veterans as College Administrators

As is well known, few veterans work in an academic or administrative position at most colleges, universities, or technical schools. Thus, there are few or no administrators at many colleges and universities who can help veterans and the remaining administrators do not understand when there is a need to help veterans. Thus, veterans have few allies among administrators to help them cope with their burdens. Accordingly, more veterans should be encouraged to become college administrators.

Veterans as Experts in the Education of Veterans

A program should be established to attract veterans to become researchers who investigate how veterans are best educated. Currently very few veterans become researchers in education. If more veterans became these types of researchers, pedagogy could be more easily developed to educate veterans.

Help from Other Sectors of Society

This book has reviewed the many reasons why some veterans do not complete, or even attend, college. In order to remedy the problems confronting veterans, higher education has a daunting task ahead of it. Clearly, more work needs to be done to help our veterans (Leverenz, 2005). Equally clear, the job facing higher education is too great for it to carry out alone. Higher education will need advice, inspiration, and assistance to fix the problems that veterans now encounter in colleges and universities.

Higher Educational Organizations. In order to get the help needed, higher education should prod other sectors of our society capable of providing assistance to do so. Higher education might seek help from educational organizations for professionals such the American Council on Education and the American Association of University Professors. Veterans service organizations could also contribute to the coordinated effort to facilitate the college education of veterans, including the following: the VA, the part of the federal Department of Education concerned with veterans, the part of the federal Department of Labor concerned with veterans, the Veterans of Foreign War (VFW), Disabled American Veterans, and the American Legion. These veterans service organizations and federal agencies typically have executives whose duties are to attend to the problems of veterans while they are being educated. These executives can routinely call for better treatment of veterans as the veterans seek a degree. Communities of faith can also call to the attention of their members those practices that incorrectly or unfairly affect veterans who are their members.

Members of Congress, Members who belong to committees that are responsible for helping veterans as well as those who are veterans, can propose legislation that might remediate the problems of veterans in higher-education settings. Finally, public sentiment for proper treatment of veterans while they are in college can be mustered if the public is informed on the range of these problems for veterans returning to school. With an effective plan and sound implementation of this plan, the higher education community might realize that its best interest lies in elimination of the Veterans Education Problem.

The Promising Future of Veterans College Education

Although American higher education has considerable work to do, the authors also recognize that the academic environment is becoming more and more veteran friendly across the nation, and the authors believe that a movement to help veterans in college is developing. Some articles that have proposed that veterans are treated well on campus today (Gruder, 2008; Heller, 2006; McDaniel, 2006; Nelson, 2006; Harmeyer, 2007; Lanigan, 2007). Accordingly, we complete this chapter with a review of recent developments that may be seen as contributing to such a movement. The developments that are next reviewed include efforts to improve the college education of veterans by: society, the military, and by higher education itself. These developments deserve recognition for how they help veterans obtain a degree and because they set an example for how things might continue to improve.

Societal Developments

The Media
Some authors have written that a military background can improve a person's character (Mettler, 2005; Mullane, 2005). In general the press has given more attention in the past few years than previously to military educational programs (Huckabee, 2008; Campus News for Veterans, 2008; see also Veterans for America. 2008). In some cases, veterans have been seen as good students to have on campus (Nelson, 2006; Walters, 2006).

Assistance to Veterans for the Costs of College
GI Bill. Congress has recognized that the GI Bill available to veterans needs to be improved. Government assistance to the education of veterans has increased dramatically in the new Post 911 GI Bill through the Veterans

Education Assistance Act (Chapter 33) effective in August of 2009 (Department of Veterans Affairs, 2008; see also Chapman, 2007; Kime, 2007; Webb, 2007; Williamson, 2008).

Tuition Assistance to Veterans by States. Besides the federal government, the following states are offering tuition waivers to qualified veterans: Connecticut, Illinois, Montana, Texas, Wisconsin and Wyoming. Each state administers its own criteria for awarding tuition assistance to a veteran, so not every veteran may be qualified for the tuition waiver.

Organizations for Veterans on Campus

Student Veterans of America, has assumed responsibility to co-ordinate campus organizations for veterans across the country (such as Omega Delta Sigma) and to provide information for veterans (Powers, 2008a; McDaniel, 2006) who are students in college and for educators of veterans (Powers, 2008b; see also Vincennes University, 2008). Wal-Mart provided support for this organization. Similarly, the recently formed Iraq and Afghanistan Veterans of America has developed an executive summary of this book, **Educating Veterans in the 21st Century,** for its membership (Campbell, 2009).

Recently an organization has been established for veterans who work in academia as professors, college administrators, researchers and staff. This organization, the Academic Veterans Organization, aims to help veterans who are students on campus through influencing administrative and educational processes in a manner different from how veterans who are students influence these processes.

National Guard Programs to Educate Service Members

Tuition Assistance. People in the military know, but it is not well known in America, that the National Guard offers wonderful opportunities for members of the Guard to get a college education. Members of the Guard have their tuition and fees paid for whenever they take college courses while they are still in the Guard. These Guard members do not have the tuition and fees paid for after they leave the Guard. However, after leaving the Guard, these Guard members become eligible for GI Bill support while they attend college. This support depends on how long they served full time while in the Guard.

Transition Assistance. Members of the Guard in every state also receive assistance that encourages them to seek college degrees. First, Guard members in every state are provided seamless transition assistance as they leave the military and return to civilian life. This assistance involves encouragement to attend college when Guard members want a college degree. Second, the families of the Guard are provided with a family Readiness Program that prepares families to help the soldiers in their families to return to civilian life (Department of Defense, 2003; Military Community Awareness, 2007; Minnesota National Guard, 2007; National Guard Family Program, 2003). Families whose soldier(s) has been attending college are provided information that their soldier needs in order to continue the pursuit of a degree. It should be noted that the staff of Transition Assistance of the Guard also help members of other branches of the service with their transition to civilian life.

Efforts To Improve Higher Education's Practices to Veterans

A Call for Quality Control in Higher Education. To begin with, the American Council on Education called upon all educators in 2007 in colleges and universities to increase quality control on what is taught in the classroom. Increases in quality are seen as possible if institutions require accountability by professors for what students learn in class (NextStudent, 2007). Such a call is consistent with efforts to improve the education of veterans in college.

School Specific Programs. Several schools have developed programs specifically for veterans returning from the war on terror and for veterans in general (Harmeyer, 2007; Heller, 2006; Lanagin, 2007). University of North Carolina provides mini courses about how to help veterans (North Carolina, 2007). Citrus College in California established a course for veterans to learn about how to make the transition from military life to college life (Quillen-Armstrong, 2007). Indiana State University has established a free semester program for veterans returning from the War on Terror (Beacon, 2008). Indiana University has established procedures for deployed Guard members to get help with academic procedures (Trustees of Indiana University, 2007). Chicago colleges and universities, along with Representative Rahm Emanuel of Illinois, have proposed policies to facilitate Iraq and Afghanistan Vets to enroll and succeed in college (Administrator of Polish News, 2008).

In 2008, Wal-Mart provided support to the American Council on Education (ACE) to award grants to 20 institutions of higher education that have developed a sound plan to help veterans in higher education (ACE and Wal-Mart Team-up, 2008). The programs were encouraged to address topics such as helping the educational process before, during, and after deployment: helping veterans make the transition to college life; treating veterans with PTSD; assisting a veterans care of families; and other issues related to the topics in this book (ACE was briefed in 2006 about the problems addressed in this book). The following institutions are some of those that were awarded a grant: Arkansas State University; Cleveland State University; Citrus College (Calif.); Florida Community College; Mississippi State; Montgomery College (Md.); San Diego Community College; San Diego State University; University of Minnesota; University of Incarnate Word (Texas). The ACE Wal-Mart Program is consistent with ACE's emphasis on higher education providing accountability for what is taught to students in colleges and universities (Council for Opportunity in Education, 2008; Next Student, 2007).

A Call for Better Interaction Between Colleges and the Military. In early April 2009 a very important conference addressed the "Ivies and the military: toward reconciliation" at the Harvard Divinity School. The relationship between the military and education was described as negative ever since the Vietnam War, as discussed in Chapter 2. This conference aimed at opening lines of communications between Ivy League institutions and the military. A by-product of this conference is to improve better treatment of veterans at these institutions.

Veteran Specific Programs. The Wal-Mart Foundation in recent years has donated substantial sum funds to help veterans in higher education in several ways. It provided support in 2008 to Severely Injured Military Veterans for their 'Fulfilling Their Dreams program." The Wal-Mart Foundation donated substantial funds to help veterans in higher education in several ways. It has provided support to Severely Injured Military Veterans for their 'Fulfilling Their Dreams program." Similar efforts to help the wounded have been conducted through the Wounded Warrior Outreach Program (Veterans for America, 2008; see also Aleethia Foundation, 2007).

A Call for Better Practices Toward Veterans and Service Members. Professors and administrators in some organizations and some states have come together to formulate better policies for the education of those with a military background as they seek a college degree. The American Association of State Colleges and Universities has recently published guidelines for how their member colleges and universities may help veterans obtain the college education that they want (McBain, 2008). A notable example of a statewide effort to help veterans that the authors know about is that of Indiana. In the past few years, research had indicated that only a few colleges and universities in Indiana had policies presented on the Web about veterans. Also, a survey found that about 30% of Indiana colleges and universities were aware that some veterans and some service members were having trouble in the various categories discussed throughout this book (Herrmann 2007a,b; discussed in Chapter 3). The Military Family Research Institute at Purdue University surveyed Indiana's higher educational institutions to determine what percentage of institutions engaged in practices that negatively affect servicemembers and veterans while in college (Sternberg, MacDermid Wadsworth, Vaughan, and Carlson, 2009)

See also a survey that demonstrated that some of Indiana's higher educational institutions fail to fully implement programs intended to help servicemembers and veterans in college (Sternberg, MacDermid Wadsworth, Vaughan, and Carlson, 2009)

The Military Family Research Institute at Purdue University surveyed Indiana's higher educational institutions to determine what percentage of institutions engaged in practices that negatively affect servicemembers and veterans while in college (Sternberg, MacDermid Wadsworth, Vaughan, and Carlson, 2009). For example, approximately 30% of Indiana's institutions requires servicemembers to reapply for admission on return from deployment and 47% do not allow servicemembers to make up coursework if deployed midsemester. Currently the Military Family Research Institute are conducting a program of providing grants, supported by the Lilly Foundation, to Indiana higher educational institutions who propose the most deserving academic programs to help servicemembers and veterans obtain a college degree.

In 2008, the Adjutant General and the Governor of Indiana called on the CEOs or their representatives of Indiana's higher educational institutions to develop a prototype of a policy that all schools might use to guide their interactions with students who are veterans or service members. A taskforce was established of the leaders of Indiana's educational institutions that developed such a prototype. This prototype consists of a series of best practices that professors and college administrators might engage in when interacting with veterans and service members (Herrmann, 2009). Table 15.1 presents a

188

summary of the best practices recommended by Indiana's higher educational leaders. A similar set of Best Practices was also developed in 2008 by the American Council on Education (Schmidt, 2008).

What Colleges and Universities Can Do To Improve Systems for Educating Veterans

This chapter proposed that complete success at educating veterans could be achieved by making systemic changes in the American higher education. Colleges and universities can contribute to improving the American system for educating veterans in four ways. First, pedagogy needs to be established that investigates and develops the methods of teaching and assessing the learning of veterans. Second, colleges and universities may adopt the mission of educating veterans. Third, colleges and universities may hire professors, college administrators, staff who are veterans. Fourth, colleges and universities may help improve the college education of veterans by encouraging other colleges and universities to embrace changes that will encourage veterans to obtain a college degree. They may also augment changes by seeking collaboration with individuals and organizations in the veterans' community, e.g., the American legion, VFW, Disabled American Veterans. In the final section of this chapter, some recent efforts to improve the college experience for veterans were reviewed.

Table 15.1
Best Practices for Support of Military and Veteran College Students

I. Designate a highly visible office with appropriate staff to serve as an institutional single point of contact for students with military affiliation
II. Ensure point of contact is knowledgeable about and sensitive to the need and experiences of service members and veterans
- Deliver student services and advise decision-makers on campus-level policies and peer-to-peer interaction for service members and veterans
II. Develop transition programming and ongoing assistance specifically designed to meet the needs of military service members and veterans
- Develop flexible orientation programs specifically for students with a military background that is appropriately in both content and timing
- Ensure that staff are knowledgeable about the counseling, advising and potential health care needs of students with a military background
- Create an efficient process for students departing for or returning from deployment or other military duty
III. Develop and communicate to students, staff, and faculty, policies and procedures unique to service members or veterans students about
- Credit articulation for military training and military experience
- Fee deferments when GI Bill or tuition assistance is delayed
- Withdrawal, course completion procedures (incompletes, partial credit) for students on deployment or on active military duty
- Absence policies related to military duty
- Fee refund procedures for military withdrawals
- Mechanisms for communication with students while deployed
- Student procedures following deployment or other military duty
- Sensitive consideration for surviving family members of students who died while in military service to include resolution of grades from the student's final semester and potential posthumous award of degree
IV. Institutions are encouraged to communicate, develop and implement additional best practices to serve military members and veterans
- Institutions with small numbers of military members and veterans maximize services by collaborating with other similar institutions
- Institutions should take advantage of opportunities for their designated staff members to meet with peers from other schools

Note: The table above is a summary of Best Practices that were written by a group of educators from Indiana's colleges and universities in the fall of 2008.

Summary

This chapter first pointed out that various organizations could do more to help veterans. The authors believe that leaders in higher education would move quickly to develop higher education programs for veterans if those outside of higher education urged higher education to make the necessary changes promptly. Our country needs a more sound decision-making process and better ways to convey opposition about a war to our government leaders—not to its veterans. A better process will ensure that veterans who seek a college degree are treated and educated with the best practices. There are some indications that a movement to help veterans with their college problems has begun.

Chapter 16
Just for Students who are Veterans

This book has the goal of providing leaders in American society, the veterans community, and in higher education with information that will lead higher education to be more accommodating to veterans. If you are a veteran who currently is in school, you likely have found parts of this book interesting. However, prior to this chapter, the knowledge presented in this book will be helpful to veterans only if professors and college administrators decide to make recommended changes that will facilitate the college experience of veterans.

This chapter presents knowledge that may enable veterans to take steps to facilitate their own college experience. This chapter is intended just for students who are veterans and who want to take steps to eliminate the problems that they are encountering in college. If you are a veteran reading this chapter, you are probably considering going to college or you are student in college. From here on, this chapter assumes you are a veteran in college. Note: If you are a reader but not a veteran who will make application for or is attending college, please realize that the word "you" is intended just for a reader who is a student and a veteran.

Purpose of this Chapter

Veterans seek civilian careers that will provide them with a good living to support themselves and members of their family. In order to qualify for the career they want, many veterans, like you, seek a college degree. If you encounter problems as you pursue a degree, know that there are actions you can take to lessen or eliminate the problem. The contents of this chapter have the purpose of describing and explaining these actions.

Initial Actions to Take

Adopt a Positive Attitude

When you encounter problems in school, remember that America wants you to get a college degree. Also, remember that the vast majority of professors and administrators at your school want you to attend and graduate from college. Additionally, know that if someone creates some obstacles or hassles you, most of the other people at your college do not want you to be treated in this manner.

So if you are encountering problems in your school see if you can solve some problems and work your way around other ones. Doing so will facilitate getting your education sooner and enable you to get on with your career. Many people, including the authors of this book, believe that educated veterans will provide America with the best possible technical knowledge and leadership.

Diagnose Your Problem

When you recognize that you are having a problem at school, ask yourself whether your problem is the same as non-veterans you know. If you decide that your problem has nothing to do with your veteran status, you can still take steps to resolve the problem. Consider whether your problem has anything to do with any of the following categories of problems discussed in this book; interacting successfully with other students and/or professors; adjusting to the culture of your campus, failing to get information about college programs that you need; financial problems; transfer problems; health problems; and finding employment on graduation.

To correct such a problem, take the following action. Go talk to a non-veteran student with whom you feel comfortable. Ask this person how to deal with the problem. If you do not receive sufficient advice, your problem might also be resolved by talking with a professor or administrator whom you trust. You may also want to talk to a counselor at your school. In some cases, you might find out how to solve your problem by reading one of the several books about adjusting to college. Many college problems are solved through reading and thinking about them.

Actions to Take If the Problem is Due to Your Veteran Status

If your problem has something to do with your veteran background, you might want to explore further action about the problem. Understand what this book has to say about veterans' problems and read the chapter that is pertinent to your problem.

Discuss the Problem with Others

Discuss the problem in detail with another veteran at your school. Discussion may help you clarify your understanding and feelings about the problem. At a minimum, discussion will at least give you a chance to blow off steam.

However, discussion of a problem with other veterans may also lead you to conclude that the problem is especially serious. Hence, you may want to do something to eliminate the problem for others beside yourself. Some problems may pertain to all veterans, so you might want to try to change the problem for the veterans at your school.

Find a professor or an administrator to advise you about what you should do about a problem. Once you have identified someone to approach about your problem, ask this person to keep your problem confidential. If he or she hesitates to agree to do so, say thanks for their time and leave. However, most professors or administrators will listen to you, try to help, and respect your request for confidentiality.

If one or more veterans agree that there is a problem and someone who you consult agrees the problem is real, then you may decide to take a further action. But before you go further with complaining about a problem, consider the negative consequences that may come from doing so.

Negative Consequences

A difficulty that veterans have is that their complaints may lead to recriminations. For example, a complaint may lead the professor who is the target of a complaint to make things difficult for the veteran who raised a complaint about him or her. Veterans may fear that a professor who is biased against them will give a lower grade than they deserve. Students may fear as well that professors in general may become biased against any veteran who makes complaints about any professor.

Complaints about administrators may also result in some difficulties. An administrator may delay in providing a service that a veteran needs. The administrator may simply not provide the service. For example, the military credits that the veteran wants transferred can sit on the administrators desk without action taken.

Taking Action

If you are willing to experience all the negative consequences that may come from taking action, there are several things you might do. Assume from the beginning of lodging a complaint that colleges and universities have a chain of command just like the military. When you speak up, then do so in a way that respects this chain and consider doing the following.

1. If your school has a professor or administrator designated to help veterans, discuss the problem with this person. Most schools today do not have a person who officially is supposed to help veterans. If this is the case at your school, find a faculty member or administrator who is a veteran.

2. If you cannot find a professor or administrator to help or who is a veteran, determine whether your school has a "certifying official" and, if so, ask this official to help you with your problem. Your school will have a "certifying official" if you and/or other veterans receive GI Bill at your school. The "certifying official" reports to the VA whether a veteran is enrolled at your school. At some schools, certifying officials are advocates for veterans and will help them resolve their problems.

3. If talking with a professor, administrator, veterans co-ordinator, or certifying official does not help with your problem, get together with other veterans and file a grievance. Nearly all schools have some kind of grievance system. However, not all schools have administrators or professors who have been designated as a person who veterans should go to and get advice about their issues.

4. On some campuses there simply is no administrator or no professor who is sensitized to the needs and requirements of veterans. Consequently, you may find that the grievance procedure is stacked against veterans. If this is he case, you may want to drop your complaint about the problem.

5. If you file a grievance and find that the grievance procedure does not work but you still want the problem resolved, report the problem to the Dean who is over the professor or administrator. If the Dean is not able to resolve the problem, consider stopping your complaint. All battles are not won despite the best intentions.

6. If you want to work further on the problem, you might discuss it with an education officer in a veteran service organization near to your school, such as with the American Legion, the VFW, or some other such organization.

7. If at this stage, you are convinced that your problem is very serious, you may want to consider transferring to a school that treats veterans better, one that is known to be veteran friendly. However, please know that another school may turn out to be just as anti-military/anti-veteran as the one you are at currently. Check with veterans at the school you are thinking of transferring to about how much anti-military/anti-veteran difficulties you might encounter there. With luck you will find a school that will appreciate veterans and which you will want to transfer to.

8. If you consider transferring, recognize that doing so is burdensome and will usually delay your education. Consequently, forgetting about the problem and staying at your school may be your best option. Only you can make that decision.

Summary

The problems that a veteran may encounter in school are like most problems. They sometimes are complex and defy simple resolution.

Problems that students encounter usually are not that complex. They can be addressed and eliminated. Sometimes it is easier to adapt to the problem and forge ahead with your education.

Problems that are due to veteran status are difficult and take time to resolve. These problems are fundamentally political and societal. It may be in your best interest to work your away around these problems and get your degree. If you decide to tackle such problems, we recommend that you consider the actions we have discussed above as you decide what to do about your problems

The authors of this book encountered a range of obstacles when they were seeking a degree and/or have learned about obstacles from veterans who recently have been seeking a college degree. We have written this book because we want you to complete your degree as efficiently as possible. We firmly believe that educated veterans belong in society where they can make the greatest contributions. By adding a college education to knowledge obtained from military training and experience, our society acquires experts with special backgrounds that can, in turn, help our nation in unique ways. When an education is provided to veterans, the nation expresses gratitude for your service. And the authors of this book also thank you for your service.

Epilogue

In Conclusion

Veterans who survive military service, with or without disabilities, possess wisdom and courage. It is in the best interest of our nation to educate as many veterans as possible so that they are available to contribute and, if need be, lead in the special way that only veterans can. In summary, a college or university can help create a better environment for educating veterans throughout America by promulgating its endorsement of the Bill of Educational Rights of Veterans.

Educational Rights for Veterans

Colleges and organizations that serve veterans, especially the Servicemembers Opportunity Colleges, have developed bills of educational rights for veterans. The bill of education rights presented in Table E.1 was influenced by all previous such bills that the authors are aware of. Some legislators have been considering how to make veterans a truly protected class legally (Columbian, 2007). Regardless of the legalities of veteran status, common decency calls for veterans to be treated fairly while they seek a college education. A Bill of Educational Rights for veterans could establish standards for how higher education should treat veterans as they seek a degree.

Responsibilities of Veterans to Colleges and Universities

With rights, come veterans' responsibilities. Veterans should expect to follow the rules of a school or university. By doing so, veterans offer an incentive to colleges and universities to adhere to the Bill of Educational Rights presented above. The responsibilities of veterans are the same as expected of any student.

Veterans must uphold a school's codes of conduct. They must respect the rights and dignity of others: and uphold academic honesty and integrity by refraining from cheating, fabrication, or plagiarism. Veterans are expected to contribute and to facilitate their learning environment, by completing readings and assignments before classes. They should attend classes, participate fully, and respect the value of materials, as well as fulfilling academic requirements in a timely manner.

Table E.1
A Bill of Educational Rights for Veterans

Rights to Certain Freedoms

Freedom from discrimination because of being a veteran

Freedom from harassment because of being a veteran

Freedom from coercion and deception when deciding whether to
matriculate at a specific school

Freedom to access one's records

Freedom to use facilities that any other student can use

Freedom from coercion and deception to enroll in a school

Freedom from coercion and deception in billing

Freedom from misinformation about scholarships and financial aid

Freedom from coercion and deception by the financial aid office

Freedom from false advertising by schools and by organizations that
claim to help veterans with their college education

Freedom to use the school's judicial process without retribution

Rights in General

Right to information about a school's programs, requirements, and
accreditation

Right to a veteran's records be kept confidential

Right to be assessed fairly for admission and course placement

Right for assessment and course placement to take account of military
training and military experience

Right to have appropriate academic support services

Right to have emergency treatment for service-connected disabilities

Right to pursue the education based in part on military background

Right to being billed by my school in the same amounts as are
non-veterans

Right to have my military credits transferred to my school in the
same amount, as they would be transferred to other schools that
have similar missions

Right to not be verbally abused by other members of the academic
community

Right to be provided an employment search for veterans that is as effective
as it is for non-veterans

References

Adams, J. A. (2000). The G.I. bill and the changing place of higher education after World War II. Presented at the annual meeting of the Association for the Study of Higher Education. Sacramento, CA., November.

Administrator of Polish News (2008). Rep. Rahm Emanuel and representatives from Chicago-area universities today announced policies that will make it easier for veterans of the wars in Iraq and Afghanistan to attend college in Illinois and succeed, *Polish news*. Tuesday, 19 August. Retrieved on March 26, 2009 from
http://www.polishnews.com/index.php?option=com_content&view=article&catid=81:news-from-chicago-wiadomoci-z-chicago&id=359:emanuel-chicago-area-universities-unveil-first-in-the-nation-plan-to-utilize-new-gi-bill-send-veterans-to-college-&Itemid=198

Aleethia Foundation (2007) The Aleethia Foundation supports recently injured troops in their rehabilitation upon returning home. Retrieved on November 22, 2008 from http://www.humanevents.com/article.php?id=23076-50k; see also http://www.aleethia.org/

Allen, B.S., (2003). *Comments welcome veterans home,* Readjustment Counseling Service, *Vet Center Voice*, 24, p. 29. US Department of Veterans Affairs, Washington, DC.

Allen, B. S. (1987). Issues that confront those from Appalachia following their wartime experiences. *Now and Then Magazine*. 4, #3. Center for Appalachian Studies and Services, East Tennessee State University, Johnson City, Tennessee.

Allen, B. S. Jr., Herrmann, D., & Giles, S. L. (1995). Vietnam as a class war: Myth or reality. *Sociological Spectrum*, 14, 299-311.

American Association of Collegiate Registrars and Admissions Officers (AACRAO) (2008) Retrieved from http://www.aacrao.org

American Council on Education (ACE) (2008) Severely Injured Military Veterans ACE supported a Fulfilling Their Dreams project in which veterans with severe injuries are assisted in their return to civilian life. Retrieved on March 20, 2009 from http://www.acenet.edu/Content/NavigationMenu/ProgramsServices/MilitaryPrograms/veterans/index.htm-69k-Cached-Similar pages

American Council on Education (ACE) (2008). ACE and Wal-Mart Team-up to Offer Veteran Grants – Education. Retrieved on March 20, 2009 from http://www.military.com/money-for-school/ace-and-wal-mart-team-up—to-offer-veteran-grants—18k

American Council on Education (ACE) (2007). Military installation voluntary education review orientation and guidelines. Retrieved on January 2003.from http://www.acenet.edu/AM/Template.cfm?Section=Search&section=PDF6&template=/CM/ContentDisplay.cfm&ContentFileID=300.

American Council on Education. (ACE) (2004). *Military programs.* Retrieved February 21, 2003 from http://www.acenet.edu/calec/military.

American Psychiatric Association (1994). *Diagnositc and Statistical Manual, 4th edition.* Washington, D.C.: American Psychiatric Association.

Anderson, D. L. (2002). *The Columbia guide to the Vietnam War.* New York: Columbia University Press.

Anderson, R. C. (2004). *Home front: The government's war on soldiers.* Atlanta: Clarity Press.

Angrist, J. D. (1993). The effect of veterans benefits on education and earnings. *Industrial & Labor Relations Review,* 46, 637-653.

Anonymous, VFW (2007a). *Applauds Disability Benefits Commission Report. Executive summary and full report.* Retrieved on September 10 http://www.vetscommission.org/reports.asp

Anonymous. VFW. (2007b). Educational attainment and war vets. *Veterans of Foreign Wars Magazine,* 94, 8-9.

Anonymous, VFW. (2001). *House votes G.I. Bill Raise, Ups Ante on Senate.* Retrieved in 2007 from http://acenet.edu/calec/military

Appy, C. (1992). *Working Class War,* University of North Carolina Press.

Armstrong, K., Best, S. & Domenici, P. (2005). *Courage After Fire: Coping Strategies for Returning Soldiers and Their Families.* Berkeley, CA: Ulysses Press.

Asch, B. J., Kilburn, M. R., & Klerman, J. A. (1999). Attracting college-bound youth into the military: toward the development of new recruiting policy options. Rand Mongraph (Number: MR-984-OSD): *RAND Distribution Services.* Retrieved on March 22, 2005 from http://www.rand.org/about/

Ashabranner, B. K., (1988). *Always to remember : The story of the Vietnam Veterans Memorial ; photographs by Jennifer Ashabranner:* Scranton, Pennsylvania: Scholastic.

Ashby, C. M. (2002). Veterans' education benefits: comparison of federal assistance awarded to veteran and non-veteran students. *Report to the Ranking Minority Member on Committee on Veterans Affairs. U.S. Senate* by the Director of Education, Workforce and Income Security, U.S. General Accounting Office.

Association of Veterans Education (2006). *Association of Veterans Education Certifying Officials. A Non-Chartered Organization* . National Headquarters Address, 9813 104th Avenue Ottumwa, IA 52501. Retrieved from   http: // www1.va.gov/vso/inde.cfm?template=viewreport&Org_ID=338-13k-Cached

Avery, C. E. (1946). Veterans' education in the universities. *Journal of Higher Education, 17,* 360.

Baars, B. J. (1992). *Experimental slips and human error: Exploring the architecture of volition.* New York: Plenum Press.

Bascetta, C. A. (2002). Military and veterans' benefits: observations on the transition assistance program. *Testimony before the Subcommittee on Benefits Committee on Veterans' Affairs, House of Representatives.* Washington, DC: General Accounting Office (GAO-02-914T).

Batteiger, R. P. (1993). Lies and Versions in Neil Sheehan's "A Bright Shining Lie." *Journal of the Vietnam Veterans Institute,* 2, issue 1.

Bauerlein, M. (2004). Liberal groupthink is anti-intellectual. *Chronicle of Higher Education,* November 12, 2004

Beacon, J. E. (2008). Proposal for one-time veteran's tuition waive. Terre Haute: Indiana State University.

Bedford, J. H. (1946). *The veteran and his future job.* Los Angeles: Society for Occupational Research.

Bensen, D. R. 1989. Treatment and prevention of alcoholism and substance abuse in the military. In. *Alcoholism & substance abuse in special populations,* G. Lawson and A. Lawson . New York: McGraw Hill.

Berger, M. C., & Hiersch, B. T. (1983). The civilian earnings experience of Vietnam-Era veterans.. *Journal of Human Resources, 18,* 455-480.

Berry, G. L. (1977). Counseling needs of disadvantaged veterans. *Journal of College Student Personnel., 18,* 406-412.

Black, T., Westwood, N. J., Sorsdal, M. N., & Michael. M. N. (2007). From the Front Line to the Front of the Class: Counseling Students Who Are

Military Veterans. In J. A. Lippincott and R. A. Lippincott, Ruth A. (Eds.) *Special populations in college counseling: A handbook for mental health professionals.* (pp. 3-20). Aleandria, VA: American Counseling Association.

Bolte, C. G. (1945). *The new veteran.* New York: Reynal & Hitchcock.

Bonior, D. D., Champlain, S. M., & Kolly, T. S. (1984). *The Vietnam veteran: A history of neglect.* New York: Praeger.

Boscarino, J. A., (2006). Eternal-cause mortality after psychological trauma: The effects of stress exposure and predisposition. *Comprehensive Psychiatry,* 47, 503-514.

Bound, J. & Turner, S. (2002). Going to War and Going to College: Did World War II and the GI Bill Increase Educational Attainment for Returning Veterans? *Journal of Labor Economics.* 20, 4, 784-816.

Brady, D. U. & Rapport, L. (1973). Violence and Vietnam: A comparison between attitudes of civilians and veterans. *Human Relations,* 26, 735-752.

Brown, P. (2006, January 12). "Since we need both, DoD and academia must reconcile." *The Orlando Sentinel.* Retrieved on 20 Jan. 2006 from http://www.orlandosentinel.com.

Brown, R. (1998). *Prejudice.* Malden, Mass.: Blackwell Publishers.

Bureau of Labor Statistics (2006). *College enrollment and work activity of 2006 high school graduates.* USDL 07-0604 Washington DC: United Sates Department of Labor.

Butchjax (2005). To the anti-military recruiters. Retrieved on September 14, 2007 from http://butchjax.wordpress.com/about/

Butler, S. (2005). The current number of veterans in the United States. *Administrative support to measurement excellence and training resource information center.* Houston, T: METRIC.

Burkett, B. G. (1998). *Stolen valor: How the Vietnam generations were robbed of its heroes and its history.* Sunnyvale, CA: Verity Press.

Buyer, S. (2004). Wall street and main street agree: Veterans give business the winning edge! *House Committee on Veterans' Affairs.* March 24. Retrieved on Jan 12, 2006 from http://veterans.house.gov/hearings/schedules108/mar04/3-24-04/witness/html.

Callahan L. F., & Pincus T. (1988). Formal education level as a significant marker of clinical status in rheumatoid arthritis. *Arthritis Rheum.* 31, 1346-57.

Campbell, P. (2009) Problems of Veterans who are students in college. Executive Summary of Educating Veterans. *Iraq and Afghanistan Veterans of America.*

Campus Antiwar Network (2003). Independent, democratic, grassroots network of students opposing the occupation of Iraq and military recruiters in our schools. Wikipedia, 2004

Campus Antiwar Network (2004). March 2004, at City College of New York, four people were arrested at a counter-recruitment protest. Wikipedia 2004.

Capps, W. (1982). *The unfinished war: Vietnam and the American conscience.* Boston: Beacon Press.

Caputo, P. (1978). *A rumor of war.* New York: Balantine Books.

Card, D. & Lemieux, T. (2001). Going to college to avoid the draft: The unintended legacy of the Vietnam War. *The American Economic Review*, Vol. 91, No. 2, Papers and Proceedings of the Hundred Thirteenth Annual Meeting of the American Economic Association. (May, 2001), pp. 97-102.

Card, J. J. (1983). *Lives after Vietnam.* Lexington, MA: Lexington Books.

Carney, C. P., Sampson, T. R., & Voelker, M. (2003). Women in the gulf war: combat experiences, exposures, and subsequent health care use. *Military Medicine, 168,* 654-661.

Carpenter, D. S. (1992). *Bright ideas: The ins and outs of financing a college education.* New York: Simon & Schuster.

Cartright, M. A. (1944). *Marching home: Educational and social adjustment after the war.* New York: Teachers College, Columbia University.

Caudell, R. (2005). *Need a lift? To Educational Opportunities, Careers, Loans, Scholarships, & Employment.* (54th edition). Indianapolis, IN.: American Legion National Headquarters. http://emblem.legion.org

Chapman, S. (2007). Is It Time to Revive the GI Bill? How much should we offer the troops? *Reason Magazine*, October 15.

Chavez, L. (2006). Discrimination Is Alive and Well. *Human Events.* 62, 19.

Clark, C. A (2004) State demographics and veteran disability. A Master's thesis in the field of government. Cambridge: *Harvard University.*

Clark, D. A. (1998). The two Joes meet—Joe college, Joe veteran. *His-*

tory of Education Quarterly, 38, 166-189.

Coeyman, M. (2001). *Basic back-to-school training. Christian Science Monitor, 93, 18.*

Cohen, J., Segal, D. R., & Temme, L. V. (1992). The impact of education on Vietnam-Era veterans. *Social Sciences Quarterly, 73*, 397.

Colloquy Live. (2005). G.I. recruiting blues. *Chronicle of Higher Education*, May 12..

Columbian (2007) *The Vietnam 'Gorilla.'* Vancouver, WA. Retrieved on September 28th from http://panther.indstate.edu:2048/login?url=http://search.ebscohost.com/login.asp?direct=true&db=nfh&AN=2W62W6408143 0012&site=ehost-live

Commission on Post-War Training and the Adjustment (1942) A statement of principles relating to the educational problems of returning soldiers, sailors, and displaced war industry workers. New York: Teachers College, Columbia University.

Congressional Research Service (2008). Report for Congress: American War and Military Operations Casualties: Lists and Statistics .

Cook, Joan M., Walser, Robyn D., Kane, Vincent, Ruzek, Josef I., & Woody, George, (2006). Dissemination and feasibility of a cognitive-behavioral treatment for substance use disorders and posttraumatic stress disorder in the Veterans Administration. *Journal of Psychoactive Drugs, 38,* 89-92.

Cooper, A. (2007). Young veterans struggle to find jobs. *Anderson Cooper Blog 360,* CNN, April 4.

Cornelius, S. L. (1993). *Leaving the military and landing on your feet.* Plantation. Florida: Distinctive Publications.

Council for Opportunity in Education (2008) ACE Launches New Veterans Initiative with help from WalMart. Retrieved from http://www.coenet.us/ecm/AM/Template.cfm?Section=November_2008&Template=/CM/HTMLDisplay.cfm&ContentID- 39k

Coyle, B. S., Wolan, D. L., & Van Horn, A. S. (1996). The prevalence of physical and sexual abuse in women veterans seeking care at a Veterans Affairs Medical Center. *Military Medicine, 161,* 588-93.

CQ Researcher (2007). GI Bill of Rights by the Roosevelt Administration and Congress. CQ Researcher, 17, 706-708.

Crawley, J. W. (2006). Young vets can't find jobs. *Potomac News.* September 14, Retrieved on June 13, 2007 from http://www.potomacnews.com/

servlet/Satellite?pagename=WPN%2FMGArticle%2FWPN_Basic Article&c=MGArticle&cid=1149188216054&path=

Creveld, M. V. (2001). Men, women and war. London: Cassell. Cronbach, L. J. (1984). *Essentials of Psychological Testing.* New York: Harper Row Publishers.

D'Avanzo, C. (2003). Application of Research on Learning to College Teaching: Ecological Examples. *BioScience, 53,* 1121–1128.

Defense activity for non-traditional education support agency. (2004). *Voluntary education fact sheet fy03.* Retrieved on June 9, 2005 from http://www.dantes.doded.mil/dantes_web/library/docs/voledfacts/FY03.pdf.

Democracy Now (2005). Campus Resistance: Students Stage Counter-Recruitment Protests Across the Country. War & Peace Report on Democracy Now radio and TV show. Hosted by Amy Goodman and Juan Gonzalez
http://www.democracynow.org/article.pl?sid=05/03/18/1450222

Department of Defense (2003) *Guide to Reserve Family Member Benefits.* Washington, D.C. Pentagon.

Department of Veterans Affairs (2008) *The Post-9/11 Veterans Educational Assistance Act of 2008* . VA Pamphlet 22-09-1 Retrieved on October 2008. from http://www.GIBILL.VA.GOV/GI Bill Info/programs.htm

Department of Veterans Affairs (2007). *38 CFR Book C Schedule for Rating Disabilities* on October 6, 2007 from http://www.warms.vba.va.gov/bookc.html

Department of Veterans Affairs (2006). *Homeless veterans.* Retrieved on September 12, 2007 from http://www1.va.gov/homeless/page.cfm?pg=1

Department of Veteran Affairs. (2005). *Federal benefits for veterans and dependents.* Washington DC: Office of Public Affairs.

Department of Veteran Affairs. (2004). *National survey of veterans.* Washington, D. C.: National Center for Information Analysis and Statistics.

Department of Veteran Affairs (1994). *National Survey of Veterans.* Washington, D. C.: National Center for Information Analysis and Statistics.

Dickson, P. & Allan, T. B. (2004). *The bonus army: An American epic.* New York: Walker and Company.

Dillingham, W. P. (1952) *Federal aid to veterans.* Gainsville: University of Florida Press.

DiLorenzo, T. J. (1997). The truth about the GI bill. *The Lighthouse.* The Independent Institute. January 1.

Diyanni, R. (1997). *How to succeed in college.* Boston: & and Bacon.

Dobbs, J. M., Hopper, C. H., & Jurkovic, G. J. (1990). Testosterone and personality among college students and military veterans. *Personality and Individual Differences, 11,* 1263-1269.

Dockery, P. H. (1997) Agents orange, white, and blue – new disclosures a combat soldiers research. *Journal of the Vietnam Veterans Institute,. 6,* 1-4.

Dolan, E. (1989). *America after Vietnam: Legacies of a hated war.* New York: F. Watts.

Donnelly, F. (2006). Today's GI bill: pay for it. *Staten Island Advance.* September 03. Retrieved on September 14 2007 from http://www.silive.com/news/advance/inde.ssf?/base/news/1157289309263610.ml&coll=1

Dovidio, J., F., Kamkami, K., & Gaertner, S. L. (2002). Implicit and explicit prejudice and interracial integration. *Journal of Social and Personality Psychology, 82,* 62-68.

Drew, D. E., & Creager, J. A. (1972). *The Vietnam-era veteran enters college.* Washington, D.C.: American Counsel on Education.

Drier, H. N. (1995). *Out of uniform: A career transition guide for e-military personnel.* New York: Career Horizons.

Drury, T. (2005). Really supporting our troops. *Buffalo Business First.* October 3. Retrieved on Jan 14, 2006 from http://buffalo.bizjournals.com/buffalo/stories/2005/1003/focus1.html.

Dyhouse, T. (2004). GI bill needs 21st century upgrade. *Veterans of Foreign Wars Magazine, 92,* 4, 1.

Eagle (2007). *For veterans with PTSD, there's help in the area.* Brian, Teas, 08/29/2007. Retrieved on September 28, 2008 from http://panther.indstate.edu:2048/login?url=http://search.ebscohost.com/login.asp?direct=true&db=nfh&AN=2W62W6231204201&site=ehost-live

Educational Policies Commission (1944). *A program for the education of returning veterans.* Washington, D.C.: National Education Association of the United States and the American Association of School Administrators.

Egendorf, A. (1985). *Healing from the War: Trauma & transformation after Vietnam.* Houghton Mifflin, Boston.

Emerson, G. (1972). *Winners and Losers.* New York: Random House.

Employer Support for the Guard and Reserve (2007). Retrieved on December 5 2007 from http: www.esgr.gov

Enzie, R. F., Sawyer, R. N., & Montgomery, F. A. (1973). Manifest anxiety of Vietnam returnees and undergraduates. *Psychological Reports, 33,* pp 446.

Eric. (2007). Homeless veterans are everywhere, but who's counting? *Classical Values*. September 8. Retrieved from September 14, 2007 from http://www.classicalvalues.com/archives/2007/09/post_449.html

Farley, J. (2005). *Military to civilian career transition guide*. Indianapolis.

Farrell, E. F. (2005). Military recruiters promise 'money for college', but recent veterans find that tuition benefits fall short. *Chronicle of Higher Education*. May 13.

Fields, S. (2006). Who say college boys are smart? Townhall. November 6. Retrieved on December 15, 2006 from http://www.townhall.com/columnists/SuzanneFields/2006/11/06/who_say_college_boys_are_smart

Figley, C. R. (1988). *The Counseling Psychologist, 16,* No. 4, 635-641 (1988)

Figley, C. R. (1978a). Symptoms of delayed combat stress among a college sample of Vietnam veterans. *Military Medicine, 143,* 107-110.

Figley, C. R. (Ed.) (1978b). *Stress disorders among Vietnam veterans*. New York: Burnner/Mazel.

Fine, B. (1947). Veterans raise college standards. *Educational Outlook, 22,* November.

Flint, T. (2000). *Serving Adult Learners in Higher Education: Principles of effectiveness*. Chicago: Council for Adult and Experiential Learning.

Fogg-Davis, H. J. (2007). Understanding Affirmative Action: Politics, Discrimination, and the Search for Justice – by J. Edward Kellough. *Governance, 20,* 545-547.

Gaines, F. P. (2004). 1945 opening the doors of opportunity: liberal education and the veterans. *Liberal Education*, Fall.

Gaul, B. (2006). Rigid, Command-and-Control Leadership? I don't Think So. *Destiny Group*. Retrieved on 10 Jan. from https://destinygrp.com/destiny/template/show_article.jsp?article_id=113.

Geiser Consent Decree (2001). Executive Order 11246, as amended to the Rehabilitation Act of 1973 and the Vietnam Era Veteran Readjustment Assistance Act. Retrieved from http://en.wikipedia.org/wiki/Eecutive_Order_11246http://en.wikipedia.org/wiki/1973_Rehabilitation_Act—29k—http://www.dol.gov/compliance/laws/comp-vevraa.htm—40k -

Gelber, S. (2005). A 'Hard-Boiled Order': the reeducation of disabled WWI veterans in New York City. *Journal of Social History*, Fall.

General Accounting Office. (1994). *Veteran's benefits: Lack of time-*

liness, poor communications cause customer dissatisfaction. GAO Document (GAOAEHS-94-179). Washington, D.C.: General Accounting Office.

George, P. (2005). Group protests Army presence at career fair. *The Daily Texan, University of Texas at Austin.* October 20th.

Geraerts, E., Kozaric-Kovacic, D., Merckelbach, H., Peraica, T., Jelicic, M., & Candel, I. (2007) Traumatic memories of war veterans. *Consciousness and Cognition: An International Journal, 16,* 170-177.

Gillman, J. (2002) Students feign death in anti-war protest. *Student newspaper at the University of Rhode Island.* 11/26/02 Section: News.

Gilroy, M. (2007). GI tuition benefits: What's right, what's wrong. *The Hispanic Outlook in Higher Education, 17,* 15-17.

Gimbel, C. & Booth, A. (1994). Does *military* combat experience adversely affect marital relations? *Journal of Marriage & Family, 56,* 691-703.

GI Rights Hotline (2007). Information to members of the military about discharges, grievance and complaint procedures, and other civil rights. Retrieved from

http://www.objector.org/girights/contact.html

GoArmy.Com (2007). Retrieved on December 4, 2007 from http://www.goarmy.com/rotc/enlisted_soldiers.jsp—63k—Cached—Similar pages—Note this

Golden, D. (2006). Foreign Students Find U.S. Colleges To Be More Forthcoming With Aid. *Wall Street Journal.* 1 Feb. 2002: 3 Jan 2006. http://opendoors.iienetwork.org/?p=2947

Goldman, P. & Fuller, T. (1983). *Charlie company: What Vietnam did to us.* New York: Balantine Books.

Greenberg, M. (2004). How the GI Bill Changed Higher Education. *The Chronicle of Higher Education.* Washington: Jun 18, 2004.50, 41; pg. B.9.

Greene, Bob, (1989). *Homecoming: When the soldiers returned from Vietnam.* New York, Balantine.

Greer, M. (2005). A new kind of war. *APA Monitor online, 36,* 4, April

Griffith, K. (2006). Young veterans face hurdles at home—Federal and local officials alarmed at unemployment rate in troops returning from Iraq. *VA Watchdog.* Retrieved on September 14 2007 from http://www.vawatchdog.org/old%20newsflashes%20AUG%202006/newsflash08-06-2006-9.htm

Grinnell, J. E. (1945) When the G.I. Goes to College. *The Journal of Higher Education. XVII,* 5, 243-246, 282.

Gruder, M. W. (2008. One state, one team; Foglesong, R. H. (2008). Four star Air Force General becomes president of Mississippi State University. *MSU Alumnus magazine.*

Hall, R. (2007). Protestors wrong on Vietnam, Then and on Iraq now. *CNS.* Retrieved on April 5, 2008

Hall, W. C. & Schweizer, P. (2005). Campus radicals vs. our vets. *National Review Online.* Retrieved Aug 29, 2005, from http://www.nationalreview.com/comment/hall_schweizer200508290810.asp

Harmeyer, E. (2007). Dartmouth President founds college service for wounded veterans. *VFW Magazine,* September, 18-19. Retrieved from http:www.vfw.org

Harris, J, T., III (2005). Higher education, College rankings and access for lower-income students. *Black Issues in Higher Education.* 21, 106.

Hass, K. A, (1988). *Carried to the wall : American memory and the Vietnam Veterans Memorial.* Berkeley: University of California Press,

Heller, J. (2006). From Combat to College War Veterans on Campus. *VFW Magazine,* . Retrieved from http://www.vfw.org

Helmer, J. (1974) *Bringing the war home: The American soldier in Vietnam and after.* New York: The Free Press.

Hemingway, M. Z. (2007). Vets winning job suits. *Federal Times,* 43, p1-5.

Henderson, J. L. (1977). Persistence and nonpersistence of disadvantaged Vietnam-era veterans in college. *Dissertation Abstracts International,* 37, 4133-4134.

Herr, M. (1978). *Dispatches.* New York: Knopf.

Herrmann, D. (2009). Indiana's Best Practices for the Higher Education of Servicemembers and Veterans. Veterans Higher Education Group. Terre Haute, Indiana.

Herrmann, D. & Gruneberg, M. (2008). SuperMemory II. New York: Strategic Book Publishing.

Herrmann, D. (2007a). *What it is like to be a veteran in college today.* Presented to the Veterans Advisory Committee on Education. Washington, D.C. May.

Herrmann, D. (2007b). A Survey of Indiana Colleges and Universities about the Problems of Members of the Guard and Reserves in College. Terre Haute, IN: Veterans Higher Education Group, May.

Herrmann, D., & Guadagno, M. A. (1997). Memory performance and socio-economic status. *Applied Cognitive Psychology,* 11, 113-120.

Herrmann, D., Raybeck, D., & Gruneberg, M. (2002). *Improving memory and study skills*. Toronto: Hogrefe and Huber.

Herrmann, D., Raybeck, & Gutman, D. (1993). *Improving student memory*. Toronto: Hogrefe and Huber.

Herrmann, D., Raybeck, D., & Wilson, R. B. (2008). College Is for Veterans, Too. The Chronicle Review, *Chronicle of Higher Education*, November 11, 2008.

Herrmann, D., Wilson, R. & Hopkins, C. (2006). A Literature Review of Sources that Pertain to Problems of Veterans in Higher Education. Terre Haute, IN: Veterans Education Association.

Herrmann, D., Plude, D., Yoder, C., & Mullin, P. (1999). Cognitive Processing and Extrinsic Psychological Systems: A Holistic Model of Cognition. *Zeitschrift fur Psychologie, 207,* 123-147.

Herrmann, D., Schooler, C., Caplan, L. J., Lipman, P. D., Grafman, J., Schoenbach, C., Schwab, K., & Johnson, M. L. (2001). The latent structure of memory: A confirmatory factor-analytic study of memory distinctions (results of the Vietnam Head Injury project). *Multivariate Behavioral Research, 36,* 29-51.

Herrmann, D., Yoder, C., Gruneberg, M., & Payne, D., C. (2006). *Applied Cognitive Psychology*. Mahwah, N.J.: Erlbaum.

Higgs (2006). *Wars and Numbers; Geocites*. Retrieved in 2006 from http://www.geocities.com/Athens/Acropolis/2321/memorialday2003/number).

Higher Education Reconciliation Act (2005). Public Law 109-171; Title VIII of the Deficit Reduction Act, was approved by conference committee and subsequently approved by the Senate on December 21, 2005, the House on February 2, 2006 and signed by the President on February 8, 2006.

History News Network. (2003). *How many American troops have died in war*. Retrieved on September 14 2007 from http://hnn.us/articles/1381.html

HistoryNet (2006). American Indian Wars | Brule Siou Spotted Tail's... Retrieved on August 15, 2006 from
http: www.historynet.com/wars_conflicts/american_indian_wars/3037126.html—58k

Hoffman, A., Roesner, N., & McCandless, S. (2005). The Validity of Memory Failure Self Reports. *Cognitive Technology. 11,* 45-53.

Hohmann, J. (2007). Bush condemns schools without ROTC programs. *The Stanford Daily*, May 18. Home of Heroes (2007).Retrieved on January 15, 2009 from http://www.homeofheroes.com..

Hopkins, C. D. & Antes, R. L. (1990) *Classroom Measurement and Evaluation* (3rd ed.) Itasca, IL: F. E. Peacock.

Hopkins, C. D. (1976). *Educational Research: Structure for Inquiry*. Columbus, OH: Chares E. Merrill.

Horne, A. D. (1981). *The wounded generation: America after Vietnam*. Englewood Cliffs: Prentice Hall. House Committee on Government Operations (1981) Office of the Inspector General, Audit of Veterans Benefit Administration. Report No. 05-01931-158. Retrieved on December 4, 2007 from http://www.google.com/search?hl=en&q=House+Committee+on+Government+Operations+%281981%29+veterans&btnG=Search

House Committee On Veterans' Affairs (2004). Subcommittee on health. Report of VA Advisory Committee on Homeless Veterans (PDF). Retrieved on December 4, 2007 from
http://veterans.house.gov/hearings/schedule108/may04/5-6-04/witness.html

House Committee On Veterans' Affairs (2001). H.R. 1291, 21st century Montgomery GI Bill enhancement act. *Hearings Before the Subcommittee on Benefits of The Committee on Veterans Affairs, House of Representatives. One Hundredth Seventh Congress, First Session*. Washington DC: House-HRG-107-6.

Howell, T. (2007). Veteran homelessness on the rise. *Military.com*. September 12, 2007 from http://www.military.com/NewsContent/0,13319,139317,00.html

Huckabee, M. (2008) Congress Should First 'Bail Out' Our Veterans. FOX Forum.

Hunter, R. & Tankovich, M. B. (2007) *The Army National Guard The You Can Guide to Paying for your College Education*, 2nd Printing. Washington, D.C.: Uniformed Services Almanac, Inc. http://virtualarmory.com

Hyer, L., Boudewyns, P., Harrison, W. R., O'Leary, W. C., Bruno, R. D., Saucer, R. T., & Blount, J. B. (1988). Vietnam Veterans: Overreporting Versus Acceptable Reporting of Symptoms. *Journal of Personality Assessment*, 52, 475-486.

Indianapolis Healing Arts Program (2006). The Art of Combat Veterans: how visual and written arts may help people with PTSD and related disorders. Terre Haute, IN: Indiana State University.

Iraq and Afghanistan Veterans of America (2008a). A new GI Bill: Rewarding our troops, rebuilding our military. *IAVA Issue report*, January.

Iraq and Afghanistan Veterans of America (2008b). A new GI Bill: Rewarding our troops, rebuilding our military. *IAVA Quick Facts*, January.

Jennings, P. A., Aldwin, C. M. Levenson, M. R., Spiro, A., & Mroczek, D. K. (2006). Combat Exposure, Perceived Benefits of Military Service, and Wisdom in Later Life: Findings From the Normative Aging Study. *Research on Aging*, 28, 115-134.

Joanning, H. (1975). The academic performance of Vietnam veteran college students. *Journal of College Student Personnel*, 16, 10-13.

Johnson, D. (2007). College students protest Iraq War at Goshen College. Goshen Indiana: *Goshen News*.

Jones, D. (2005). *Web extra: combat trains workplace leaders*. Asbury & Park Press. March 28. Retrieved on Jan 1, 2006 from http//www.app.com/apps/pbcs.dll/article?AID=/20050328/BUSINESS/

Jowers, K. & Kauffman, T. (2007). Ruling strengthens vets' rights in federal job-bias claims. *Army Times*, 67, p25-25, 1/4p.

Judge, J. (2004). Where do soldiers come from? *Washington Peace Letter*. 40, August/September. Retrieved Jan 15, 2006 from http://www.washington-peacecenter.org/articles/0408pl.wheresoldiers.html.

Karnow, S. (1983). *Vietnam: a history*. London: Penguin Books.

Keane, T. M. (1998). Psychological effects of military combat. *Adversity, Stress, and Psychopathology*, pp. 52-65. New York: Oxford University Press.

Kime, S. (2007a). Updating the Montgomery GI Bill. *Committee on House Veterans Affairs Subcommittee on Economic Opportunity*, 110th Congress. October 18.

Kime, S. (2007b). Why Veterans get Second-Class treatment. Retrieved on January 8, 2008 from http://newscomet.com/

Kime, S. (2006). Transition assistance and educational benefits: Congressional testimony. *Committee on House Veterans Affairs Subcommittee on Economic Opportunity. Congressional Quarterly*, Inc. March 22.

Kime, S. F. (2005). *Voluntary Military Education: A Strategic Perspective*. Washington, D.C.: Servicemembers Opportunity Colleges.

Kingsbury, A. (2007). American Council on Education's new pilot program for wounded veterans. *U.S. News & World Report*. 143, 71-71.

Kingston, M. H. (2006). *Veterans of War, Veterans of Peace*. Kihei: Koa Books.

Kirsch, I., Braun, H., Yamamoto, K., & Sum, A. (2007). *Perfect Storm:*

Three forces changing our nation's future. Princeton, N.J.: Educational Testing Service; can also be retrieved from http://www.ets.org/research/pic

Klein, R. E. (1989). *Personal and family income of veterans and non-veterans.* Washington, D. C.: Department of Veterans Affairs.

Klein, R. E. (1985). *School enrollment among male veterans and non-veterans 20 to 34 years old.* Washington, D. C.: Office of Information Management and Statistics.

Klein, R. (1981) *Wounded men, broken promises.* NewYork: Macmillan.

Kovic, R. (1984). *Born on the fourth of July.* New York: Pocket Books.

Kubany, E. S., Haynes, S. N., & Abueg, F. R. (1996). Development and validation of the trauma-related guilt inventory (TRGI). *Psychological Assessment, 8,* 428-444.

Landau, E. (2002). *Veterans Day: Remembering Our War Heroes.* Berkeley Heights, NJ : Enslow Publishers.

Lane. C. (2005). Law Schools Challenge Rule Requiring Universities to Give Equal Access or Risk Losing Funding. *Washington Post.* May 3, Page A02.

Langbert, R., & Wells, W. (1982). *Education and income characteristics of male war veterans and non-veterans.* Washington, D. C.: Office of Reports and Statistics.

Lanham, S. L. (2005). *Veterans and families guide to recovering from PTSD.* Annandale, VA: Purple Heart Service Foundation.

Lanigan, K. (2007). Operation education. *VFW Magazine,* September, 20-21.

Lavela, S. L., Weaver, F. M., Smith, B. & Chen, K. (2006). Disease Prevalence and Use of Preventive Services: Comparison of Female Veterans in General and Those with Spinal Cord Injuries and Disorders. *Journal of Women's Health, 15,* 301-311.

LawMemo (2006). US Supreme Court unanimously upholds Solomon Amendment. March 06. Retrieved on May 15, 2007 from http://www.law-memo.com/blog/2006/03/us_supreme_cour_4.html

Lederman, D. (1997). Colleges that bar the military won't lose most student aid. *The Chronicle of Higher Education*: 02/21. Retrieved on December 22, 2007 from http:chronicle.com/che-data/articles.dir/art-43.dir/issue-24.dir/24a03401.htm—20k—Cached—Similar pages—Note this

Lehrer, J. (2002). Protesting war with Iraq. *Online News Hour; Online*

Focus. PBS.

Leisner, B. A. (1995). Learning needs of hospitalized veteran patients: Developing a tool for practice. *Patient Education and Counseling, 25*, 151-162.

LeShan (1992). *The Psychology of War: Comprehending its Mystique and its Madness.* Chicago: Noble Press.

Leverenz, N. A. (2005). Not doing enough for our veterans. *AlterNet.* Retrieved on Jan 8, 2006 from http://alternet.org/story/27818/.

Lewin, T. (1990). Harvard Protesting R.O.T.C. Rejection Of Homosexuality. *New York Times,* June 15.

Lipsett, L. & Smith, L. F. (1949). Veterans carry through on operation "education." *Journal of Educational Research, 42,* 395-397.

Likar, L. L., Panciera, T. M., Erickson, A. D., & Rounds, S. (1997). Group education sessions and compliance with nasal CPAP therapy. *Chest, 111,* 1273-1277.

Love, L. L. & Hutchison, C. A. (1946). Academic Progress of Veterans. *Educational Research Bulletin, 25,* 223-226.

Maclean, A. (2005). Lessons from the cold war: Military service and college education. *Sociology of Education, 78,* 250.

Maclean, L. & Roller , W. (2005). Students Protest Military Recruitment. The Golden Gate [Express] Online, San Francisco State University. March 9.

Macpherson, M. (1984). *Long time passing.* Garden City, NY: Doubleday.

Magruder, L. (2005a). What hypocrisy! a short history of "therapy" remarks after 9/11.Vietnam Veterans for Academic Reform. *The University of Kansas Student Auxiliary.* Retrieved on December 15 2006 from http://v-v-a-r. org/.

Magruder, L. (2005b). Turning their backs—again. Vietnam Veterans for Academic Reform. *The University of Kansas Student Auxiliary.* Retrieved on December 15, 2006 from http://v-v-a-r.org/.

Magruder, L. (2005c) Vietnam and the Media. Vietnam Veterans for Academic Reform. *The University of Kansas Student Auxiliary.* Retrieved on December 15, 2006 from http://v-v-a-r.org/.

Magruder, L. (2003). Manifesto against leftist tyranny. Vietnam Veterans for Academic Reform. *The University of Kansas Student Auxiliary.* Retrieved on December 15, 2006 from http://v-v-a-r.org/.

Magruder, L. (2002). How the campus lied about Vietnam. Vietnam Veterans for Academic Reform. *The University of Kansas Student Auxiliary.* Retrieved on December 15, 2006 from http://v-v-a-r.org/.

Malkin, M. (2008). It's time we quit coddling anti-military militants. *Home News Tribune Online* 03/13/08

Malladi, S. (2005). Students protest army presence. *Badger Herald, University of Wisconsin,* Thursday, February 17, 2005

Mangan, K. S. (2005). Affirmative Action and Military Recruiting Spur Debate at Law-School Meeting. *Chronicle of Higher Education*, A19-A19.

Manguno-Mire, G., Sautter, F., Lyons, J., Myers, L., Perry, D., Sherman, M., Glynn, S., & Sullivan, M. (2007). Psychological Distress and Burden Among Female Partners of Combat Veterans With PTSD. *Journal of Nervous and Mental Disease, 195,* 144-151.

Maraniss, D. (2004). *They Marched into Sunlight...1967.* New York: Simon & Schuster.

Marklein, M. B. (2007). Complex GI Bill makes for a rocky road from combat to college. *USA TODAY*, December 26.

Marley, D. F. (1998). *Wars of the Americans: A chronology of armed conflict in the new world, 1492 to the present.* Santa Barbara, CA: ABC-CLIO.

Mason, P.H.D. (1990). Recovering from the war: A woman's guide to helping your Vietnam vet, your family, and yourself. New York: Penguin.

Massey, D. S. (2000). *Higher Education and Social Mobility In the United States* 1940-1998. Paper presented at the AAU Centennial Meeting, Washington D.C. April 17.

Mayer, R. E. (1999). *The promise of educational psychology: Learning in the content areas.* Upper Saddle River, NJ: Prentice Hall.

Maze, R. (2007a). Vets' disability claims keep piling up. St. *Louis Area Iraq War Veterans.* Retrieved on December 7, 2007 from http://stliraqwarvets.wordpress.com/2007/06/01/vets%e2%80%99-disability-claims-keep-piling-up/

Maze, R. (2007b). Many hiring managers snubbing vets. *Federal Times*, 9/10/2007, Vol. 43 Issue 29, p1-20.

McBain, L. (2008). When Johnny [or Janelle] comes marching home: National, state, and institutional efforts in support of veteran's education. *Perspectives: American Association of State Colleges and Universities*, Summer Issue.

McDaniel, L. (2006). Campus Veterans Clubs Boost Camaraderie and

Careers. *VFW Magazine*, 25 Jan. Retrieved on January 15, 2008 from https://www.vfw.org/inde.cfm?fa=news.magDt&dtl=2&mid=2148>.

McKeachie, W.J. (1999). Teaching Tips : Strategies, Research, and Theory for College and University Teachers. Boston: Anker.

McIntire, S. A. & Miller, L. A. (2007). *Foundation of Psychological Testing: A Practical Approach.* Thousand Oaks, CA: Sage.

McLay, R. N. & Lyketsos, C. G. (2000). Veterans have less age related cognitive decline. *Military Medicine*, 165, 622-625.

McNemar, Q. (1969). *Psychological Statistics*, 4th Edition. New York: Wiley.

Mears, B. (2005). Pentagon, law schools square off. *CNN News*. 6 Dec. 2005. Retrieved on January 5,. 2006 from http://www.cnn.com/2005/LAW/12/06/scotus/recruiters/.

Mehrabian, A. (1969). Significance of posture and position in the communication of attitude and status relationships. *Psychological Bulletin*, 71, 359-392.

Melymuka, K. (1999). "Why military veterans make great it leaders." *CNN News*. Retrieved Jan 8, 2006 from http://www.cnn.com/TECH/computing/9905/28/vets.idg/.

Mettler, S. (2005). *Soldiers to citizens: The GI Bill and the Making of the Greatest Generation.* Cambridge: Oxford Univ. Press.

Miami Times. (2005). *To cut veterans' program would be a disgrace.* Miami, Fla.: Mar 16-Mar 22, 200, .82, 29; pg. 2

Military Community Awareness (2007). Positive parenting. Retrieved from http://WWW.guardfamily.org See also http://www.lifeskillsused.com

Mindy, A., & Lester, D. (1994). Attitudes toward war in veterans. *Psychological Reports*, 75, 314.

Minnesota Online Veterans (2007). Retrieved on March 21 2007 from http://www.acenet.edu/AM/Template.cfm?Section=For_the_Record&Templa
Minnesota National Guard (2007a) Family readiness programs that include information on going to college. Retrieved on January 15, 2008 from http://www.minnesotanationalguard.org/education

Minnesota National Guard (2007b). *A Family Reintegration Program.* Retrieved on Septermber 28th, 2007 from http://www.minnesotanationalguard.org/returning_troops/btyr_overview.php—24k

Moore, K. D. (1989). *Classroom Teaching Skills: A Primer.* Random House,

New York.

Mullane, L. (2005). Soldiers and scholars: what the military and higher education can teach each other. *The American Council on Education.* Retrieved on September 1, 2007 from http://www.acenet.edu/AM/Template. cfm?Section=Search&template=/CM/HTMLDisplay.cfm&ContentID=11193.

Muran, E. M., & Motta, R. W. (1993). Cognitive distortions and irrational beliefs in post-traumatic stress, anxiety, and depressive disorders. *Journal of Clinical Psychology, 49,* 166-176.

National Coalition for Homeless Veterans. (2007). *Facts and media.* Retrieved on September 12, 2007 from http://www.nchv.org/background.cfm

National Guard Family Program (2003). Staying Together. Retrieved on January 15, 2008 from

http://www.guardfamily.org; see also http://www.lifeskillused.com

National Veterans Foundation (2007). *Home Page: Veterans helping veterans.* Retrieved on March 22, 2007 from http://www.nvf.org/?q=

National Veterans Legal Services Program (2007). *Veterans Benefit Manual.* Retrieved on October 24, 2007 from

http://www.nvlsp.org/Information/inde.htm

National Veterans Training Institute (1994). *The resource center: helping build your information network.* Denver, Colorado: U. S. Department of Labor.

NAVPA (2006). National association of veterans ' program administrators. Retrieved on March 21 2007 from

http://www.navpa.org/web_membership.htm—26k—Cached –Similarpages.

NAVREF. (2006). National association of veterans ' research and education foundation. Retrieved on March 21, 2007 from   http://www.navref. org/—14k—Cached -Similarpages

Nelson, S. S. (2006). Governor wants more veterans in state's colleges. *The Orange County Register.* CA.

Next Student (2007). American Council on Education Meeting: Questions on Accountability. 13 February. Retrieved on January 15, 2008 from http://www.nextstudent.com.

Nilsen, W. R. (2001) Veterans' employment and training service. Flexibility and accountability needed to improve service to veterans. Report to the Subcommittee on Oversight and Investigations, Committee on Veterans' Affairs, House of Representatives. Washington DC: General Accounting Office (GAO-01-928)

Nisbett, R. E. (2003). *The geography of thought*. New York: Free Press.

North, O. (2005) [Anti] Military Operations. *Freedom Alliance*, July 21. Retrieved on March 21, 2007 from http: www.military.com/Opinions/0,,Freedo mAlliance_072105,00.html—37k -

North Carolina University (2007). Seminars on how veterans are a protected class. Retrieved on December 11, 2008 from http://www.ncsu.edu/ equal_op/education/oeo_programs.html).

Nursing Standard (2007). Men who have served in the armed forces at high risk of suicide. *Nursing Standard*, 21, p17-17. Retrieved from http://www.nursing-standard.co.uk/inde.asp

O'Brian, T. (2003). *The things they carried*. Broadway Books.

O'Donnell, M. A. (2002). *The G.I. bill of rights of 1944 and the creation of America's modern middle class society*. New York: St. John's University.

Office of Academic Affiliations (2005). General military service history. Retrieved from http://www.vba,va.gov/oaa/pocketcard.

Olson, K. (1974). *The G.I. bill, the veterans, and the colleges*. Lexington, Kentucky.

Paige, C. (2007). Home from America's wars, yet homeless in its suburbs. The Boston Globe. September 14, 2007 from http://www.boston.com/ news/local/articles/2007/08/12/home_from_americas_wars_yet_homeless_ in_its_suburbs/

Parade (2008). The fight for ROTC. November 30th.

Parente, R., & Herrmann, D. (2003). *Retraining cognition*. Austin, Teas: Pro Ed.

Partnership for veterans education (2006). Retrieved on March 15, 2007 from http://veterans.house.gov/hearings/schedule109/sep06/9-27-06a/ NorbertRyan.html-36k

Pathway Home (2007). Pathway home for the Care of Combat Veterans. Retrieved on January 19, 2009 from http://www.va.gov/OPA/fact/returning_vets.asp..

Pedan, E. (1987). *An analysis of unemployment among male war veterans*. Washington, D. C.: Office of Information Management and Statistics.

Penn foster College (2007) A complaint about transfer credits. Home web site. Retrieved on December 20, 2007 from http://www.pennfostercollege.edu/inde.html?semkey=Q092370

Penzenstadler, N. (2007) Students (from the University of Wisconsin at Madison) join D.C. war protest. *The Badger Herald*, University of Wisconsin.

Peter, H. M. (1975). Effects of open admission on the academic adjustment of Vietnam veterans. *Journal of College Student Personnel*, 16, 14-16.

Peterson's College Planner (2007a). *National Call to Service and Education Benefits: GI Bill Education Benefits.* A Nelnet Company. All Rights Reserved. Retrieved from http://www.petersons.com/common/article. asp?id=1667&path=ug.pfs.advice&sponsor=1

Peterson's College Planner (2007b). *Did You Know? Free Information Article: College Education for Veterans.* Retrieved on December 20, 2007 from http://www.petersons.com/choosetoprosper.com/college-for-veterans.html-10-k-Cached

Petrovic, K. (2006). Anti-military sentiments persists on elite campus. *VFW.* Retrieved Jan 16, 2006 from https://www.vfw.org/inde.cfm?fa=news. magDt&dtl=1&mid=2766

Pierre, R. E (2003) Students Across U.S. Mount Antiwar Protests. Published on Thursday, March 6, *Washington Post*

Post 9/11 (2009) Veterans Education Assistance Act (Chapter 33), signed into law on June 30, 2008 to take effect August 1, 2009. http://www.gibill.va.gov/S22/Post 911

Powell, G. J., & Doan, R. E. (1992). Combat and social support as variables in perceived symptomatology of combat-related post traumatic stress disorder. *Psychological Reports, 70,* 1187-1194.

Powers, J. T. (2008a) *Campus Kit for Colleges and Universities..* Student Veterans of America. Retrieved from www.studentveterans.org.

Powers, J. T. (2008b) *Campus Kit for Student Veterans.* Student Veterans of America. Retrieved from http//www.studentveterans.org.

Price, C. W. (1980). Preliminary study of the scholastic progress of veteran with honorable and general discharges. *Psychological Reports,* 47, 1174.

Public Broadcasting System (2007). Classical Values. Retrieved on September 8, 2007 from http://www.classicalvalues.com/archives/2007_07.html

Quillen-Armstrong, S. (2007). Course to help transition veterans into civilian life. July 5., Community College Times Web site: Retrieved on July 16, 2007 from http://www.communitycollegetimes.com/article. cfm?ArticleId=417.

Rentz, E. D., Martin, S. L., Gibbs, D. A., Clinton-Sherrod, M., Hardi-

220

son, J. & Marshall, S. W.. (2006). Family Violence in the Military: A Review of the Literature. *Trauma, Violence, & Abuse, 7,* 93-108.

Reston, J. (1997). Education programs available to enlisted personnel and veterans. *Black Issues in Higher Education, 14,* 38-42

Roca, V. & Freeman, T. W. (2001). Complaints of impaired memory in veterans with PTSD. *American Journal of Psychiatry, 158,* 1738-1739.

Roche, J. (2000). *The Veteran's Survival Guide: How to File and Collect on VA Claims.* Washington, D.C.: Brassey's Incs.

Rogers, C. R. & Wallen, J. L. (1946) *Counseling with returned servicemen.* New York: McGraw Hill.

Rollins, P. C. (1993) Behind the Westmoreland Trial of 1984. *Journal of the Vietnam Veterans Institute,* 2, No. 1.

Rollins, P. C. & Yates, J. E. (1995). *Journal of the Vietnam Veterans Institute,* Volume 4, November 1, 1995.

Rosenzweig, Y. (2002). Harvard joins national anti-war protest. *The Record, Harvard Law Journal,* Issue date: 10/10/02 Section: News.

Ross, D. B. (1969). *Preparing for Ulysses: politics and veterans during World War II.* New York.: Columbia University Press

Roth-Douquet, K. & Schaeffer, F. (2006a). AWOL: *The Unexcused Absence of America's Upper Classes from Military Service—and How It Hurts Our Country,* New York: Collins.

Roth-Douquet, K. & Schaeffer, F. (2006b). Those who serve. *Blueprint,* 2, 16-20. Rye, D. (2001). *The complete idiots guide to financial aid for college.* Indianapolis, IN: Alpha Books.

Sailer, S. (2004). Comparison of IQ of Veterans and nonveterans by State. *Sailer Archives.* Retrieved on August 8, 2006 from http://www.vdare.com/sailer/inde.htm

Santolli, A. (1981). *Everything we had. New York*: Random House.

Schlachter, G. A. (1998). *Financial Aid for Veterans, Military Personnel and Their Dependents, 1998-2000.* Redwood City, CA: Reference Service Press. Eric # ED291315

Schmidt, P. G. (2009). Our student veterans. Edmonds Community College and Washington Department of Veterans Affairs..

Schnurr, P. P., Rosenberg, S. D., & Friedman, M. J. (1993). Change in MMPI scores from college to adulthood as a function of military service. *Journal of Abnormal Psychology, 150,* 479-483.

Schram, M. (2008) *Veterans under siege: How America Deceives and dishon-*

ors those who fight our battles. New York: St. Martins. Retrieved on September 14 from http://www.veteransforamerica.org/home/vfa/

Serow, R. C. (2004). Policy as symbol: title ii of the 1944 GI B*ill. Review of Higher Education. 27,* 481.

Severo, R. & Milford, L. (1990). *The Wages of War: When America's soldiers came home – from Valley Forge to Vietnam.* New York: Touchstone.

Servicemembers Opportunity Colleges (SOC). (2007a). Retrieved on Aug 25, 2007 from http://www.soc.aascu.org/

Servicemembers Opportunity Colleges (2007b). *Veterans Education Bill of Rights.* Presented to the Veterans Affairs Committee on Education, May 16.

Servicemembers Opportunity Colleges. (2004). *What is SOC?* Retrieved on February 5, 2005, from http://www.soc.aascu.org/socgen/WhatIs.html.

Shepard, B. (2003). *A war of nerves: Soldiers and psychiatrist in the twentieth century.* Cambridge: Harvard University Press.

Sherman, M. D., Zanotti, D. K. & Jones, D. E. (2005). Key Elements in Couples Therapy With Veterans With Combat-Related Posttraumatic Stress Disorder. *Professional Psychology: Research and Practice*, 36, 626-633.

Shuckra, D. (2006). Retaining adult learners: what works? *The American Council on Education.* September 3, 2007 from http://www.acenet.edu/AM/Template.cfm?Section=Search&template=/CM/HTMLDisplay.cfm&ContentID=22087.

Sinner, C. (2008) 16 arrested in anti-war protest; More than 200 protesters joined in the march around the University campus Thursday. *Macalester College Minnesota Daily,* University of Minnesota, Minneapolis.

Slavin, R. E. (1995). *Cooperative Learning: Theory, Research, and Practice*, Second Edition. MA: Allyn & Bacon.

Smilkstein, R. *(2002). We're Born to Learn: Using the Brain's Natural Learning Process to Create Today's Curriculum.* Corwin Press.

Smilkstein, R. (1991). A Natural Teaching Method Based on Learning Theory. in Gamut: *A Forum for Teachers and Learners.* Seattle Community Colleges, Seattle, Washington.

Snyder, L. B. (2002). Cashing in on the GI. bill. *Soldiers..* 57, 22.

Sparks, R. A. & Cadli, M. (2002). *Debt free college.* New York: Penguin, Sparta/Gannett, S. (2008). Rutgers students march on Route 18, down N street. *Rutgers University*, New Brunswick, New Jersey.

Spaulding, C. D. J., Eddy, J. P., & Chandras, K. V. (1997). Gulf war syndrome: Are campus health officials prepared to cope with Persian Gulf veterans. *College Student Journal, 31, 317-322.*

Stand Down (2007). Stand Down for Homeless Veterans. Retrieved from on January 5, 2008 from http://www.navy.mil/search/display.asp?story_id=3061

Stanley, M. (2003). Policy as Symbol: Title II of the 1944 G.I. Bill. *Quarterly Journal of Economics.* Cambridge: May. 118, 2, 671.

Stanley, M. (2000). Essays in program evaluation, *Harvard University,* 132 pages; AAT 9988626

Steigmeyer, R. (2009, February 21) From combat to college: A tough transition that few understand. Wenatchee World. Retrieved from http://wenatcheeworld.com/article/20090221/NEWS04/702219970

Sternberg, M., MacDermid Wadsworth, S., Vaughan, J., & Carlson, R. (2009). The higher education landscape for student service members and veterans in Indiana. West Lafayette: Military Family Research Institute at Purdue.

Stever, J. A. (1996). The veteran and the neo-progressive campus. .*Academic Questions, 10,* 41-52.

Storzbach, D., Campbell, K. A., Binder, L. M., McCauley, L., Anger, W., K., Rohlmann, & D. S., Kovera, C. A. (2000). Psychological differences between veterans with and without gulf war unexplained symptoms. *Psychosomatic Medicine, 62,* 726-735.

Strange, R. (1974). Psychiatric perspectives of the Vietnam veteran. *Military Medicine, 139,* 96-98.

Straus, R. (2005). Vet-to-vet counseling heals new and old soldiers. Columbia News Service, Nov 1.

Stiglitz, J. E. & Bilmes, L. J. (2008) *The Three Trillion Dollar War: The True Cost of the Iraq Conflict.* New York: Norton, W. W. & Company.

Students for a Democratic Society (SDS) (2008). Press release anti Iraq in schools around the nation. Retrieved April 8, 2008 from http://www.en.wikipedia.org/wiki/Students_for_a_Democratic_Society_(2006_organization)—66k –

Sullivan, K., Krengel, M., Proctor, S. P., Devine, S., Heeren, T. & White, R. F. (2003). Cognitive functioning in treatment-seeking gulf war veterans: pyridostigmine bromine use and PTSD. *Journal of Psychopathology &*

Behavioral Assessment, 25, 95-103.

Teachman, J, (2005). Military service in the Vietnam era and educational attainment. *Sociology of Education, 78,* 50.

Thirtle, R. M. (2001). *Educational benefits and officer-commissioning opportunities available to U.S. military servicemembers.* Santa Monica, CA: RAND Corporation. Retrieved on January 15, 2006 from http://www.rand.org/publications/MR/MR981.

Thompson, J. (1997) Teaching the Vietnam War to Generation X. *Journal of the Vietnam Veterans Institute,* 6, No. 1-4.

Thorn, R. G. & Payne, S. L. (1977). Ethical judgments of armed service veterans attending college. *Psychological Reports, 41,* 337-338.

365 Gay.Com (2007). Yale Students Protest Military Recruiters On Campus Retrieved on October 15, 2007 from http://www.365gay.com/Newscon07/10/100207yale.htm

Tick, E. (2005). *War and the Soul Healing our Nation's Veterans from Post-traumatic Stress Disorde*r. Wheaton, Ill: Theosophical Publishing House.

Tiet, Q., Finney, J., & Moos, R. H. (2006). Recent sexual abuse, physical abuse, and suicide attempts among male veterans seeking psychiatric treatment. *Psychiatric Services,* 57, 107-113.

Todd, W. E. (1949). *Rehabilitation and education for veterans of World War II.* Stanford University Bulletin, Dissertation Abstracts, ser 8(35).

Traina, T. (2004). Appeals court rules colleges can ban recruiters from campuses. *Heretical Ideas.com.* Retrieved on October 8, 2006 from http:hereticalideas.com/?p=2582-25k-Cached-Similarpages-Notethis

Trewyn, R.W. (1994). Discrimination Against Veterans by the Federal Agency Charged With Protecting Veterans' Rights. *Journal of the Vietnam Veterans Institute,* 3, 22-36.

Trewyn, R. A. & Stever, J. A. (1995). Academia: Not so hallowed halls for veterans. *Journal of the Vietnam Veterans Institute, 4,* 63-75.

Trustees of Indiana University (2007) Military reservists called to active duty.

Ensure a deployed guard person gets funds or credits called for.

Tucker, J. (2006). *War of nerves: Chemical welfare from World War I to al-Qaeda.* Cambridge: Harvard University Press.

U.S. Census Bureau (2003). *U.S. armed forces and veterans.* U.S. Census Bureau, Public Information Office. Special Edition. Retrieved Jun 1, 2004 from http://www.census.gov/prod/2003pubs/02statab/defense.pdf.

U.S. Census Bureau. (2001). *Current population survey.* Publication Office. Retrieved Jun 1, 2004 from http://www.census.gov.

U.S. Census Bureau. (2000). *The graduates: Educational attainment.* Retrieved Jun 1, 2004 from http://www.census.gov/prod/2003pubs/02statab/defense.pdf.

U.S. Department of Labor (2006). *Elaws—employment laws assistance for workers and small businesses—USERRA Advisor.* Retrieved in 2006 from http://www.dol.gov/elaws/userra.htmport.

U.S. Department of Veterans Affairs (2004). *EEO progress report.* Retrieved on September 12, 2007 from http://www.google.com/search?hl=en&q=U.S.+Department+of+Veterans+Affairs+%282004%29&btnG=Search

VA Watchdog (2006). *VA Watchdog.com.* Retrieved on September 12, 2007 from http://www.yourvabenefits.org/sessearch.php?q=homeless&op=and

Van Devanter, L & J.A. Furey., Eds., (1991). *Visions of War, Dreams of Peace: Writings of women in the Vietnam War.* New York: Warner.

Veterans Administration (2006a). *A Brief History of the VA.* Office of Construction & Facilities Retrieved on January 15, 2007 from http:www.va.gov/facmgt/historic/Brief_VA_History.asp—19k

Veterans Administration (2006b). *History of the Department of Veterans Affairs. Retrieved on January 15, 2007 from* http: www.va.gov/facmgt/historic/Brief_VA_History.asp—19k

Veterans Administration. (1991). *Federal benefits for veterans and dependents.* Washington, D. C.: Veterans Administration.

Veterans' Employment & Training Service (VETS) (2006). *Partnership for veterans education.* Retrieved on December 14, 2007s from http:veterans.house.gov/hearings/schedule109/sep06/9-27-06a/NorbertRyan.html—36k

Veterans Information Service (2003). *What every veteran should know.* East Moline, Ill: Library of Congress.

Veterans for America (2008) About veterans for America. Retrieved on November 22 from http://www.veteransforamerica.org/home/vfa/

Veterans Museum & Memorial (2004). Retrieved on December 5, 2007 from http://www.veteranmuseum.org/

Vincennes University (2008) *Military Education Program Handbook: Arkansas Edition.* Vincennes, Indiana. Retrieved on December 2008 from http://www.vinu.edu

Vietnam Era Veteran Readjustment Act (1974) 38 U.S. C. Sect. 2021, et seq,

Walters, A. K. (2006). State contributions to veterans education benefits. *Chronicle of Higher Education, 52*, 18.

Washton, N. S. (1945) A veteran goes to college: Opinions of a soldier who has been a college teacher. *Journal of Higher Education*, 16, No. 4 (Apr., 1945), pp. 195-196,226

Webb, J. (2007). Introducing a sweeping expansion of the education. *US Fed News Service, Including US State News*. Washington, D.C.: Jan 4.

Webb, R. W. & Atkinson, B. H. (1946). The Veteran is in College. *The Journal of Higher Education. XVII, 5*, 238-242, 282.

Wector, D. (1944). *When Johnny comes marching home*. Boston: Houghton Mifflin.

Weller, W. W. (1944). *The veteran comes back*. New York: Dryden Press.

Wenger, D., Rufflo, M., & Bertalan, F. J. (2006). ACME project, internet-based systems that advocate credit for military experience and analyze options for veterans in career transition. *Proceedings of the IEEE International Conference on Advanced Learning Techniques*, IEEE The Computer Society.

Wikipedia (2006). Indian Wars—Wikipedia, the free encyclopedia. Retrieved on December 5, 2007 from

http: //www.en.wikipedia.org/wiki/Indian_Wars-77k-Cached-Similar-pages

Wilkes-Edrington, L. (2007). First battle: serve in military. Net battle: finish college. *The Missourian*. Retrieved on September 14 2007 from http://www.columbiamissourian.com/stories/2007/05/26/first-battle-serve-military-net-battle-finish-col/

Williamson, V. (2008) A New GI Bill: *Rewarding our Troops, Rebuilding our Military*. Iraq and Afghanistan Veterans of America, issue report.

Wilson, K. M. (2006). Report on VA's education benefit programs and the Administration's views on the Total Force GI Bill concept. *Presented to the Committee on Veterans' Affairs Subcommittee on Economic Opportunity, U.S. House of Representatives.*

Wilson, R. (2006). Professor Charges Bias Over War Injuries. *Chronicle of Higher Education*; 9/1/2006, 53, 23-23.

Wilson, R. B. (2003). *Indiana State University's Veterans Handbook*. Terre Haute, IN: Indiana University Press.

Winter, G. (2005). From Combat To Campus On the G.I. Bill. *New York Times* (Late Edition (East Coast)). New York, N.Y.: Jan 16,p. 4A.8

Wisconsin Department of Veterans Affairs (2007). *Wisconsin G.I. Bill Tuition Remission Program*. Retrieved on October 24 from http://dva.state.wi.us/Ben_education.asp

Yates, J. E. (1993). Hello Miss American Pie (An essay for Veterans Day, 1992). *Journal of the Vietnam Veterans Institute*, 2, No. 1.

Yates, J. (2004) Examining the myths of the Vietnam War. A conference held at Simmons College by the RADIX Foundation, *Journal of the Vietnam Veterans Institute*, 26-29 July.

Yehuda, R., Keefe, R. S. E., & Harvey, P. D. , Levengood, R. A., et al. (1995). Learning and memory in combat veterans with posttraumatic stress disorder. *American Journal of Psychiatry*, *152*, 137-139.

Young, A. (2005). Bureaucratic tangle delays education payments to veterans. *Knight Ridder/Tribune News Service*. November 1.

YouTube (2003). Anti war protest of college students in Austin, Texas.

Zahn, P. (2007). Epidemic of mental illness in U.S.. military? War and women. *Paula Zahn Now*. Retrieved Dec 3, 2007 from http://panther.indstate.edu:2048/login?url=http://panther.indstate.edu:2920/login.asp?direct=true&db=nfh&AN=32U0942688305CNPZ&site=ehost-live.

Appendices

Appendix 14-A

Veterans-Friendly Rating Scale for Higher Educational Institutions

Rate your college or university for how often it addresses each of the following practices that encourage a veteran to attend and complete a college degree. My college or university

1. promotes a public image as holding generally positive attitudes toward veterans.
    Never Rarely Sometimes Often Always

2. directs faculty to not openly advocate anti-military attitudes and anti-veteran attitudes in class (discussion of these attitudes is permitted in courses that are concerned with politics, government, and the military).
    Never Rarely Sometimes Often Always

3. teaches faculty how to read the countenance of veterans and to distinguish veterans from non-veterans who are similar in age
    Never Rarely Sometimes Often Always

4. directs faculty and students to not say rude, disrespectful and slanderous things about veterans.
    Never Rarely Sometimes Often Always

5. provides assistance to veterans with their transition from military life to civilian and college life.
    Never Rarely Sometimes Often Always

6. does not require veterans to spend all of their GI Bill to pay for tuition and fees in the early months of a semester.
    Never Rarely Sometimes Often Always

7. calculates a veteran's financial aid without subtracting GI Bill from the financial aid that a veteran could receive; to ensure that veterans are just as eligible to get loans and grants as non-veteran students.

Never Rarely Sometimes Often Always

8. calculates a veteran's financial aid without subtracting costs of living from the financial aid that a veteran could receive; to ensure that veterans are just as eligible to get loans and grants as non-veteran students.

Never Rarely Sometimes Often Always

9   guides veterans to apply for scholarships that are appropriate to their background.

Never Rarely Sometimes Often Always

10. establishes scholarships that are tailored to the background of veteran students.

Never Rarely Sometimes Often Always

11. helps veterans with a family to support with finding financial assistance.

Never Rarely Sometimes Often Always

12. provides veterans with a hassle-free program for a thorough transfer of military training and experience into academic credits.

Never Rarely Sometimes Often Always

13. provides credit for physical education that veterans receive in the military.

Never Rarely Sometimes Often Always

14. if you are in the Guard or Reserve, provide credit for work completed in part of a semester before being deployed.

Never Rarely Sometimes Often Always

15. provides special programs designed specifically to help veterans shift from the learning style appropriate for military training to the learning styles required to succeed in college.

Never Rarely Sometimes Often Always

16. enables veterans to continue to major the specialty they acquired while in the service.

Never Rarely Sometimes Often Always

17. addresses particular disabilities.

Never Rarely Sometimes Often Always

18. has a program for veterans to find employment that is appropriate to a veterans education and background.

Never Rarely Sometimes Often Always
19.   addresses the particular health concerns of veterans where these concerns may be due to military service.
Never Rarely Sometimes Often Always

Your branch of service _____

Number of years in military service _____

Name _____

Appendix 14-B

Veteran Higher Education (VHE) Index of Colleges and Universities

Developing a *Veteran's Higher Education* (VHE) Index for Your Institution

If your institution does not have a VHE index and you want to generate one, you might follow these directions.

A school can develop a system to determine how veterans feel about the way that the school treats them. The questionnaire presented in Appendix 14-A is one way that a school may assess how well it treats veterans. Below is a **Veterans Friendliness/Unfriendliness Questionnaire** that can be administered considerably faster than the one used in Appendix 14-A. This questionnaire is faster for two reasons. It asks only ten questions, only half the number of questions used in the questionnaire in Appendix 14-A. Additionally, the questions used in the **Veterans Friendliness/Unfriendliness Questionnaire** require a "yes" or "no" response for each question; a decision that can be made much faster than can be done with the questionnaire in Appendix 14-A questionnaire that requires the use of a five point rating scale (Never, Rarely, Sometimes, Often, Always).

Veteran Friendliness/Unfriendliness Questionnaire

Directions for Completing the Questionnaire

You should answer each question by circling either the "yes" or "no" alongside of the question. For purposes of this questionnaire, statements in opposition of a war are not necessarily anti-military and anti-veteran. However, statements that indicate that our military has behaved badly might be anti-military and anti-veteran. The veteran has to use judgment in deciding whether someone is making prejudicial comments.

1.	Yes	No	Are there protests against the military on your cam pus presently?
2.	Yes	No	Were there protests against the military on your campus last year?
3.	Yes	No	Was your campus a site of protests against the mili tary during a previous American conflict?
4.	Yes	No	Have you had a student, faculty member, or admin istrator say anti-veteran insults to you?
5.	Yes	No	Do you know a veteran at your institution who has reported that a student or an administrator says anti-veteran things to them?
6.	Yes	No	Do you know a faculty member who clearly treats veterans with as much or more respect than he or she treats non-veteran students?
7.	Yes	No	Does your institution have any programs designed specifically for veterans?
8.	Yes	No	Has your institution given you sufficient transfer credits for military training and experience, according to the ACE system and/or other systems?
9.	Yes	No	Does your financial aid office seek financial aid appropriate for you while knowing you are a veteran.
10.	Yes	No	Do you have an advisor or advisors who take account of your military background when providing you with advice.

Administration of a *Veteran's Higher Education* **(VHE) Index for Your Institution**

Ask the veterans at a particular institution to complete the Veterans Friendliness/Unfriendliness Questionnaire. Only veterans who study at an institution should be allowed to complete this questionnaire. Employees or non-veteran students of an institution should not be allowed to complete the questionnaire.

Scoring the Veteran's Friendliness/Unfriendliness Questionnaire

A veteran indicates the degree of friendliness or unfriendliness of a school by his or her answers to the **Veteran's Friendliness/Unfriendliness**

Questionnaire. The friendliness of responses to this questionnaire score value for yes or a no responses varies across the ten questions in the questionnaire. A "no" answer to any of the first five questions indicates that, according to the veteran respondent, the school engages in friendly actions toward veterans. A "yes" answer to any of the second five questions indicates that, according to the veteran respondent, the school engages in friendly actions toward veterans.

A veteran regards a school as friendly if that veteran answers six or more questions that indicate the school engaged in friendly actions. A veteran regards a school as unfriendly if that veteran's answers indicate the school engaged in six or more unfriendly actions.

The VHE index can vary from +1 to –1. A VHE index is calculated by subtracting the number of unfriendly actions from friendly actions and then by dividing this difference by 10. A positive VHE Index occurs when the number of friendly actions exceeds the number of unfriendly actions. A negative VHE Index occurs when the number of unfriendly actions exceeds the number of friendly actions. The index is zero if the veteran does not view his or her school as friendly or unfriendly. A veteran can have only one kind of score that is either a friendliness score, an unfriendliness score or a zero score.

The table below (1, 14B) lists the possible VHE Index scores according to the possible combination of friendly and unfriendly answers that a veteran may provide on the questionnaire and an index associated with each yes friendly and unfriendly response pair.

Table 14B.1
The Veteran's Higher Education Index According to
The Number of Friendly and Unfriendly Answers

```
10 friendly and  0 unfriendly = an index of  +  1.0
 9 friendly and  1 unfriendly = an index of  +   .8
 8 friendly and  2 unfriendly = an index of  +   .6
 7 friendly and  3 unfriendly = an index of  +   .4
 6 friendly and  4 unfriendly = an index of  +   .2
 5 friendly and  5 unfriendly = an index of       0
 4 friendly and  6 unfriendly = an index of   -   .2
 3 friendly and  7 unfriendly = an index of   -   .4
 2 friendly and  8 unfriendly = an index of   -   .6
 1 friendly and  9 unfriendly = an index of   -   .8
 0 friendly and 10 unfriendly = an index of   -  1.0
```

Interpreting a Veteran's VHE

A user of the scores on the **Veteran's Friendliness/Unfriendliness Questionnaire** may draw conclusions about how a veteran regards his or her school as friendly or unfriendly about veterans. A professor, administrator, or veteran may conclude that a veteran regards his or school is friendly if the veteran's index is .2, .4, .6, .8, or 1.0; larger indices may be interpreted as indicative of more friendliness than smaller indices. Similarly, a professor, administrator, or veteran may conclude that a veteran regards his or her school as unfriendly if the veteran's index is .-2, .-.4-, .-6, .-8, or -1.0: larger negative indices may be interpreted as indicative or more unfriendliness than smaller indices.

The validity of a VHE index attributed to a school by a veteran may be evaluated in different ways. Some of the smaller index values might be regarded as too small to be interpreted as valid. The usefulness of a VHE index may be evaluated on the basis of experience with the indices of different veterans in the past. The appropriate used of a school's index can be evaluated on the basis of on the basis of experience with the indices of different veterans in the past. Over the years administrators will get a sense of indices that correspond with veterans problems on campus. Some VHE values will suggest that an index of a certain level corresponds to serious events. .

The validity of an index can also be evaluated on the basis of statistical criteria (Hopkins & Antes, 1976, 1990; MacNemar, 1969). Nevertheless, a friendly index of .6, .8 or 10 probably indicates something that merits inquiry among veterans and others at the school by an administrator or professor at the veteran's school because the veterans index suggests that the veteran feels that the school is doing something right. An unfriendly index of -.6, -.8 or -10 indicates something that merits inquiry by an administrator in order to determine what the veteran feels the school is doing wrong.

Scoring A School's Average Veteran's Friendliness and Unfriendliness.

A school's overall Veterans Higher Education (VHE) index may be derived by summing the individual indices of veterans and by dividing the sum of these indices by the number of veterans making ratings. A school may be regarded as at least somewhat friendly if it has a VHE that is positive. A school may be regarded as at least somewhat unfriendly if it has a VHE index that is negative. Schools may regard as neither friendly nor unfriendly if its mean ratings are not consistently different from zero.

The validity of a mean VHE index may be evaluated in different ways. Administrators or professors may decide that very small means are not worth worrying about, although previous experience may suggest when the magnitude of a mean VHE index is large enough to be of concern about the current adjustment of veterans at that school

The validity can be evaluated on the basis of statistical criteria. Nevertheless, statistical validity may not always be sufficient for drawing conclusions about the adjustment of veterans at a school. A mean unfriendly index of .4 or higher suggests that veterans' experiences at the school merits inquiry by an administrator. A friendly index of .4 or higher also merits inquiry by an administrator in order to determine what veterans think the school is doing right.

A Comparison of the Veteran's Friendliness of Different Schools.

Some schools may want to compare how each other treats veterans by comparing their VHE indices. A comparison of mean VHE indices of two or more schools requires evidence that the comparison of the VHE of the schools is reliable (Hopkins & Antes, 1976, 1990; MacNemar, 1969). A conclusion about whether the difference in the mean VHE indices of two or more school's mean friendly or unfriendly responses are reliably different from each other is a matter of experience with veterans and their VHE mean indices at particular schools Nevertheless, a difference of two means that is .6 or higher suggests that veterans experiences at the two schools merit inquiry by administrators and professors. At a minimum, a difference in the means VHE indices of .6 also merits inquiry by an administrator in order to determine what one school has led veterans to conclude that they are treated better than veterans are treated at another school.

Appendix 14-C

The Shortcomings of the VA Website Concerning Information Needed by Veterans Who Want to Attend College or Complete College

The VA Website provides much information that is useful to veterans. However, the VA web site fails to meet its standards for information quality when it comes to those veterans who want to seek a college degree. As explained below, the VA web site gives little information for veterans who want to go to college. Veterans who are interested in going to college receive so little information to critical questions. Here are the shortcomings of the site for veterans who want to seek a college degree.

The VA web site says a lot about GI Bill, how a veteran may qualify for it, and how to apply for it. In contrast, the VA web site says nothing to solve several financial problems that veterans may encounter in college. The VA web site says nothing about:

1. what to do if his or her college or university applies the "Means test" regarding GI Bill. The site says nothing about what a veteran may do if his college or university subtracts his GI Bill payments from the total financial aid when calculating the veteran's financial aid.
2. what he or she can do if his or her higher educational institution does not count cost of living in their total possible financial aid
3. what he or she can do if his or her higher educational institution subtracts the veteran's previous year's military salary from the total possible financial aid—despite the fact that the veteran no longer receives that salary.
4. how veterans can apply for scholarships

5.   how veterans with families can get support for their spouse and children while in college.

The VA web site says a lot about a veteran's educational benefits in general. However it says nothing about:

1.   how veterans can get a fair transfer of ACE credits at their higher educational institution—In other words, the VA web site says nothing about how veterans may appeal decisions that they feel incorrectly deny them transfer credit for their ACE credits.

2.   how a veteran may appeal decisions to not give him academic credits or give him too few of the academic credits that were merited on the basis of ACE evaluations.

3.   those colleges and universities that deal with ACE credits incorrectly, that is, about which schools are likely not to give a fair transfer of ACE credits. The VA says it has a policy of providing disclaimers on products that may claim VA approval but it does not provide veterans with the names of which schools do not give a fair transfer of ACE credits.

The VA web site says that veterans have educational benefits but says nothing about

1.   the kinds of educational programs that veterans might want to get involved in while in college.

2.   what veterans should learn in study skills that have designed specifically for veterans so that they may adopt the learning styles required to succeed in college.

3.   how a veteran can arrange to major or minor (MOS related) in the specialty that they acquired while in the service.

4.   what a veteran might do if an educational program at their school fails to take account of his or her veteran background

The VA web site says nothing that might prepare veterans for social interactions that they might have in college about

1.   what a veteran might do if insulted by a professor in higher education.

2.   what to do if the campus community appears to be hostile to veterans

The VA web site does say that it indicates which colleges or universities the VA approves. However, it says nothing about:

1. what are the criteria that can lead to approval or disapproval. In other words, there is no explanation about what qualifies a school as a veterans-friendly institution

2. what to do if an institution is not listed with a history of approval or disapproval.

3. which of the many forms should be completed by a veteran who wants to attend college.

The VA web site does say that vocational rehabilitation is available to veterans who have a service-connected disability. However, it says nothing about:

1. whether a veterans rehabilitation counselor is able to advise a disabled veteran about which college or university he or she should attend and can impart reasonably developed skills, knowledge, and abilities.

2. which colleges and university health services provide assistance with service connected disabilities

3. does not explain how disabled veterans who complete college may be directed to appropriate employment.

The VA web site does not indicate which colleges or universities have health services appropriate for veterans. The VA web site does not say

1. which colleges or universities provide vocational rehabilitation for veterans who have a service-connected disability?

a. which colleges or universities have a program designed to help student veterans find employment consistent with their health needs after graduating with a college degree.